Medieval and Renaissance Series
Number 3

MEDIEVAL

AND

RENAISSANCE STUDIES

Proceedings of the Southeastern Institute
of Medieval and Renaissance Studies
Summer, 1967

Edited by John M. Headley

The University of North Carolina Press · Chapel Hill

To

M. M. C., B. J. B., and B. P. G.

*whose invaluable assistance contributed to the success
of the Institute's third session.*

Foreword

The essays included in this volume were originally presented as public lectures during the third session of the Southeastern Institute of Medieval and Renaissance Studies held on the campus of The University of North Carolina at Chapel Hill from July 17 to August 24, 1967. They are offered here to permit their wider circulation and to serve as a record of the activities of the Institute. A description of the aims of the Institute and a list of seminars and participants appear in the Appendix.

The present volume represents the combined interest and activity of several individuals and groups. The Institute is supported by a grant from the Ford Foundation and functions as part of the Duke-University of North Carolina Co-operative Program in the Humanities. Special thanks are due to the Joint Central Committee of the Co-operative Program whose members under the chairmanship of Professor James L. Godfrey of The University of North Carolina have provided guidance and aid to all the activities of the Institute. The editor is particularly grateful for the assistance of Professor John L. Lievsay, Co-Chairman of the 1967 Institute and Chairman for the 1966 and 1968 sessions; and for the advice and aid of the other members of the Institute Committee: Professors Ray Petry, S. K. Heninger, and Dale B. J. Randall of Duke University and Professors O. B. Hardison and John Keller of The University of North Carolina. Finally, the editor wishes to express the gratitude of the Institute Committee as well as his own personal appreciation for the generous co-operation and interest evinced at all times by the Senior Fellows.

J. M. H.
Chairman, 1967 Institute
Chapel Hill, N.C.

Contents

Foreword *vii*

 I *Metaphor As Cosmic Correspondence*
   by S. K. Heninger, Jr. 3

 II *The Treaties of the Carolingians*
   by François L. Ganshof 23

 III *French Attitudes Toward Literary Criticism*
   by W. L. Wiley 53

 IV *1367: The Founding of the Spanish College*
   at Bologna
   by Berthe M. Marti 70

 V *The Alliterative* Morte Arthure, *the*
   Concept of Medieval Tragedy, and the
   Cardinal Virtue Fortitude
   by Robert M. Lumiansky 95

 VI *Medieval Landscape Painting:*
   An Introduction
   by François Bucher 119

 VII *Circumstances and the Sense of History*
   in Tudor England: The Coming of the
   Historical Revolution
   by Arthur B. Ferguson 170

 VIII *The European Significance of*
   Florentine Platonism
   by Paul Oskar Kristeller 206

Appendix: Statement of Objectives; List of
   Seminars and Participants 231

[ix]

MEDIEVAL
AND
RENAISSANCE STUDIES

I

Metaphor As Cosmic Correspondence

S. K. Heninger, Jr.
Duke University, Durham, North Carolina

The problem that I am concerned with in this lecture is fundamentally an epistemological problem. The renaissance poet lay under the injunction to purvey truth—as Philip Sidney said, "to knowe, and by knowledge to lift up the mind from the dungeon of the body to the enjoying his owne divine essence."[1] So I am interested in where the poet sought truth, what he accepted as ultimate reality, and how he tried to express this truth in ways intelligible to his readers. Since truth was almost ineffable—because of its comprehensiveness, its subtlety, and its complexity, it was divine—the poet had the enormous task of making explicit what was essentially implicit. This was the special function of poetry, however, to make known the unknown, to make understood the unknowable—as Shakespeare said, to "give to airy nothing a local habitation and a name"; in the words of Milton, to "justify the ways of God to men." This talent for truthful statement is what made the poet holy, a *vates*. But this role carried the onus of making verbally carnate a truth that was otherwise tenuous and elusive.

To perform this task, the poet resorted to metaphor, to the comparison between two things, one known and one unknown, with the intention of explaining the unknown in terms of the known. It is in this broad sense that I use the word "metaphor." By it I mean all figurative comparisons—similes, hyperboles, allegories, symbols. By "metaphor," to repeat, I mean any comparison between two things—objects, ideas, emotions, and any combination of these—any comparison between two things, one

[3]

known and one unknown, by which the poet seeks to explain the unknown in terms of the known.

To give a simple example, if I wished to explain a knight's performance in battle, something which you as audience do not yet know about, I might compare him to a lion, something with which you are familiar. I might say, "He was a lion in the fight," a formal metaphor. Or I might construct a formal simile, "He fought like a lion"; or a hyperbole, "He was more ferocious than a lion"; or an allegory, probably a beast-fable, "The lion fought ferociously," where the lion in the allegory stands for the knight; or a symbol, "The lion of chivalry fought bravely"; or perhaps I might use just a connotative word without resorting to a formal figure of speech, "He fought with leonine ferocity." For my present purposes, I shall consider all of these as examples of metaphor, as a comparison between two things whereby an unknown, the actions of the knight, is explained in terms of a known, the lion's traditional ferocity.

When we turn to renaissance criticism and look for contemporary statements about the poet's ultimate reality and his means of expressing it, we find two persistent themes. One of these themes evolves from Plato, and the other from Aristotle. The first, the Platonic theme, identifies the poet as a maker under divine influence and derives his title from the Greek word ποιεῖν, to fashion, to make. By creating poetry, the poet reproduces the creative act of νοῦς, the divine mind that conceived the idea for our universe and had the power to execute it.[2] The second theme, the Aristotelian theme, defines poetry as μίμησις, the imitation of life. And though the poet has the sensitivity to see beauty and the license to idealize, there is no doubt that the data of his imitation must be the objects of our physical world.[3]

It can be seen at once that the epistemological assumptions of these two themes are antithetical. A doctrine of poet as creator does not accord with a doctrine of poem as imitation. The contradiction is so manifest, and so central to poetics, that George Puttenham began his *Arte of English Poesie* (1589) with recognition of this very point. Although the passage is fairly long, I think it worthwhile to quote his opening sentences:

A Poet is as much to say as a maker. And our English name well conformes with the Greeke word: for of ποιεῖν to make, they call a maker *Poeta*. Such as (by way of resemblance and reverently) we may say of God: who without any travell [travail] to his divine imagination, made all the world of nought. . . . Even so the very Poet makes and contrives out of his owne braine, both the verse and matter of his poeme. . . . And nevertheless without any repugnancie at all, a Poet may in some sort be said a follower or imitator, because he can express the true and lively of every thing [which] is set before him, and which he taketh in hand to describe: and so in that respect is both a maker and a counterfaitor: and Poesie an art not only of making, but also of imitation.[4]

Here we have the two themes neatly counterposed. The Platonic theme looks to a godhead for its impetus and seeks its truth in a suprasensible world of ideas, what Plato called the world of being. By deduction, the poet might bring down from this unchanging, noncorporeal world some notion of the permanent essences that reside there, and might make this truth intelligible to his fellowmen. In contrast, the Aristotelian theme insists that poetry begin with the facts of our physical environment and seek to devise an all-inclusive statement that will be true in every instance, what Aristotle called a universal. By induction, the poet constructs a general truth that is viable among his fellowmen. The antithesis is that between revelation and science. We are all familiar with this perennial crux in intellectual history.

These divergent opinions of wherein lies truth are irreconcilable as philosophical systems. According to either epistemology, however, the poet was perforce a cosmic philosopher, one who "sees into the life of things," if I may open the door to an intruder. The poet was in a continuous tradition extending from the earliest Greek philosophers: Thales, Pythagoras, Empedocles, Parmenides—all of whom had expressed themselves in meter.[5] And it was the unique triumph of renaissance poetics to fuse these two concepts of ultimate reality, or at least to make

[5]

them congruous. The poet as maker fashioned his poem out of the materials of his own sense experience. As Puttenham asserted: "They [the poets] were the first observers of all naturall causes & effects in the things generable and corruptible, and from thence mounted up to search after the celestiall courses and influences, & yet penetrated further to know the divine essences."[6] The poet's description of reality, as Sidney argued, was not the limited factuality of history, nor the tenuous abstraction of philosophy; but rather it was an imitation of life which started with the imperfect and ephemeral brazen world and by poetic imagination transmuted this to a golden world of superreality.[7] Whether the poet began with the unrelated experiences of actual life, and by the coadunating faculty of his imagination arrived at a timeless verity; or whether he started with the eternal ideas of Plato's world of being, and purveyed them in the sensible form of objective correlatives in the physical world, he was dealing with the same truth. Poetry was ποίσις, a fashioning of random data into a significant statement of universal relevance. It was μίμησις, the imitation not of apparent or of fragmentary, but of ultimate reality.

For the nonce I should like now to leave poetics, and turn to the discipline of physics, by which I mean, of course, the study of physical nature, as the Greeks used the word "physics." What I shall deal with is the orthodox physics inherited from the middle ages, the conservative physics as yet unrevolutionized by the new scientists of the sixteenth and seventeenth centuries, the traditional physics accepted almost without question by every major poet through Milton. When we take a synoptic view of renaissance physics, we find here also a dichotomy, two opposing ways of considering nature. Each of these two ways is distinct, but they are not mutually exclusive. The same mind could consider the same reality in both ways; in fact, in the greatest poetry this is exactly what happens—the poet gives an interpretation of reality which incorporates both views of nature. But that is getting ahead of my argument, so let me proceed to define these two ways of considering nature.

One way is what I shall call the physical view. This is the

way more familiar to us today. Through his senses, the poet perceived the physical world and described it in terms of the dimensional time-space continuum. Quantity and color and smell and feel—these are the components of reality described in this way. Fire, for instance, is flickering and red and warm—its physical appearance.

The other way of considering reality is what I shall call the conceptual view. And this way may be difficult for us to appreciate because it is not scientific, in the modern sense. But it was easily familiar and wholly justifiable to the renaissance poet. The conceptual view of reality considers the components of our environment in an abstract way as concepts rather than physical objects. It stresses the innate qualities of things, and the relationships between things. Fire considered conceptually, for instance, has the qualities hot and dry, and is the opposite of water, which is cold and wet.

An illustration will, I hope, clarify the difference between physical reality and conceptual reality. I have reproduced two woodcuts, Figures 1 and 2, each of which depicts the arrangement of the four Elements. Figure 1, the first that I should like to examine, is from Sebastian Munster's *Cosmographia*. This reproduction comes from an edition printed at Paris in 1568, although the woodcut had appeared regularly in every edition since the first at Basle in 1544. It shows, quite obviously, the stratification of the Elements: Water and Earth at the bottom, Fire uppermost, and Air in-between. Then come the heavens, with the Sun and Moon prominently displayed to indicate their eternality. And from the empyrean, God surveys His creation. This diagram indicates the spatial arrangement of the Elements. These are the Elements disposed as our senses perceive them. This diagram illustrates, in fact, the orderly arrangement of the physical world as God created it in that busy six days before He rested.

But it was possible, and indeed frequent, to present a different arrangement of the Elements, a scheme depicting their conceptual reality. Let us look now at Figure 2. This is a woodcut from Oronce Finé's *De sphaera mundi,* printed at Paris in 1542. It is a tetrad arrangement of the four Elements, a concept that had originated with the Pythagoreans and had received full enunciation by Empedocles. It emphasizes not the spatial organization of the Elements, but rather their inherent qualities and their relationships one to another.

In the diagram, we see the four Elements: Fire, at the top; Air, at the right; Water, at the bottom; and Earth, on the left. Each of these Elements partakes of two among the four basic qualities: heat, indicated in the upper right-hand corner; moisture, indicated in the lower right-hand corner; cold, indicated in the lower left-hand corner; and dryness, indicated in the upper left-hand corner. For each Element, one quality is dominant—i.e., *summa*—and one quality is recessive—i.e., *remissa* —but this part of the concept is not important to us. What is important, however, is that adjacent qualities may combine— as labeled, *combinatio possibilis*—and in fact, do combine in each of the Elements. But qualities that are opposite one another in the diagram cannot combine, and this fact is labelled *combinatio impossibilis*. For example, at the top dryness and heat combine to produce Fire; but dryness and moisture, the diagonal opposite of dryness, cannot combine. Similarly, an Element can accord with its neighbor, since they share a common quality, so that Fire can accord with Air, a compatibility that is labeled *simbolisantia*. But an Element cannot agree with its opposite in the diagram—for example, Fire cannot agree with Water—a discord that is labeled *contraria*. This discord between opposites produced an outward thrust, Empedoclean hate, which tended to disrupt this conceptual arrangement of four distinct entities. But around the periphery of the diagram the accord existing between neighbors provided a counteractive force, Empedoclean love, which held the four Elements within a single system, a cosmos.

Notice that in this diagram there is no such thing as physical space, dimensional space. Space is designated only to represent a relationship between two portions of the concept. The diagram illustrates the *conceptual* reality of the four Elements:

[8]

their qualities, their interrelationships, and their incorporation into a stable system, a cosmos.

This concept of Elemental reality is quite different from the physical configuration of Elemental reality in Figure 1, although both deal with the same facts. These two distinct views of reality correspond roughly to the two halves of the chain of being, the realm of spirit and the realm of matter, which man joins together in his central position on the great chain. With the angels and God, man shares the ability to perceive conceptual reality by exercising his mind; by employing his senses, man perceives physical reality, which comprises animals, plants, and stones. Just as the whole man must incorporate both halves of the chain, however, both spirit and flesh, so truth, the poet would say, must incorporate both conceptual and physical reality.[8]

It is interesting to note that on the page in Finé's textbook opposite Figure 2 there is another diagram showing the spatial arrangement of the four Elements. I have reproduced this woodcut as Figure 3, and it warrants a quick look. Comprising our planet in the center are Earth and Water; in the outermost circle is Fire; and in-between is Air, somewhat sophisticated here, as was commonplace, by division into three layers: at top the *suprema aeris regio,* the upper region of Air; next the *media regio,* the middle region, which, being cold, congealed the Air into clouds, as you see; and finally the *infima regio,* the lower region. Finé was aware of both the physical and the conceptual reality of the Elements, and he elucidated both.

Often the same diagram amalgamated the two views of reality, the physical and the conceptual, into the same schema. For example, if I may expand from the four Elements to the universe at large, in Figure 4, a woodcut from Johann Eck's edition of Aristotle's *De caelo,* printed at Augsburg in 1519, we see the familiar spatial arrangement of the Elements at the center: Earth in the very middle, then, ranging outwards, Water, Air, and Fire. Next are the spheres of the seven planets, arranged in spatial order, from the Moon, through Mercury, Venus, the Sun, Mars, and Jupiter to Saturn. Then the sphere of fixed stars, which contains the signs of the zodiac; the cristal-line sphere; and finally the *primum mobile,* which is bounded by the infinite *empireum immotum,* the immobile empyrean —which should stretch out indefinitely, of course, but here is crudely confined by the borders of the diagram. To stress that this is a physical representation, a time-space continuum, the period of revolution is indicated at the right for each of the celestial spheres. The sphere of Mercury, for example, turns in *unus annus,* one year; that of Mars in *duo anni,* two years; that of Saturn in *triginta anni,* thirty years; and so forth.

But there are also attempts to represent conceptual reality in this diagram. On the left-hand side, for example, printed within each sphere is the musical note which that planet was supposed to play in the universal harmony—*hypate* for the Moon, *parhypate* for Mercury, *lychanos* for Venus, and so on. In the upper-left corner of the diagram within the box is this label: *Pythagorae octochordos lyra, proslambanomenos terra* (the eight-chorded lyre of Pythagoras, with earth playing the lowest note). This portion of the diagram, of course, is intended to represent the Pythagorean notion of universal harmony, with each planet contributing its individual but complementary note to the total consort. This is conceptual reality; in fact, everyone agreed that human ears, being imperfect, could not hear the music of the spheres. And to validate the non-corporeality of this idea, in the upper-right corner of the diagram a little angel —labeled *intelligentia assistens,* the assisting intelligence—places his helping hand on the outermost sphere, thereby applying motion, the physical form of God's will, to the primum mobile, whence this motion is transferred in a physical manner by friction down through the other spheres. Notice how this angel becomes an entrepreneur between conceptual and phys-ical reality, how he provides a bridge between the abstract and the concrete. Though the angel resides in the empyrean, in the infinite and eternal, he turns the primum mobile, the finite and temporal; thereby he transmutes God's will into physical fact.

I should like now to examine another diagram which com-bines components of both physical and conceptual reality. Fig-

FIGURE 1. Sebastian Munster, *La Cosmographie universelle* (Paris, 1568), p. 1.

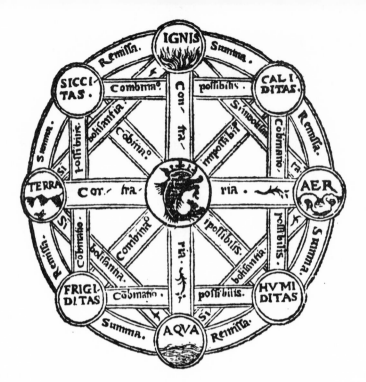

FIGURE 2. Oronce Finé, *De sphaera mundi* (Paris, 1542), fol. 2.

FIGURE 3. Oronce Finé, *De sphaera mundi* (Paris, 1542), fol. 1ᵛ.

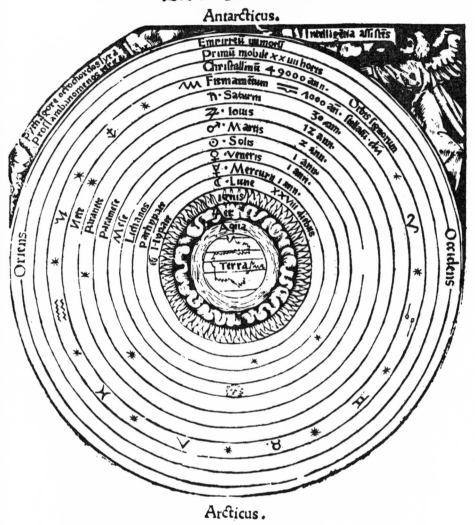

FIGURE 4. Aristotle, *De caelo*, ed. Johann Eck (Augsburg, 1519), fol. 29ᵛ.

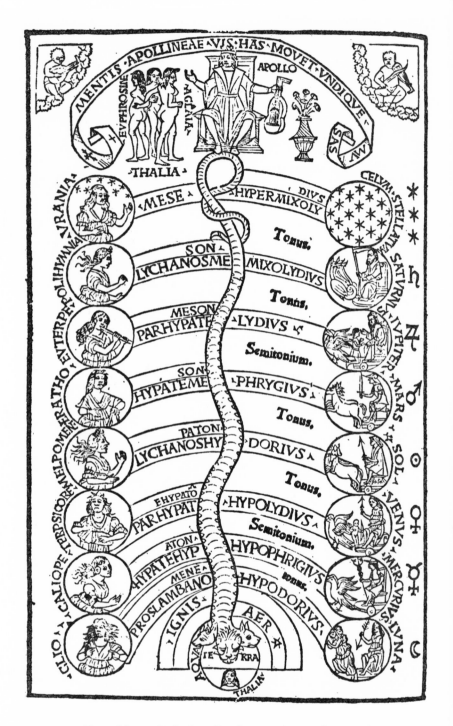

FIGURE 5. Franchinus Gafurius, *De harmonia musicorum instrumentorum opus* (Milan, 1518), fol. 94ᵛ.

FIGURE 6. Robert Fludd, *Utriusque cosmi . . . historia* (Oppenheim, 1617), title page.

FIGURE 7. Isidore of Seville, *De responsione mundi* (Augsburg, 1472), fol. b3ᵛ.

ure 5 is an illustration from a handbook of music by Franchinus Gafurius, printed at Milan in 1518. It also, like the last diagram, represents the universe in toto. At the very bottom are the four Elements in spatial arrangement: Terra, Aqua, Aer, and Ignis. Then rising in order are the spheres of the seven planets, and the sphere of fixed stars at the top, making a total of eight spheres in order to demonstrate a concept which I shall come to in a moment. The planets are labeled in the right-hand margin by both names and astronomical symbols, and are also indicated mythologically by the circular vignettes of the appropriate god or goddess. Already we are out of the realm of simple physical reality. Indeed, although this diagram depends structurally upon the physical facts, its emphasis is rather upon conceptual reality, as befits a treatise on music. The diagram is primarily concerned to demonstrate the music of the spheres, the universal harmony, and therefore the musical note which each planet plays is prominently displayed. Exactly eight celestial spheres are indicated to accommodate the octave, the diapason of musical notes. Moreover—and here we depart completely from physicality—each celestial sphere is further identified with one of the Muses, depicted in the circular vignettes on the left. To provide the necessary number of nine, Earth is identified with Thalia at the bottom. And reigning over all is Apollo at the top, attended by the three Graces and advertised by a banner which proclaims, "The power of the Apollonian mind completely controls these Muses." The intention is clear: each Muse, each note, each planet, though playing an individual part, contributes concordantly to a larger whole, represented in the single figure of Apollo. The concept thereby demonstrated is the ancient theme of unity in multeity. And although the components of the diagram begin in physical reality, they evolve into conceptual reality, so that the final statement is much more than a physical description of the universe. The diagram demonstrates that the consort of the Muses led by Apollo is immeasurably more beautiful than any single note or any harmonizing of single notes, just as infinity is immeasurably greater than any possible summation of finite parts.

Since the poet, by profession, was committed to an imitation of reality, he had to face the epistemological problem. And since a metaphor is an attempt to explain the unknown in terms of the known by means of a comparison, constructing a metaphor brings to crisis the epistemological decision. The metaphor-maker must decide on what is known, what can be taken for granted, what is actual. His metaphor must be grounded in a cosmology acceptable both to himself and to his reader.

To bring the intimate relationship between poetics and physics into focus—and this is the raison d'être of my discourse —I should like to examine a French encyclopedist's definition of metaphor in conjunction with an English physician's diagram of the universe. I shall juxtapose a passage in Pierre de la Primaudaye's *French Academie,* as R. Dolman translated it in 1601, with the title page of Robert Fludd's *Utriusque cosmi . . . historia,* printed at Oppenheim in 1617. The verbal statement by La Primaudaye is a perfect gloss for Fludd's diagram; or I could say that Fludd's diagram is a perfect illustration for La Primaudaye's statement. I am not suggesting that Fludd had La Primaudaye consciously in mind—in fact, I think that circumstance unlikely—but I am saying that each, by his own means, expressed the same renaissance commonplace.

First, I shall look at Fludd's title page, Figure 6, since we can easily see its continuity with the other diagrams that we have examined and can readily establish familiarity with it. The most striking feature of the engraving is the human figure with outstretched limbs, and the sphere which circumscribes him is the microcosm. Starting at the center, we have the four Elements, indicated by the four humours to which they correspond. Not labeled, though certainly intended, is *bilis* at the very center, correspondent to Earth; then *pituita,* or phlegm, correspondent to Water; then *sanguis,* correspondent to Air; and finally *cholera,* correspondent to Fire. Then come the seven spheres of the planets; and the outermost limit of the microcosm is a sphere of fixed stars which contains the constellations designating the twelve signs of the zodiac, each of which controls a part of the body. Encircling the microcosmos is a

depiction of the macrocosmos, attended by some obvious difficulty in the visual representation. First must come the four
Elements, and they are indicated by four spheres—but these
four spheres are unlabeled because the engraver could not
bring himself to situate the four Elements so far removed from
the geometric center of the diagram. Here physical reality is
interfering with the representation of conceptual reality. But
certainly those first four unlabeled spheres of the macrocosm
are intended for the four Elements. Then come seven spheres
for the planets and a final sphere of fixed stars, in exact correspondence to the microcosmos. Outside this is the empyrean,
depicted in an imaginative way to suggest its infinity; and in
the upper right, to suggest its eternality, a strange creature representing Time, winged and hoofed and with an hour-glass on
his head, pulls a rope which rotates the finite universe below
him. This strange emblem of Time is reminiscent of the angel
turning the primum mobile in Eck's diagram (Figure 4)—but
here he is mythological and pagan, rather than Christian; somehow renaissance, rather than medieval. Anyway, in Fludd's
engraving the infinite and eternal empyrean is rendered more
imaginatively than in Eck's woodcut.

But the comparison I wish to make is not between Fludd
and Eck, but rather between Fludd and La Primaudaye. I
have mimeographed for you the passage from *The French
Academie*, and ask that you note how aptly it applies to Fludd's
title page: "The learned and venerable antiquitie figureth, and
maketh the universall world (to be) one, and threefold. . . .
For there is the uppermost world of all, which Divines name,
the Angelicall, and philosophers call the intellectuall world:
which (as *Plato* saith) was never yet sufficiently praised. Then
is there the celestiall world, or that of the spheres, which suc-
ceedeth and is next the first: and the third and last is the ele-
mentarie world which we inhabite, under the concavitie of the
moone."[9] Both verbal statement and visual representation convey the same data, the same notion. In a nearby passage glossed
"The originall of allegorical sense," La Primaudaye then goes
on to state how these worlds are made one, are integrated into

a single system, by the perfect correspondences between their parts: "For even as the three worlds being girt and buckled with the bands of concord doe by reciprocall liberalitie, interchange their natures; the like doe they also by their appellations." And therefore one world can be used to explain another; it can serve as the known to explain the unknown, and thereby fulfill the role of metaphor. As La Primaudaye says, "And this is the principle from whence springeth and groweth the discipline of allegoricall sense."[10]

In yet another paragraph from the same section of his encyclopedia, La Primaudaye describes a fourth world, what Fludd's engraving had labeled the microcosmus, and asserts that the same correspondences are valid for the little world of man: "Moreover besides these worlds, which we have also distinguished, there is also another a fourth, wherein may likewise be found all that which subsisteth in the others. And this is (man). . . . it is a common use in schooles to teach, that man is a little world, and that within him the bodie is composed of the elements."[11] In renaissance thought the microcosm-macrocosm analogy was considered a truism, and that is why it turns up so frequently. But other cosmic correspondences were equally self-evident metaphors.

In fact, La Primaudaye's "Allegoricall sense"—what we have called metaphor—is not an arbitrary construct of a poet's mind, but rather the discovering of pre-existent correspondences. The poet by means of verbal statement makes manifest what a diagram may show by visual statement. For example, Figure 7, taken from an edition of Isidore of Seville's *De natura rerum* printed at Augsburg in 1472, is a tetrad arrangement of the four Elements comparable to Finé's in Figure 2. Not only the Elements are interrelated, however, but also the four seasons of the year and the four humours of the human body. We have the cosmoi not only of the physical world, *mundus,* but also of *annus* and of *homo,* of the year and of man. And the point of the diagram is the exact correspondence between these three cosmoi: Fire, for example, is correspondent to summer in the year and to choler in man, because each partakes of the basic qualities *siccus* and *calidus,* dry and hot. Such a concept is a veritable mine of poetic metaphors, and Spenser used them all in the December ecologue of *The Shepheardes Calender.* As E. K. summarized it in the Argument:

He proportioneth his life to the foure seasons of the yeare, comparing hys youthe to the spring time, when he was fresh and free from loves follye. His manhoode to the sommer, which he sayth, was consumed with greate heate and excessive drouth caused throughe a Comet or blasinge starre, by which hee meaneth love. . . . His riper yeares hee resembleth to an unseasonable harveste wherein the fruites fall ere they be rype. His latter age to winters chyll and frostie season, now drawing neare to his last ende.

The poet in his effort to express the truth, if we take Spenser as the prototype, does not fabricate a meaning by his own whim, but rather seeks to reveal the eternal relationships maintained by a Christian God or a pagan Nature. Reading the book of nature is the poet's first task, then, and interpreting its contents in a significant and pleasing manner is his aim. In this vein, Philip Sidney concluded: "Of all Sciences . . . is our Poet the Monarch."[12]

But after the poet has decided upon his truth and then turns to the business of expressing it, he still must make decisions. He may express himself consonant with either of the two ways that we have distinguished, in terms of physical reality or in terms of conceptual reality. And we have poetry of both sorts. As an example of metaphor in terms of physical reality, Marlowe gives a wholly sensual description of Hero's buskins. We not only see, but even hear, this footwear:

> Buskins of shells all silvered used she,
> And branch'd with blushing coral to the knee,
> Where sparrows perch'd, of hollow pearl and gold,
> Such as the world would wonder to behold;
> Those with sweet water oft her handmaid fills,
> Which, as she went, would cherup through the bills.
> *(Hero and Leander,* 31-36)

Although the metaphor is submerged, Marlowe is telling us something about Hero's natural beauty and potential fecundity by associating her with sea-creatures and sparrows. And he also says something about the artifice which she has used to enhance her native endowments: the shells are silvered, the sparrows are made of pearl and gold, and they chirrup by an artificial device. But the point I wish to make is that this comparison per se is between physical things only and stays on the physical plane. The unknown buskins are explained to us in terms of sea-animals and birds visually described. Physicality, of course, is the proper context for Marlowe's sex symbol.

Conversely, however, a poet may express himself wholly in terms of conceptual reality. As an example, in sharp contrast to Marlowe's lines is this opening of a poem by Walter Raleigh:

> Give me my scallop-shell of quiet,
> My staff of faith to walk upon,
> My scrip of joy, immortal diet,
> My bottle of salvation,
> My gown of glory, hope's true gage;
> And thus I'll take my pilgrimage.
> ("The Pilgrimage," 1-6)

There is almost no physical content in this passage, nothing for the senses to perceive. As the poet prepares to make a pilgrimage, he collects about him those necessities for the journey: peace of mind, faith, joy, hope of salvation, hope of glory. The scallop-shell has no physical qualities to make it an acceptable symbol of quiet; in fact, the roaring of a shell when held against the ear militates against the metaphor. But because the scallop-shell designated a pilgrim to St. James of Compostella, it suggested the notion of peace acquired through penance. Similarly for the other items—the scrip of joy, bottle of salvation, and gown of glory—they are not conveyed as physical entities. They are concepts. Only the staff of faith ventures into the realm of physicality; the staff is a symbol of faith because, conceptually, faith supports the pilgrim on his difficult journey to heaven, just as, physically, a staff supports a traveler on the highway. This last metaphor functions on both the physical and the conceptual planes, and, I think, is thereby the most expressive of the list.

For the most successful poetry is that which somehow combines and interfuses physical and conceptual reality, so that the poetic statement is relevant in either context. Only the most consummate poets have consistently managed this feat, and yet this is the distinctive mark of the greatest poetry—indeed, the special function of poetry, to show the interdependence of conceptual and physical, of ideal and real, of divine and mundane.

For examples of this supreme metaphor we turn, of course, to the supreme masters. First, I should like to consider a passage from Shakespeare, from Ulysses' famous argument in *Troilus and Cressida* for the necessity of order in the commonwealth. There the inclusive metaphor is a comparison between the ordered celestial spheres and the ranks of human society. As Ulysses asserts:

> The heavens themselves, the planets and this center,[13]
> Observe degree, priority, and place.
> (I, iii, 85-86)

He then goes on to define the responsibilities of the king, who should exercise the strongest authority in human society, in terms of the Sun, who holds the mid-most position as number four among the seven heavenly planets:

> And therefore is the glorious planet Sol
> In noble eminence enthroned and sphered
> Amidst the other, whose medicinable eye
> Corrects the ill aspects of planets evil,
> And posts like the commandment of a king,
> Sans check to good and bad.
> (I, iii, 89-94)

The king is like the Sun in his physical aspects of brilliance and power, and he sits in the midst of his courtiers as the Sun sits in the middle of the planets. But this comparison is effective also because of its conceptual significance, because the Sun represents the concepts of goodness, beauty, and truth in the

Platonic tradition, the concepts of divinity and providence in the Christian tradition, and the concept of beneficent cosmic control in the Aristotelian tradition. For Ulysses, the comparison of king to Sun explains the necessary but neglected social order in terms of the well-known relationships in the celestial realm. The microcosm of human society and the macrocosm of the celestial spheres are shown to be correspondent, interdependent.

I shall give one other example of metaphor which assimilates both physical and conceptual reality, this one Spenser's description of Lucifera's House of Pride in Book I of *The Faerie Queene*. Note how carefully Spenser builds up the image, as though he were constructing a visual representation, a diagram:

> A stately Pallace built of squared bricke,
>   Which cunningly was without morter laid,
>   Whose wals were high, but nothing strong, nor thick,
>   And golden foile all over them displaid,
>   That purest skye with brightnesse they dismaid:
>   High lifted up were many loftie towres,
>   And goodly galleries farre over laid,
>   Full of faire windowes, and delightfull bowres;
> And on the top a Diall told the timely howres.
>   (I, iv, 4, 1-9)

The basic comparison here is between pride and a false facade. The inherent flaws of pride, and consequently its deceptive appearance, are conveyed as physical description: the squared brick, but laid without mortar; the walls that are high, but not strong and thick; the golden foil, that glisters to the detriment of the pure sky; the towers that rise haughtily; and so on. The metaphor is fully realized as a physical image. But also the metaphor is fully realized as a concept. The mind goes behind the visual representation and perceives the concept of pride as false display.

Consequently, the passage has relevance to pride of the body or to pride of the spirit. In fact, with a bit of ingenuity we can trace the relevance of the poetic statement for each of the worlds that La Primaudaye and Fludd enumerated. The bricks and mortar place this palace firmly in the mundane region of the four Elements, and without a doubt it is an allegory of the human body, the microcosm, just as another castle, the House of Alma in Book II of *The Faerie Queene,* is a detailed account of the human body. This House of Lucifera is a negative example in Spenser's moral primer, just as the House of Alma is an exemplar of acceptable behavior. Next, the glistering foil and lofty towers threaten the supremacy and the order of the heavens; and the sun-dial in the last line which marks the passage of time, while an effective physical detail which adds to the concreteness of this diagram, also conveys the notion that all herein is subject to time, all herein is mortal. Pride is a universal fallacy that brings mutability, decay, death. Spenser here restates in his own terms the theme of man's fall as a universal principle. Finally, we must recall that Lucifer presides over these premises, a feminine Lucifer who personifies cosmic pride. Though now fallen, Lucifera once resided in the empyrean. Pride has wrought havoc even in the highest heaven. We have, then, the flaws of pride revealed as an omnipresent threat that lurks in the microcosm of the human body, in the macrocosm of God's created world, and even in the pure spirit of the suprasensible empyrean. This metaphor amply reveals the correspondences between the various portions of our universe.

To conclude, the doctrine of metaphor as cosmic correspondence depends upon an orthodox view that our world is made up of separate but interrelated parts—that it is a *uni*verse. Moreover, it depends upon the assumption that each of these parts in its interior organization is analogous to each of the other parts, that a single pattern of order subsists throughout all levels of creation. In such a self-contained and co-ordinated arrangement, the poet could readily find a comparison by which to explain the unknown. Metaphors lay in great abundance ready to everyone's hand, and the poet's particular talent was to discover them, his particular task to reveal them. When the notion of *uni*verse broke down, however, when the new scientists displaced the four Elements from the center of our world and removed its finite boundaries, the poet could no longer rely upon natural metaphors; he no longer had a ready-made supply of incontrovertible comparisons. He then had to contrive his own comparisons, and a known by which to explain an unknown was hard to come by. This change in epistemology, I believe, is the best way to define the phenomenon commonly known as metaphysical poetry. It was this carelessness with metaphor that prompted Dr. Johnson's strongest censure of the metaphysical poets: "Their thoughts are often new, but seldom natural. . . . The most heterogeneous ideas are yoked by violence together."[14] Uncertainty about ultimate reality has become increasingly manifest in poetry since the renaissance.

But that is another tale, and I shall save it for another occasion.

NOTES

1. *An Apologie for Poetrie* (London, 1595), in *Elizabethan Critical Essays,* ed. G. Gregory Smith (2 vols.; Oxford, 1904), I, 161.

2. For a contemporary version of this theme, cf. William Webbe:

> They [the ancients] supposed all wisdome and knowledge to be included mystically in that divine instinction wherewith they thought their *Vates* to be inspyred. . . . And *Cicero* in his *Tusculane* questions [I, xxvi] is of that minde, that a Poet cannot expresse verses aboundantly, sufficiently, and fully, neither his eloquence can flowe pleasauntly, or his wordes sounde well and plenteously, without celestiall instinction: which Poets themselves doo very often and gladlie witnes of themselves, as namely *Ovid* in 6. *Fasto: Est deus in nobis; agitante calescimus illo,* etc. [VI, 5] (*A Discourse of English Poetrie* [1586], in *Elizabethan Critical Essays,* I, 231-32).

And then Webbe makes a reference to Spenser's *Shepheardes Calender,* where the line from Ovid is used as the emblem for the October eclogue.

3. For a contemporary version of this theme, cf. Philip Sidney: "There is no Arte delivered to mankinde that hath not the workes of Nature for his principall object, without which they could not consist." Then Sidney lists the various arts and suggests how they expound nature. He continues:

> Onely the Poet, disdayning to be tied to any such subjection, lifted up with the vigor of his owne invention, dooth growe in effect another nature, in making things either better then Nature bringeth forth, or, quite a newe, formes such as never were in Nature (*Apologie for Poetrie,* in *Eliz. Critical Essays,* I, 155-56).

4. Ed. Gladys D. Willcock and Alice Walker (Cambridge University Press, 1936), p. 3. For a discussion of Fracastoro's handling of the problem, see J. E. Spingarn, *A History of Literary Criticism in the Renaissance* (2nd ed.; Columbia University Press, 1908), pp. 31-34.

5. Cf. Sidney, in *Eliz. Critical Essays,* I, 152.

6. *Arte of English Poesie,* p. 9. Notice the tell-tale vocabulary: "generable and corruptible," which is Aristotelian, and "divine essences," which is Platonic.

7. *Eliz. Critical Essays,* I, 163 ff.

8. It might be tempting to correlate these two views of reality with the two themes in criticism that I defined earlier. Because of the historical development of Platonism and Aristotelianism, however, this could be misleading—indeed, could even suggest a correlation that is exactly reversed. One might expect the spiritual view to be associated with Platonism, and the material view with Aristotelianism. But if anything, the opposite is the case. Because of its assimilation into scholasticism, Aristotelianism with its logic and analysis would more likely suggest a tendency toward conceptual reality. Whereas Platonism, with its interest in numbers, became the justification for scientific examination of physical reality. This latter development is extremely complex; but because of its interest, I shall briefly sketch the major trend. Platonism had absorbed Pythagoreanism—vide the *Timaeus*—which held that number was not only the organizing principle, but also the substance of reality. Qualities were expressed as integers, and relationships between things were numerical ratios. These numbers, in the beginning, were considered to be abstractions, comparable to Platonic essences. But in the renaissance, as the new science rejected the Aristotelianism of the schools, the Pythagorean concept of number was resurrected as justification for measurement, for a system of knowledge built upon quantities rather than qualities. This was the impetus for a science derived primarily from observation and experiment.

9. *The Third Volume of the French Academie* (London, 1601), p. 64.

10. The remainder of La Primaudaye's paragraph, though too long to read aloud, is well worth quoting in a note:

> For it is certaine that the ancient fathers could not conveniently have represented one thing by other figures, but that they had first learned the secret amitie and affinitie of all nature. Otherwise there could be no reason, why they should represent this thing by this forme, and that by that, rather then otherwise. But having the knowledge of the universall world, and of every part thereof, and being inspired with the same spirit, that not onely knoweth all things, but did also make all things: they have oftentimes, and very fitly figured the natures of the one world, by that which they knew to be correspondent thereto in the others. Wherefore the same knowledge, and the grace of the same spirit is requisite for those, who would understand, and directly interpret such significations and allegoricall meanings (*ibid.*, p. 67).

11. *Ibid.*, p. 68.

12. *Eliz. Critical Essays*, I, 172.

13. I.e., our planet, earth.

14. In the essay on Cowley, quoted here from *The Works of Samuel Johnson*, ed. Arthur Murray (12 vols.; London, 1816), IX, 20.

II

The Treaties of the Carolingians

François L. Ganshof
Professor Emeritus, University of Ghent, Belgium

I intend to investigate how the Carolingians managed to conclude their treaties. Let us first of all start with a definition.
I think we can give the word treaty the following one: an agreement between states, peoples, tribes, or rulers.

The treaties about which we will be concerned were concluded by the rulers of the *Regnum Francorum,* belonging to
the Carolingian dynasty, between 751 and 887.[1] They were
very numerous. To study them, we have but few immediate
sources at our disposal: some full texts and a few fragments of
agreements concluded between Carolingian rulers, after the
death of Louis the Pious in 840, when the unity of the Frankish
monarchy had ceased to exist. With the exception of these
documents, we can only have recourse to narrative sources,
especially to the so-called Royal Annals, to the Annals of Saint-
Bertin, the Annals of Fulda, the Annals of Xanten, the Annals
of Saint-Vaast,[2] and also, in a lesser extent, to the *Vita Karoli*
of Einhard and the biographies of Louis the Pious by Thegan
and by the so-called "Astronomer" as well as to the *Historiae*
of Nithard.[3] Such information as can be gathered from these
narratives is occasionally inaccurate and often inexplicit.

Let us begin by setting apart a certain number of treaties
which were basically nothing more than simple acts of submission pronounced vocally to a victor, this not having been
preceded by any negotiations worth mentioning.

We naturally know several of these for the Saxons; when
vanquished by Charlemagne,[4] one or the other fraction of this
population submitted to the king of the Franks. The chieftains

of these tribes promised to be faithful and to submit, and sometimes bound themselves to pay tribute, even reinforcing their
promises by an oath; they delivered hostages which fully se-
cured their submission.[5] As their promises nevertheless were
often transgressed, it happened that the hostages were abandoned to the conqueror.[6] The act of submission itself might
have been expressed by a gesture of the hands.[7]

A great number of such acts of submission to Charlemagne
or to Louis the Pious and more often to their successors, the
kings of *Francia Orientalis,* were accomplished in the name
of Slav populations by their chieftains. These acts were regu·
larly followed by new upheavals and these again by renewed
submissions—the mention of which in the sources is repeated
with tedious regularity. As to the main features of these acts of
submission, they are generally the same as those of the Saxon
tribes.[8] It may be noted that for the chieftains of certain Slav
populations, a gesture of the right hand appears also to have
meant submission; maybe in expectation of a parallel gesture
by the victor attesting the restoration of peace.[9] Vassalage having found its way from *Francia Orientalis* to the neighboring
Slav populations, toward the end of the period considered here,
Moravian and Slovenian chieftains confirmed the re-establishment of their subjection—indeed purely formal—by becoming
vassals of the Germanic king.[10]

The Avar chieftains also accomplished similar acts of submission.[11] These seem to present distinctive features similar to
those of the Slavs.[12]

In the northwest of the *Regnum Francorum,* the Breton
chieftains have rendered their submission in a way not very
different from what we have met so far. They had rebelled
against the Carolingian monarchs whose subjects they theoretically were, but Frankish military operations had suppressed the
rebellions successfully. The surrender of the Breton chieftains
was expressed by a gesture of the hands[13] accompanied by oaths
and by the delivery of hostages.[14] No other features may be de-
tected before about 846.[15]

Things were no different with the Basques or Gascons, the inhabitants of sub-Pyrenean and Pyrenean regions.[16]

The acts of submission which have just been mentioned created, confirmed, or modified legal connections between the Carolingian monarchs on the one hand and non-Frankish peoples, tribes, or rulers on the other. On this ground it is necessary to recall them. However, these were one-sided acts, accomplished by the representatives of these peoples, these tribes, these rulers. The Carolingian monarchs only accepted these unilateral acts of submission and occasionally drew as a consequence of them the restoration of peace. These acts were not agreements and therefore cannot be considered as regular treaties.

We will at present pass on to genuine treaties, in which both parties, namely a Carolingian ruler and another party, pledged themselves to one another to perform definite engagements. I believe that among these treaties one should distinguish agreements of various kinds.

First, there are those treaties concluded by the Carolingians with states, peoples, tribes, or rulers, either foreign or imperfectly submitted to Frankish authority. Among these contracting parties, some made use of writing for acts of this kind, whereas others did not.

The following group of treaties are those to which we have already pointed: they were concluded between Carolingian rulers; here we must draw a line between the agreements resulting in a partition and the others.

Finally, we have the agreements concluded between Carolingian rulers and the Norman pirates, later the Norman invaders, or, in other terms, with the Vikings.

The main features peculiar to these various types of agreements compel me to choose one treaty or in certain cases two treaties to illustrate each one of these groups occasionally, as necessary, referring to other treaties of the same type. I mean to keep to this plan except as to what concerns the treaties with the Vikings.

[25]

I will begin with the treaties concluded by the Carolingians with states, peoples, tribes, or rulers using little or no writing. Here we meet with the Danes.[17] Denmark was then a rather incoherent kingdom; supreme power was contested by various families, backed themselves by their own dependents.[18] Charlemagne wisely held aloof from those disputes and civil wars, whereas Louis the Pious was imprudent enough to allow himself to be mixed up with them. However, since the time of Charlemagne, conflicts with the Frankish realm had been caused by incidents along the border in the south of Jutland, where the Danish territory bordered on Saxony which had been conquered by the Franks. Denmark was also a close neighbor to the country of the Abodrites, a Slav population, then a faithful ally of the Carolingian emperor. There were also raids of the Danish fleets against Frisia for which Charlemagne and his successors, rightly or wrongly, held the kings to be responsible.

More than once, in the time of Charlemagne and of Louis the Pious, the Danish kings took the initiative in negotiations that resulted in agreements which were supposed to create a state of lasting peace; however, new incidents never failed to occur. A stroke of luck has given us better information about the treaty of 811 than what we know about the others. This is the one we will now consider.

The new king of Denmark, Hemming, was desirous to put a stop to the tenseness of relations which had existed between his uncle and predecessor Godfried and the Emperor Charlemagne.[19] As early as 810 he declared his peaceful intentions; a Danish envoy and Charlemagne agreed to conclude peace. However, the final conclusion was to take place on the border. It was a hard winter which made all ways of approach impassable. There was all the same a meeting involving perhaps one or two envoys of each party who concluded a truce until springtime. They reinforced their engagements by an oath of a peculiar kind. It was not a solemn oath, but rather one that was sworn on their weapons, in this case, I suppose, on the sword.[20]

When spring had made the roads less difficult, the negotiations took place on the border, at the river Eider. Each party was represented by twelve men of high rank; the names of most of them are known to us. On the Frankish side they were counts, members of the Empire's high aristocracy (*Reichsaristokratie*), led by count Wala, a cousin of the emperor and at that time his trusted advisor; among the Danish *primores,* there were two brothers of the king. Negotiations took place no doubt about boundaries, lines of communication, and various incidents, and peace was concluded: *pax confirmatur.* No text tells us how. Nevertheless, we know that oaths were taken which gave more force to the reciprocal promises; the representatives of each party pledged their honor according to their own peculiar rules:[21] the Danes were pagan; the Franks evidently had to swear on a *res sacra,* a relic, a Gospel-book, etc.; no other oath would have been considered valid.

It appears likely that Charlemagne, in the course of the next sitting of the diet—the Empire's general assembly—held at Aachen, made a statement corroborating the peace which had been settled. In November, near Aachen, the emperor received an embassy from Hemming bringing him presents and "making declarations of peace" (*verba pacifica*).[22] That was also a kind of ratification.

A written text seems to have been entirely absent. We may however admit that a brief note about the facts, a *notitia,* deprived of any legal authority, was written down on the Frankish side; the writer of the Royal Annals has probably made use of such a document.

In 804 and in 809, similar negotiations at the frontier had been planned and even undertaken; they had not led to any positive results.[23] There were others again under Charlemagne in 813,[24] and under Louis the Pious in 825.[25] In both cases the occasion was the accession to power of new kings in Denmark; as a result of those negotiations, peace was confirmed again in a sworn statement. The agreement of 825 seems to have been confirmed by both parties at the diet held at Ingelheim in 826. In the meantime, there had been in 814, in 815, in 817, and in 822 several attempts to negotiate on the part of various Danish kings who were fighting one another. Louis

[27]

the Pious took no heed of them with the exception of Heriold who became converted to Christianity and was the most unfortunate of all the pretenders.[26]

In 828, negotiations on the frontier took place again between the delegates of the Danish kings and those of the emperor. Although hostages had been exchanged so as to insure the safety of the representatives of both parties, a violent incident created by the Danish pretender Heriold put an end to the meeting. In spite of the excuses presented by the kings of Denmark[27] there was once again a state of tension.

When negotiations were resumed once more, they seem to have given up the meetings on the border. It was at Thionville, on the Moselle, in 831, and at Chalon-sur-Saône in 839, each time in the frame of an assembly, that Louis the Pious received embassies of the Danish rulers and that the agreements of peace were renewed; in 839, envoys of the Frankish emperor even proceeded later on to the court of Horick the Danish king in order to receive or most likely to exchange oaths that were meant to confirm the agreements and to insure an everlasting peace.[28] Much later, in 873, it was at Burstädt, near Worms, on the Rhine, that the envoys of the Danish king Sigfried concluded an agreement with Louis the German and it was at Metz, on the Moselle, that the envoys of Halbdeni, Sigfried's brother, did the same. Those agreements aimed at guaranteeing their respective frontiers and at insuring freedom of trade and free traffic to the merchants of both realms. The representatives of the Danish kings swore on their swords that the kings would never show themselves hostile to Louis the German, and they begged him to adopt their lords as his sons. It was decided that delegates of both parties should meet on the Eider, which still was the border between the Danish and the Frankish kingdoms, and that they should confirm the treaty and settle the boundaries on the spot. And so things were done.[29]

The Carolingian kings had also concluded treaties with Danish chieftains, who, after having lived as Vikings, had managed to settle in a more or less remote corner of the *Regnum Francorum* and to act there as lords. So did Rorik who governed an important part of Frisia since 850. He submitted to Lothair I and II, but we do not know under what circumstances nor how things happened.[30]

Let us now turn to the treaties of the Carolingians with states, populations, or rulers to whom the use of writing was common practice.

We have thought it best not to include here a study on treaties between the Carolingians and the Holy See. The magnitude of the subject and the peculiar characteristics of the negotiations undertaken and of the agreements concluded have led us to keep this research in store for another publication.

We will also set aside, but only for a short time, the other great powers, namely Byzantium, the Caliphate of Bagdad, and the emirate of Cordova.

We encounter a certain number of treaties concluded by Pepin III with the duke of Aquitaine[31] or with the king of the Lombards,[32] by Charlemagne with the duke of Bavaria,[33] by Charlemagne, Louis the Pious, and Lothair I with the Lombard dukes of Benevento,[34] by Charlemagne and Louis the Pious with local potentates of Moslem Spain,[35] and by Charles the Bald with Breton chieftains.[36] For the king of the Lombards it is known that there was a written document,[37] for the dukes of Benevento it is almost certain, considering the importance of written texts in their form of government.[38] In all other cases the standard of civilization allows a conjecture, but no more.

The agreements concluded by the Carolingians with these peoples or with their rulers had mostly been preceded by negotiations, which often did put an end to a conflict. As a rule those agreements were reinforced by oaths[39] confirming obligations of faithfulness or of nonaggression toward the Carolingians. Hostages were very frequently promised and delivered to them[40] and it happened that tributes had to be paid to them.[41] In the case of the duke of Bavaria, Tassilo III, and in the case of the Breton chieftains after 846, the co-contractors of the Carolingian monarchs were obliged to become their vassals or to renew the bonds of vassalage if they already existed, but had been violated.[42]

The treaties with Byzantium, with the emir of Cordova, or indeed even with the Caliph of Bagdad deserve to be studied more thoroughly.

It is known that in Byzantium, the imperial coronation of Charlemagne had been considered a usurpation which had created tension in their relations.[43] Nevertheless, contacts were established. In 802, the Empress Irene sent an ambassador entrusted to endeavor to conclude peace with Charlemagne whereas the Frankish emperor in his turn sent an embassy to Constantinople with the same purpose.[44] The Basileus Nikephoros who had dethroned Irene and succeeded her received the embassy and in return sent one to the western monarch. In 803, Charlemagne delivered to those Byzantine ambassadors before they left him, a written scheme of a treaty meant to secure peace, as well as a personal letter; both documents were intended to be submitted to the Basileus Nikephoros.[45]

We know nothing of their contents, but it is very likely that the scheme of a treaty implied the acknowledgement of the fact that henceforth two Roman empires[46] coexisted. That was asking too much from the sole legitimate emperor, that of Byzantium. He gave no answer and tension grew into an armed conflict.[47] Nikephoros, who had a very difficult time in the East, gave way under the Frankish pressure[48] and, in 810, he sent the "spatarios" Arsafios to carry messages, both written and verbal, to Pippin, King of Italy and son of the Western Emperor. Pippin being deceased, it was his father who received Arsafios at Aachen.[49] In a letter to the Emperor Nikephoros that has been preserved, Charlemagne declared that the messages of the Basileus were agreeable to him because they were inspired by the wish to conclude a lasting peace. He added that they were in accordance with what he himself had expected and wished for since the dispatch of his letter of 803. We are ignorant of the exact contents of these messages but they provided the possibility of peace.[50]

What occurred was a preliminary and temporary agreement

on principles, between the opposing parties, just as we have seen one concluded in 810 between Charlemagne and the King of Denmark. There are other examples of this way of acting.

The preliminary agreement must have dealt with the recognition of the imperial title and with the surrender by the Frankish emperor of those territories which he had occupied in Venetia.[51] At the beginning of 811 Arsafios was able to regain Constantinople. Charlemagne, in his turn, also sent three ambassadors, Haito, bishop of Basel, Hugh, count of Tours, and the Lombard Aio, bearers of the above mentioned letter for the Basileus.[52] Charlemagne knew now what should appear in the treaty and his ambassadors could give Nikephoros all necessary information and the guarantees which he needed to play his part in the conclusion of peace.

In 812, the Frankish ambassadors returned from Constantinople, accompanied by three Byzantine ambassadors, Michel, Metropolitan of Philadelphia, the "protospatarios" Arsafios, and the "protospatarios" Theognostos, appointed by Michel I Rangabé, son and successor of Nikephoros.[53]

With their arrival in Aachen the final phase of the conclusion of the treaty began.[54] Its first act took place in the still existing glorious Palatine Chapel. After the ambassadors of the Basileus had made their offering of presents to Charlemagne,[55] they received from him the authentic copy of the treaty (*scriptum pacti, foederis* or *pacti conscriptio, pacti descriptio*) intended for their master,[56] after it had previously been deposited on the high altar.[57] We are ignorant of its form, except for one point: it had been subscribed by the emperor (by a stroke in the monogram); it also bore the subscriptions of bishops and high placed laymen.[58] We are also ignorant of the contents of this copy of the treaty; but certain indications allow us to believe that Charlemagne acknowledged the fact that there were henceforth an oriental empire and an occidental empire in peace with one another and that he pledged himself not to contest the authority of the Basileus concerning territories subject to him.[59] There may even have been a disposition explicitly pertaining to Venetia which the Western emperor renounced on condition that a tribute should be paid to him.[60]

We may admit that this engagement was necessary for the Byzantine ambassadors to recognize, in the name of the Basileus, Charlemagne as an emperor. They did so—in accordance with the rites in use at Byzantium—pronouncing in the honor of Charlemagne, in the Greek language, the "lauds" in which he was given the titles "imperator" and "basileus" (ἰμπεράτωρ and βασιλεύς).[61]

It is possible that both parties confirmed their engagements by an oath or that they got their agreement confirmed in that way by a proxy; this however is doubtful.[62]

Other points concerning both parties may also, on that occasion, have been subject to a settlement,[63] after which the Byzantine ambassadors proceeded on their way home. Passing through Rome, they received, in St. Peters Church, very likely from the hands of Pope Leo III, a second copy of the treaty bearing his subscription.[64]

Although the performance of this ceremony had been a legal act of capital importance and although it had constituted an essential element toward the re-establishment of peace, it did not constitute the final conclusion of the treaty.

For this treaty to be perfectly concluded, one thing was still missing: the delivery to Charlemagne of the *foederis conscriptio,* of the *pacti descriptio,* that means the authentic copy of the treaty which was intended for him. In the spring of 813, Charlemagne addressed an embassy to Michel I. It was composed of Amalarius, Bishop of Trier, and of Peter, Abbot of Nonantola.[65] They were bearers of a letter from the occidental emperor to the oriental emperor, which we possess; in this exceptional occasion, the words *Romanum gubernans imperium* had been omitted in the imperial title so as not to hurt the feelings of the Basileus.[66] Charlemagne expressed his satisfaction about the re-sults obtained; but he asked that, according to an agreement (*convenientia*) he had made with the Byzantine ambassadors, a copy of the treaty, set up for his sake and drafted in Greek, bearing the subscription of the emperor, of members of the high clergy, of patricians and other personalities of high rank, be previously deposited on the altar and then presented by the Basileus to his ambassadors.[67]

One will notice the strict parallelism between the ceremonial of the delivery in Aachen and in Constantinople and between the form of both instruments.[68] The content of the copy given to the Frankish ambassadors could not be identical, but it had to be parallel to that of the copy given to the Byzantine ambassadors. Each of both copies had indeed to include that which would interest its addressee, that is to say engagements taken toward himself by his contracting partner.

The wish expressed by Charlemagne was of course granted. However, Byzantine ambassadors, the "spatarios" Christopher and the deacon Gregory, accompanied the Frankish ambassadors on their return journey; it is to Louis the Pious, who had just succeeded his father, that they handed over the *descriptio et confirmatio pacti et foederis* which the new oriental emperor, Leo V, the Armenian, addressed to him.[69] It was the final act which created the treaty: henceforth there was a *foedus firmissimum* between the Carolingian and the Byzantine emperors.

Subsequently, in 814 and 815, Louis the Pious and Leo V again exchanged acts of confirmation of the treaty as well as declarations of friendship. In 824 and in 827, Michel II sent embassies to Louis the Pious to confirm the treaty, but although they were well received, there is no trace of an exchange of documents.[70] In 839, ambassadors of the Emperor Theophilos brought to Louis the Pious presents and a letter from their master confirming the treaty and assuring the western emperor of his friendship; the letter of Louis which they brought back to Constantinople must have contained a parallel confirmation and parallel assurances.[71] These successive confirmations do not imply that the treaty of 812-14 would have had only a temporary authority: confirmations were supplementary guarantees which at that time one thought it useful to take and to renew.

After the treaties concluded with Byzantium, we must say

a few words about the treaties concluded with the Omayades, emirs of Cordova, the supreme authority in Moslem Spain.[72]

Part of the northeast of Spain, with the important city of Barcelona, had been conquered by the armies of Charlemagne.[73] During his reign and the reign of his successors, military expeditions ordered by the Emir of Cordova tried vainly to get these territories back again into Moslem Spain. But there were also truces and attempts to conclude peace. In 810, Charlemagne received an embassy from the Emir al-Hakam I and, following a proceeding which we have seen applied before, they most likely concluded a preliminary agreement on fundamental questions.[74] In 812, at Aachen, after negotiations with a new embassy of Cordova, this time the parties concluded a truce of three years.[75]

In 815, Louis the Pious refused to renew it, probably after a raid directed by a cousin of the Emir against the so-called "marca hispanica."[76] In 817, Abd al-Rahman, in the name of his father the Emir al-Hakam I, sent a new embassy which seems to have been equally unsuccessful: the Moslem ambassadors, received by the emperor at Compiègne, had to wait during three months in Aachen for a decision of Louis the Pious, and then they simply were dismissed.[77] Abd al-Rahman II, when himself Emir of Cordova, tried once more to establish lasting peace by a treaty with his neighbors of *Francia Occidentalis:* ambassadors, charged with this mission (*pacis petendae foederisque firmandi gratia*) were received with honor by Charles the Bald in Reims in 847 and dismissed with equal honors however without, as it appears, any understanding having been found possible.[78]

Sixteen years later, matters changed. Charles the Bald, in the autumn of the year 863, received at Verberie, on the Oise, an ambassador of the Emir Muhammad I, bringing presents to him, as well as a most friendly letter, proposing the conclusion of a treaty of peace. He was welcomed with benevolence and invited to reside in Senlis at the expense of the Treasury. Charles the Bald received him with great honors in an audience granted when he took leave, at Compiègne on the 1st of July,

864. He offered him presents and Frankish ambassadors were to accompany him and offer presents to his master.[79] Most probably they also were commissioned to present the Emir with a copy intended for him of an agreement concluded with his ambassador, or to negotiate and, if possible, to make a treaty with the Emir himself. It seems, in fact, that one should admit that either at Compiègne or at Cordova some sort of agreement was reached as to a long truce or to a pact of nonaggression.[80]

The Frankish ambassadors did not come back from Cordova to Compiègne until the autumn of 865, bringing, on behalf of the Emir, magnificent gifts for Charles the Bald: there were camels loaded with beds and tents, precious pieces of cloth and of silk, and rich perfumes.[81] The importance of the gifts makes it most likely that the ambassadors also were able to hand the king a copy personally dedicated to him of the treaty between himself and the ruler of Moslem Spain.

It is well known that Charlemagne, like his father Pepin III, kept up relations with the Abbassid Caliph of Bagdad. On several occasions he sent embassies to the great Harun al-Rasjid, and they negotiated with him; Charlemagne himself received ambassadors coming from Bagdad. The purpose of these negotiations, or at least one of the purposes, was the state of the Christians of Palestine, of their monasteries, hospitals, or other foundations and of the pilgrims on their way to the Holy Land.[82] These negotiations appear to have been effective; but nothing proves that they resulted in the conclusion of a treaty. Most probably, in 807, after such negotiations had been carried on in an atmosphere of good will, the Caliph had the courteousness to give the Holy Sepulchre to the Western Emperor—a donation which was well understood to be purely honorary.[83] The texts do not allow us to believe that this was anything more than a gracious unilateral deed of the Moslem monarch: we find no element suggesting that an agreement on the subject may have been reached.[84]

The same thing happened again when Charlemagne endeavored to appease the Moslem potentates of Northern Africa with respect to the Christians of these regions and probably also the traveling pilgrims. Perhaps no treaty was concluded, but some results were reached.[85]

In 831, at Thionville, negotiations led by an embassy of the Caliph of Bagdad, Abdallah al-Mamun, with Louis the Pious appear to have succeeded; they ended indeed in the concluding of a treaty creating or restoring peaceful relations.[86]

We know nothing about the way in which treaties with the Caliph of Bagdad or the North African emirs may have been concluded.

We can now pass on to agreements concluded between Frankish emperors and kings, heads of states which were in fact independent since the death of the Emperor Louis the Pious in 840. The series opens with the alliance concluded by his two younger sons, Louis the German and Charles the Bald as well as by their armies, against their eldest brother, the Emperor Lothair I, at Strasbourg in 842.[87] Agreements of that kind became more numerous and took a number of characteristic features, as the result of conferences which the Frankish emperor and kings held together from time to time, after 844.[88]

Those *conloquia* or *conventus* were meant to maintain or to restore between the brothers (Lothair I, Louis the German, and Charles the Bald) the bonds of brotherhood and affection (*fraternitatis et caritatis iura*);[89] later on the sons of Lothair— the emperor Louis II, Lothair II, and Charles—the sons of Louis the German—Carloman, Louis the Younger, Charles— and the son and grandsons of Charles the Bald—Louis the Stammerer, Louis III, and Carloman—were parties in similar meetings and in the agreements which followed them.[90] One may maintain that after the invasion of *Francia Occidentalis* by Louis the German in 858, the rule of brotherhood (*fraternitas*) had ended. The subsequent assemblies and agreements had a different spirit.

The agreements which we are now considering had been prepared by representatives of the aristocracy as well as by the rulers and their nearest advisers, some agreements even being submitted to the approval of the *populus,* which means in fact a greater number of members of the aristocracy, present and under arms. The result is that most of these agreements of which part or the whole of the text has been preserved differ appreciably in their structure from the agreements with foreign powers. However, as the contracting parties were the Frankish rulers, we have to include these treaties in our study.

The treaty which I have chosen as an example is the second treaty of Meersen, concluded in that Carolingian "palace," near Maastricht, on the Meuse, by Lothair I, Louis the German, and Charles the Bald in 851.[91] The text has been preserved, but without the protocol. However we have an introduction to the text *(inscriptio)* which I believe to be old and perhaps contemporary. It says, and the text of the agreement confirms it, that the kings have drawn up these arrangements after having consulted the important ecclesiastics and high placed laymen, and that they pledged themselves to maintain these arrangements between themselves and toward their *fideles,* that is in fact toward the aristocracies of the different kingdoms.[92] This is confirmed by the *Annales Bertiniani.*[93]

The proper text consists in eight articles.[94] The first five include the arrangements which the contracting partners promise to observe towards one another: renunciation of all hostile actions; to abstain from all intrigues and conspiracies; reciprocal aid *et consilio et auxilio;*[95] precautions and, in case of need, action against the "errants" guilty of reprehensible acts; collective action against criminals, excommunicated people, culprits of kidnapping or incest, originating from one of these kingdoms and refugees in another. The next three articles contain arrangements that the three rulers have agreed to promulgate. And so in that capacity they are integral parts of the agreement. But they might just as well have appeared in capitularies if these rulers had published any. These articles were inserted in the interest of the Church or of the secular aristocracy and they were very likely inspired by the "great" ecclesiastics or laymen who took part in the deliberations. They concern the respect which the rulers owe to the rights of their *fideles,* and the assistance due by these to their ruler *vero*

[37]

consilio et sincero auxilio; the respect for the decisions and the interests of the Church; the measures to be taken against those who wilfully will be ignorant of those dispositions or who will fight them. The authentic copies of the act containing these articles bore the subscriptions of the emperor and of the two kings in the form of monograms.[96]

Emperor and kings proceeded later to the notification of the *populus* as to what they had decided with the advice and consent of their *fideles*. Each one set about it using his own personal formula for his *adnuntiatio*.[97] Lothair, with little else, was content to proclaim the unanimity of the three brothers. Louis and Charles promised to maintain in the future this unanimity, as well as the promises they had made; Charles alone explicitly notified his audience of one disposition: that which concerned the rights of the *fideles* and the assistance due by them to the king; it was for his *fideles* and for himself that this had the greatest importance.[98]

All treaties concluded between Carolingians from 842 to 880 have many common features. However neither before, nor during, nor after the regime of the *fraternitas* have they been prepared exactly in the same way, had exactly the same form, or comprised exactly the same elements. It has happened for instance that before the negotiations proper took place, preliminary negotiations were led by itinerant envoys (*missi discurrentes*).[99] Some treaties were emphasized with oaths.[100] Nearly all of them have *adnuntiationes*. Some of these are rather lengthy; in one case it is said that they had been pronounced in vernacular, which probably has happened more than once; in two cases the word *adnuntiatio* has been omitted.[101] At the *conventus* of Koblenz in 860 the engagements of the emperor and the kings were guaranteed by important ecclesiastics and by lay *optimates* of the three "dominations."[102] I merely point out such differences.

On the other hand, I wish to draw attention to the peculiar features proper to those treaties which produced a partition; the most important, but not the only ones were the treaty of Verdun in 843 and the treaty of Meersen in 870;[103] whereas the first divided the whole empire, the second divided the kingdom of Lothair II, roughly between the Rhine on the East, the Scheldt and the middle course of the Meuse on the West. In both cases and after many conflicts, discussions, and negotiations, the immediate result was a *descriptio,* that is to say in this case a statement of the abbeys, chapters, counties, and royal estates which existed in the territories to be divided.[104] It was indeed important that each party interested in the partition receive an equivalent share of these elements so as to assure him personal revenues of similar importance and possibilities to reward his followers with more or less equivalent values.

It is on the bases of such *descriptiones* that Lothair, Louis the German, and Charles the Bald in 843, Louis the German and Charles the Bald in 870 proceeded to divide the territories over which they had disputed. The text of the treaty of Verdun has not been preserved; as to the treaty of Meersen, we have only the fraction of the statute containing the composition of the two lots.[105]

The three brothers who had in 843 concluded the treaty of Verdun confirmed their engagements by oaths. The sources do not allow us to assert that the same formalities were observed for the treaty of Meersen; indeed, the parties had already pledged themselves under oath to proceed to the partition.[106]

We now have to say a few words about agreements concluded by some Carolingian rulers with the Normans who devastated *Francia Occidentalis* and later *Lotharingia.*[107] These agreements were entirely different from the treaties which were concluded with the kings of Denmark;[108] the Norman adventurers were independent of the kings, at least in fact. The most important of these agreements were concluded in 845, in 866, and in 877, by King Charles the Bald and in 886 by the Emperor Charles the Fat; they bought, at a very high price, the Normans' departure from certain parts of *Francia Occidentalis.*[109] Perhaps[110] there were similar cases of buying them off in 853 and in 882.[111] In 877 and 884, high personalities of the kingdom[112] operated a similar buying off.

Only twice could Charles the Bald conclude with the Normans treaties of another kind: in 860 and 861, he engaged as his mercenaries at a very high price the Normans who were infesting the basin of the Somme, so that they should fight other Normans fixed in the islands of the Seine. In 873, thanks to a military success, Charles the Bald compelled the Normans, besieged in Angers, to evacuate their position.[113] In 862, Robert the Strong, Count of Anjou, had been able to enlist Normans, who had just left the Seine, in order to fight as his allies against Solomon, Duke of Brittany.[114]

In Lotharingia, Lothair II, in 864, engaged a Norman band as mercenaries at a great cost; in 882, the Emperor Charles the Fat paid a heavy sum for the withdrawal of the "Great Norman Army" from the entrenched camp of Asselt on the Meuse.[115]

Little is known about the way these treaties were concluded and especially about the form in which the parties committed themselves to it. But we do know that a considerable amount of precious metal, as a rule silver, had to be paid to the invaders within a fixed period; we quote a series of examples: 7,000 pounds of silver in 845, 3,000 and 5,000 pounds of silver in 860-61, 6,000 pounds of silver in 862,[116] 4,000 pounds of silver in 866, 5,000 pounds of silver in 877, more than 2,000 pounds of silver in 882,[117] 12,000 pounds of silver in 884, and 700 pounds of silver in 886. In 860 and in 877, it was specified how the weighing must be done, and, in 866 and 884, the weighing had to be done with Norman weights, which could make the total amount still higher.

Sometimes, deliveries in gold,[118] in kind,[119] and even in 882 and in 886, a whole region to be ransacked[120] came to be added to the precious metal. The concluding of such treaties was preceded by long negotiations and were sometimes accompanied by an exchange of hostages.[121] There is no question of any writing: everything was verbal, including the settlement of the agreement. But the setting up of notices on the Frankish side is probable; such notices may well have also been the source of what the Annals report as to the way in which the kings taxed their subjects to pay their tributes to the Normans.

In this short account I cannot systematically find out and analyze all the common features to be found in Carolingian treaties.

In conclusion I wish to point out certain features which seem to have been rather common. Among these is the fact that a first phase of negotiations frequently, though not always, led as we have seen to a preliminary and temporary agreement; a second phase would later result in the concluding of the treaty. Another fact is the length of this second phase which would sometimes last for months or even years. Another characteristic is related to the negotiators: when the negotiation took place in *Francia,* the Frankish ruler or, as the case may be, the Frankish rulers played their own personal part, which was important. One must not underestimate the part played by the king's advisors and indeed, occasionally also by aristocratic "pressure groups."

When the negotiations had to do with distant foreign powers (Byzantium, Cordova) the ambassadors must have been allowed a certain liberty of action for concluding the treaty once the basic decision of the first phase was established. The use, by either part, of *missi discurrentes,* that is to say itinerant ambassadors,[122] or even of messengers at the disposal of the ambassadors, could indeed only be possible for "close" negotiations (for example in 870 between Charles the Bald at Aachen and Louis the German at Regensburg). Finally, as to what concerns the treaties proper, at least those which had been put down in writing, it must be remembered that one had not yet reached the single unique text, produced in as many copies as there are parties; one very likely made use of parallel but distinct texts for each of the parties.[123]

Perhaps these few general statements might be accepted as the result of our research.

NOTES

1. That means since the accession to the throne of Pepin III as a king until the overthrow of Emperor Charles III the Fat. For the Merovingian period, see my article, "Les traités des rois mérovingiens," *Tijdschrift voor Rechtsgeschiedenis. Revue d'histoire du droit*, XXXII (1964); it completes my study, "Merovingisches Gesandtschaftswesen" in *Aus Geschichte und Landeskunde. Forschungen und Darstellungen Franz Steinbach gewidmet* (Bonn, 1960). Likewise for the Carolingian period, the present article completes my study: "Les relations extérieures de la monarchie franque sous les premiers souverains carolingiens," *Annali di Storia del Diritto*, V-VI (1961-62, published in 1964).

2. F. Kurze (ed.), *Annales Regni Francorum* (Scriptores Rerum Germanicarum in usum Scholarum [Hanover, 1895]); F. Grat, J. Vielliard, S. Clemencet, L. Levillain (eds.), *Annales de Saint-Bertin* ("Société de l'histoire de France" [Paris, 1964]); F. Kurze (ed.), *Annales Fuldenses* (Script. Rer. Germ. [Hanover, 1891]); B. von Simson (ed.), *Annales Xantenses et Annales Vedastini* (Script. Rer. Germ. [Hanover, 1909]).

3. Einhard, *Vita Karoli*, ed. O. Holder-Egger (Script. Rer. Germ. [Hanover, 1911]); Thegan, *Vita Hludowici imperatoris*, ed. G. H. Pertz (MG., SS. II) pp. 585-604; Anonymous (the so-called Astronomer), *Vita Hludowici imperatoris* (MG., SS. II) pp. 604-48; Nithard, *Historiarum libri IIII*, ed. E. Müller (Script. Rer. Germ. [Hanover, 1907]).

4. We will limit ourselves to those acts of submission which are described or at least explicitly mentioned in the texts. This remark applies to the Saxons and to all the other populations who happen to be mentioned in this paragraph.

5. *Ann. R. Franc.*, reign of Pepin III, a°758; reign of Charlemagne, a^is 772, 775, 776, 777 (1st text), 779, 782, 785, 794, 795, 797 (1st text), p. 16-17, 34-35, 40-43, 46-47, 48, 54-55, 62-65, 70-71, 96-97, 100; *Annales Laureshamenses*, ed. G. H. Pertz (MG., SS. I), p. 37, a° 797; *Ann. R. Franc.*, a°798 (1st text), p. 104.

6. *Ann. R. Franc.* (1st text), a°776 (events of 775), p. 44: the Saxons had "omnes obsides suos dulgtos et sacramenta rupta."

7. *Ann. R. Franc.* (1st text), a°776, p. 46: the Saxons "reddiderunt patriam per wadium omnes manibus eorum . . . et sub dicione domni Caroli regis et Francorum subdiderunt." *Ibid.*, a°777, p. 48: the Saxons "secundum morem illorum omnem ingenuitatem et alodem manibus dulgtum fecerunt. . . ."

8. Reign of Charlemagne: *Ann. R. Franc.*, a^is 789 (Wilzes) pp. 86-87; *Annales Mettenses priores*, ed. B. von Simson (Hanover, 1905), a°803, p. 90; *Chronicon Moissiacense*, ed. G. H. Pertz, rev. ed. (MG. SS. II), a°806, p. 258 (Sorbes), a°812, p. 259 (Wilzes). Reign of Louis the Pious: *Ann. R. Franc.*, a^is 816 (Sorbes), 820 (Slavs of Carniola & of Carinthia), pp. 143-44, 153; *Ann. Bert.*, a° 839 (Sorbes called Colodiques), p. 35. Reign of Louis the German: *Ann. Bert.*, a°844 (Abodrites), p. 48; *Annales Xantenses* (see above n. 2), a°845 (Abodrites), p. 14; *Annales Fuldenses*, a^is 848 (Tchechs), 856 ("Daleminzier"), 862 (Abodrites), 864 (Moraves), 869 (Tchechs), 874 (Sorbes and "Susler"; Moraves), 877 (Linons and "Susler"), 884 (Moraves and Slovenes), p. 37, 47, 56, 62, 69, 81, 82-83, 89-90, 113.

9. *Chronicon Moissiacense*, a° 812 (see n. 8): Sed et illi Wilti dextras dederunt et obsides obtulerunt et promiserunt se dare partibus imperatoris Karoli. *Annales Fuldenses*, a°869 (see n. 8): Behemi dextras sibi a Carlomanno dari petunt et accipiunt.

10. *Annales Fuldenses* (Continuatio Ratisbonensis), a°884, p. 113: . . . Zwenti-

baldus dux . . . homo, sicut mos est, per manus imperatoris efficitur, contestatus illi fidelitatem iuramento et usque dum Karolus vixisset, numquam in regnum suum hostili exercitu esset venturus. Postea veniente Brazlavoni duce, qui in id tempus regnum inter Dravo et Savo flumine tenuit suique miliciae subditus adiungitur. . . .

11. *Ann. R. Franc.*, a°796, pp. 98-101; *Ann. Mett. pr.* (see n. 8), a°803, p. 90; *Ann. R. Franc.*, a^{is} 805, 811, pp. 119-20, 135.

12. J. Déer, "Karl der Grosse und der Untergang des Awarenreiches," in *Karl der Grosse*, ed. W. Braunfels *et al.* (Düsseldorf, 1965), I, 764-71, rightly insists upon these acts of submission. However, I believe that in the words "manibus imperatoris se contradidit" by which the *Ann. Mett. pr.* indicate the submission of the Tudun to Charlemagne in 803, one must not necessarily understand the commendation into vassality (Déer, *op. cit.*, p. 771); there is indeed no question of an oath of fealty.

13. Astronomer, c. 30, p. 623, a°825: . . . tota cum eo Brittannia victa succubuit et manus dedit, ad quascumque conditiones imperator vellet denuo servitura.

14. Reign of Charlemagne and of Louis the Pious: *Ann. R. Franc.*, a^{is} 786, 799, 818, pp. 72-73, 108-9, 148; Astronomer (see n. 3), c. 30, p. 623, a°818; Ermoldus Nigellus, *In honorem Hludowici*, ed. E. Faral (Paris, 1932), III, v. 1748-51, a°818; *Ann. R. Franc.*, a^{is} 824, 825, 826, pp. 164-65, 167, 169; Astronomer, c. 39, pp. 628-29, a°825. Reign of Charles the Bald: *Ann. Bert.*, a°837, p. 22.

15. See below, n. 36 and 42.

16. Reign of Charlemagne: Astronomer, c. 2, pp. 607-8 (allusion to 769), c. 5, p. 609, a°790; c. 18, pp. 615-16, a°813 (Louis the Pious as King of Aquitaine). Reign of Louis the Pious: *Ann. R. Franc.*, a° 816, p. 144. Reign of Charles the Bald: *Chronicon Fontanellense*, a°850, ed. Dom J. Laporte ("Mélanges publiés par la Société de l'histoire de Normandie"), XV, 1951, p. 83.

17. The so-called treaties with other populations, unwritten or hardly making use of writing, were really, as we have seen, plain acts of submission.

18. General orientation in the works of L. Musset, *Les peuples scandinaves au moyen âge* (Paris, 1951), pp. 61-63, and *Les invasions. Le second assaut contre l'Europe chrétienne* (Paris, 1965), pp. 8-11, 18-27, 107-46, 206-68. The most important work as far as the facts are concerned seems to be V. La Cour, "Danmarks aeldste Konger," in K. Fabricius, *Danmarks Konger* (Copenhague, 1944).

19. In 804, King Godfried, with his army, took position at Schleswig, but did not attack; *Ann. R. Franc.*, h.a°, p. 118. In 808, Godfried, allied to the Linons, the "Smeldinger" and the Wilzes, attacked the Abodrites, allies of Charlemagne, then got a line of fortifications built in order to obstruct the south of Jutland against the Franks, *ibid.*, h.a°, pp. 125-26. To face Danish attacks, Charlemagne got a fortified outwork built at Itzehoe, on the Stoer, a tributary stream of the lower Elbe, *ibid.*, h.a°, pp. 129-30. A Danish fleet having devastated Frisia and the news spreading that King Godfried had assembled an army to invade Saxony, in 810, Charlemagne took position with his troops on the Aller, tributary of the low Weser; but since Godfried had been murdered by one of his armed retainers, the attack did not take place; *ibid.*, h.a°, p. 131.

20. *Ann. R. Franc.*, a°810, p. 133: Godofrido Danorum rege mortuo Hemmingus, filius fratris eius, in regnum successit ac pacem cum imperatore fecit. *Ibid.*, a°811, p. 134: Condicta inter imperatorem et Hemmingum Danorum

regem pax, propter hiemis asperitatem, quae inter partes commeandi viam claudebat, in armis tantum iurata servatur. . . .

21. *Ann. R. Franc.*, a°811, p. 134 (follows immediately the last words of the preceding note): . . . donec redeunte veris temperie et apertis viis, quae inmanitate frigoris clausae fuerunt, congredientibus ex utraque parte utriusque gentis, Francorum scilicet et Danorum, XII primoribus super fluvium Egidoram in loco qui vocatur . . . [name omitted], datis vicissim secundum ritum ac morem suum sacramentis pax confirmatur. Primores autem de parte Francorum hii fuere: . . . [eleven names]; de parte vero Danorum inprimis fratres Hemmingi, . . . [two names] deinde ceteri honorabiles inter suos viri . . . [seven names]. . . . One will notice that the envoys, both Danish and Frankish of whom the name is mentioned, are less than twelve in number.

22. *Ann. R. Franc.*, a°811, p. 134 (follows immediately the preceding note): Imperator vero pace cum Hemmingo firmata et placito generali secundum consuetudinem Aquis habito. . . . *Ibid.*, h.a°, p. 135; Charlemagne came back from Boulogne-sur-Mer and reached Aachen in November: Obviarunt et venienti legati Hemmingi regis, Aowin et Hebbi, munera regis et verba pacifica deferentes. . . .

23. *Ann. R. Franc.*, h.a^is, pp. 118-19, 128.

24. *Ann R. Franc.*, a°812, p. 137: Harioldus et Reginfridus reges Danorum missa ad imperatorem legatione pacem petunt et fratrem suum Hemmingum sibi remitti rogant. *Ibid.*, a°813, p. 138: Missi sunt . . . quidam Francorum et Saxonum primores trans Albim fluvium ad confinia Nordmannorum, qui pacem cum eis secundum petitionem regum illorum facerent et fratrem eorum redderent. Quibus cum pari numero-nam XVI erant-de primatibus Danorum in loco deputato occurrissent, iuramentis utrimque factis pax confirmata et regum frater eis redditus est.

25. *Ann. R. Franc.*, a°825, p. 168: at the assembly held in Aachen . . . etiam et filiorum Godefridi de Nordmannia legatos audivit ac pacem, quam ibidem sibi dari petebant, cum eis in marca eorum mense octobrio confirmari iussit. *Ibid.*, a°826, p. 169: at the assembly of Ingelheim Danish envoys appeared again: . . . legati quoque filiorum Godofridi regis Danorum, pacis ac foederis causa directi.

26. *Ann. R. Franc.*, a^is 814, 815, pp. 141, 142; Thegan, *Vita Hludowici*, a°815, c. 14, p. 593; *Ann. R. Franc.*, a^is 817, 819, 821, 822, 823, 826, 827, pp. 145 & 147, 152, 156-57, 159, 162-63, 169-70, 173.

27. *Ann. R. Franc.*, a° 828, p. 175: Interea cum in confinibus Nordmannorum tam de foedere inter illos et Francos confirmando quam de Herioldi rebus tractandum esset et ad hoc totius pene Saxoniae comites simul cum markionibus illo convenissent. . . . Then comes the relation of the incident and of its consequences. The Danish kings are the filii Godofridi.

28. *Ann. Bert.*, a°831, p. 4: . . . Necnon missi Danorum eadem[=pacem,] exorantes uenerunt et, foedere firmato, ad propria repedarunt. *Ibid.*, a°839, pp. 34-35: . . . Direxit et Horicus missos ad imperatorem, quendam uidelicet cuius consiliis prae cunctis fidere et omnia agere uidebatur, et cum eo nepotem suum, munera gentilitia deferentes, pacis amiciciaeque artius stabiliusque gratia confirmandae. Quibus hilariter susceptis atque muneratis . . . and farther: Sed et legati imperatoris ad Horich pacis gratia directi receptis sacramentis, indissolubilem pepigerunt.

29. *Ann. Fuld.*, a°873, pp. 78-79: . . . Venerunt quoque illuc [=to Bürstadt] Sigifridi Danorum regis legati pacis faciendae gratia in terminis inter illos et Saxones positis et ut negotiatores utriusque regni invicem transeuntes et mer-

cimonia deferentes emerent et venderent pacifice; quae omnia rex ex sua parte rata fore promisit. . . . [In Metz] Halbdeni frater Sigifridi regis etiam suos ad eum nuntios misit eadem postulans, quae frater suus postulaverat; videlicet ut rex legatos suos ad fluvium nomine Egidoram, qui illos et Saxones dirimit, mitteret et illi eisdem occurrentes pacem ex utraque parte omni tempore stabilem confirmarent. Obtulerunt quoque idem nuntii gladium regi pro munere aureum habentem capulum, obnixe flagitantes ut rex dominos suos, supradictos scilicet reges, in loco filiorum habere dignaretur, et illi eum quasi patrem venerari vellent cunctis diebus vitae suae. Iurabant etiam iuxta ritum gentis suae per arma sua, quod nullus deinceps de regno dominorum suorum regnum regis inquietare aut alicui in illo laesionem inferre deberet; quae omnia rex gratanter accepit et postulata se facturum esse spopondit.

30. *Ann. Fuld.*, a°873, p. 78.

31. Pepin and Duke Waifarius. *Ann. R. Franc.*, a°760 (2ᵈ text), p. 9.

32. Pepin and King Aistulfus. *Ann. R. Franc.*, aˡˢ 755, 756 (both texts), pp. 12, 15.

33. Charlemagne and Duke Tassilo III before his dismissal in 788. *Ann. R. Franc.*, 781, 787, pp. 58-59, 74-79.

34. Charlemagne and Duke Arichis, *Ann. R. Franc.*, a°787 (1st text; 2nd text: a°786), pp. 73-75, and later Charlemagne and Duke Grimoald II, *ibid.*, a°812, p. 137, Paschasius Radbertus, *Vita Adalhardi*, c. 29, ed. G. H. Pertz (MG., SS. II), p. 527 (Adalhard, cousin of the emperor, was his representative); cf. O. Bertolini, "Carlomagno e Benevento," in *Karl der Grosse* (see above, n. 12), I, 668-71. Louis the Pious and Grimoald II, *Ann. R. Franc.*, a°814, p. 141. Lothair I and Duke Sikonolf, *Ann. Bert.*, a°844, p. 46.

35. Charlemagne (and Louis the Pious, King of Aquitaine, after 781) on one side and on the other side, the wali of Barcelona or Saragossa, *Ann. R. Franc.*, a°777 (chiefly the second text), pp. 48-51; the local chieftains of Gerona (perhaps Christians), a°785, *Chron. Moissiac.* (M.G. SS. I), p. 297; the wali of Huesca, shortly after 790, Astronomer, c. 5, p. 609; the wali of Barcelona, *Ann. R. Franc.*, a°797, pp. 100-101; the wali of Huesca, *ibid.*, a°799, pp. 108-9; the wali of Saragossa and of Huesca, *ibid.*, a°809, p. 130. On these agreements of which we miss the details and which had but a limited range of influence, see P. Wolff, "L'Aquitaine et ses marches," in *Karl der Grosse* (see above, n. 12), I, 270-81.

36. These treaties were concluded after defeats had been suffered by Charles the Bald; they contain territorial and other clauses favorable to the Breton chieftains and less important provisos in favor of the king of *Francia Occidentalis*. Treaties with Duke Nominoë, *Ann. Bert.* a°846, p. 52; with King Erispoë, *ibid.*, 851 & 856, p. 63-64 et 72; with King Salomon, *ibid.*, 863, 864, and 867, pp. 96, 113, 136-37; with Vuigo, son of the latter, *ibid.*, 873, p. 193. See our chapter XXI, "Les royaumes francs et l'empire du traité de Verdun à la déposition de Charles le Gros," in F. Lot, C. Pfister, F. L. Ganshof, *Les destinées de l'empire de 395 à 888* (2nd ed.; Paris, 1940-41), pp. 540, 541, 543, 547, 551.

37. *Liber Pontificalis*. Vita Stephani II, 248 (XXXVII) and 252 (XLVI), ed. L. Duchesne, I, (Paris, 1955, reprint of the edition of 1886), I, 451 and 453.

38. It is at least the impression given by a quick examination of the collections containing charters of the dukes and private charters issued in the eighth and ninth centuries. On the charters of the dukes see R. Poupardin, "Etude sur la diplomatique des princes lombards de Capoue, de Bénévent et de

Salerne," *Mélanges d'archéologie et d'histoire*, 21 (Ecole Française de Rome, 1901).

39. Lombards; Benevento 787 (in terminis); Bavaria; Brittany.

40. Aquitains; Lombards; Benevento 787 (in terminis) 814 (probably); Bavaria.

41. Benevento; Brittany 863 and 864.

42. Bavaria 787, Brittany: 851 Erispoë; 863 Salomon; 873 Vuigo.

43. Concerning the conflict, its various phases and the negotiations which it involved, it may be enough to refer to P. Classen, "Karl der Grosse, das Papsttum und Byzanz," in *Karl der Grosse. Lebenswerk und Nachleben*, ed. W. Braunfels *et al.* (Düsseldorf, 1965), I, 594-98, 600-604; F. Dölger, "Europas Gestaltung im Spiegel der fränkisch-byzantinischen Auseinandersetzung des 9. Jahrhunderts," in the collected studies of this scholar, *Byzanz und die europäische Staatenwelt* (Ettal, 1953), pp. 323-27; R. Folz, *Le couronnement impérial de Charlemagne* (Paris, 1962), pp. 193-96, 202-5; G. Ostrogorsky, *Geschichte des byzantinischen Staates* (2nd ed.; Munich, 1952), pp. 150-51, 160-61. See also my study cited above n. 1, *in fine*, pp. 47-50.

We will not look into the negotiations carried out previously by Charlemagne with Byzantium and in particular not into those which took place in 786 and 798: indeed, they did not lead to the concluding of any treaty.

44. *Ann. R. Franc.*, a°802, p. 117.

45. *Ann. R. Franc.*, a°803, p. 118.

46. Considering that the general agreement on principles reached in 810 implied the acknowledgment of the imperial title of Charlemagne and that he himself declared at the time that the agreement was in accordance with what he had hoped for since 803. See above, p. 30 and n. 50. Classen, *op. cit.*, p. 598, sees things in the same way.

47. This armed conflict took place in the Adriatic, in Dalmatia and Venetia. Classen, *op. cit.* p. 601, thinks that the only cause of it was the contest for supreme authority on Venetia. We, on the contrary, think that it was caused both by this rivalry and by "the problem of the two emperors" (the "Zweikaiser Problem" of Ohnsorge). The fighting was moreover interrupted by a truce concluded at the end of 807 or in the beginning of 808; it was probably renewed, but ended in 809: *Ann. R. Franc.*, aᵢₛ 807 and 809, pp. 124 and 127.

48. Especially after two Byzantine defeats in the Adriatic: the failure of the attempted landing at Comacchio in 809 followed by vain endeavors by the commander of the fleet to conclude peace with Pepin, king of Italy, and still more the conquest of Venetia, including the isles of the Laguna, by Pepin, king of Italy. The attacks of Pepin against Dalmatia remained useless *Ann. R. Franc.*, aᵢₛ 809 and 810, pp. 127 and 130; see also the *De administrando imperio* of Constantine Porphyrogenetos, c. 28 ed. G. Moravcsik and R. J. H. Jenkins (Budapest, 1949), pp. 118 ff. (= ed. Bekker [Bonn, 1840]), p. 124.

49. *Ann. R. Franc.*, a°810, p. 132: . . . duasque legationes de diversis terrarum partibus, unam de Constantinopoli, alteram de Corduba, pacis faciendae causa adventare narratur. p. 133: . . . Imperator Aquasgrani veniens mense Octimbrio memoratas legationes audivit pacemque cum Niciforo imperatore et cum Abulaz rege Hispaniae fecit. Nam Niciforo Venetiam reddidit. . . .

50. The letter has been edited by E. Dümmler, *Epistolae variorum Carolo Magno regnante scriptae*, nr. 32 (MG. [in-4°], *Epistolae*, IV, 546-48). At the end of this letter, Charlemagne announced to Nicephoros the sending of his own ambassadors with the aim of promptly leading new negotiations. The tone

of the letter is cordial, but it contains nothing concerning the clauses of the agreement to be concluded.

51. Imperial title: the acknowledgment of the imperial title of Charlemagne in 812 was of course a consequence of the general agreement on principles that was reached in 810 or early in 811. Venitia: see above, n. 48 and 49.

52. *Ann. R. Franc.*, a°811, p. 133. The annalist explicitly mentions the fact that the Frankish ambassadors were sent to the East "pacis confirmandae gratia."

53. *Ann. R. Franc.*, a°812, p. 136: Niciforus imperator . . . moritur. Et Michahel gener eius imperator factus legatos domni imperatoris Karoli, qui ad Niciforum missi fuerunt, in Constantinopoli suscepit et absolvit. Cum quibus et suos legatos direxit, Michahelem scilicet episcopum et Arsafium atque Theognostum protospatharios, et per eos pacem a Niciforo inceptam confirmavit.

54. See the last sentence of the text quoted in the preceding note.

55. This is only mentioned in the *Annales Xantenses*, a°812, ed. B. von Simson (Hanover, 1909), p. 4: cum honorificis vel imperialibus muneribus. The fact is in accordance with the custom of the time; see our article cited above, n. 1 *in fine*, pp. 37-39.

56. *Ann. R. Franc.*, a°812, p. 136, after the passage reproduced in n. 53: Nam Aquisgrani, ubi ad imperatorem venerunt, scriptum pacti ab eo in ecclesia suscipientes. . . . Both other expressions referring to this instrument figured in the letter addressed in that year by Charlemagne to the Eastern emperor; see further, n. 58.

57. In his letter to the Byzantine emperor (see n. 58), Charlemagne begs that the copy of the treaty designed for him should be deposited on the altar beforehand (see further, n. 58 and n. 67); given the parallel between the ceremonies of Aachen and of Byzantium, one must admit that *in ecclesia* in the Annals (see n. 56) implies the depositing on the altar.

58. Letter of Charlemagne to Michel I, a°813, *Epistolae variorum*, n°37 (MG [in-4°], *Epistolae*, IV, pp. 555-56): . . . susicpiendo a nobis pacti conscriptionem, tam nostra propria quam et sacerdotum et procerum nostrorum subscriptione firmatam . . . illa, quam nos fecimus et tibi misimus, pacti descriptio.

59. That is what the beginning of the letter previously recalled allows us to believe. The *intitulatio* and the *inscriptio* give the same imperial title to Charles and to Michel (*imperator et augustus*). Further Charles congratulates himself on having reached that: . . . diu quaesitam et semper desideratam pacem inter orientale atque occidentale imperium stabilire . . . dignatus est. He also declared that in this respect "quicquid de hoc ex nostra parte faciendum fuit, fecimus," and he adds: "vosque similiter de vestra parte facere velle non dubitamus. . . ." See on the significance of the treaty: B. Paradisi, *Storia del diritto internazionale nel medio evo. L'età di transizione* (2nd ed.; Naples, 1956), pp. 145-48.

60. The giving up of Venitia had already been made the subject of the general preliminary agreement of 810 (see above, n. 49); it would be extremely surprising that Byzantium should not have claimed the insertion of a clause in the treaty. The tribute is mentioned by Constantine Porphyrogenetos, *De administrando imperio, loc. cit.* (See above, n. 48).

61. *Ann. R. Franc.*, a°812, p. 136, after the passage reproduced in n. 56: . . . more suo, id est Greca lingua, laudes ei dixerunt, imperatorem eum et basileum appellantes. According to the Roman tradition, these lauds were considered as having constitutive power; H. Kantorowicz, *Laudes Regiae* (Berkeley and Los Angeles, 1946), p. 77, n. 38.

62. It is only attested by a source of the end of the ninth century and of

mediocre authority, the Poeta Saxo, *Annales de gestis Caroli Magni imperatoris* IV, vers 293-94, ed. P. von Winterfeld (MG. [in-4°]), *Poetae*, IV, 53: Foedus et inter se fidei pacisque tenendae Iurando partes firmarunt protinus ambe.

63. Theophanes, AM 6304, ed. C. de Boor (Leipzig, 1883), I, 494, tells us that Michel I, ἀπέστειλε δε καὶ πρός Κάρουλον βασιλεά τῶν Φράγγων περί εἰρήνης καὶ συναλλαγῆς εἰς Θεοφύλακτον, τόν υἱόν αὐτοῦ. If Anastase ed. de Boor, quoted above, II, 332, has translated rightly συναλλαγῆς by *contractu nuptiarum*, it should have concerned the preparation of a marriage between the Byzantine emperor's son, no doubt with a daughter of Charlemagne. But the word means normally "agreement" in general; if such is the meaning of the context, the Byzantine chronicler only reports that Michel I desired to associate his presumed heir to the throne with the agreement between himself and Charlemagne. See F. Dölger, *Regesten der Kaiserurkunden des oströmischen Reiches* (Munich, 1924), I, n°385.

64. *Ann. R. Franc.*, a°812, p. 136.

65. *Ibid.*, a°813, p. 137.

66. In the *intitulatio* of the letter, Charlemagne wears the title Karolus divina largiente gratia imperator et augustus idemque rex Francorum et Langobardorum.

The exceptional character of the omission of the Roman title, is proved by the fact that the *Romanum gubernans imperium* subsisted in the *intitulatio* of the diplomas of Charlemagne.

67. Letter, n°37 (see above, n. 58): . . . ita et memorati legati nostri foederis conscriptionem tuam et sacerdotum patriciorumque ac procerum tuorum subscriptionibus roboratam, a sacrosancto altari tuae manus porrectione suscipiant; et Deo iter illorum properante, ad nos deferant . . . and later: Quapropter rogamus dilectam et gloriosam fraternitatem tuam, ut si tibi illa, quam nos fecimus et tibi misimus, pacti descriptio placuerit, similem illi-Grecis litteris conscriptam et eo modo quo superius diximus roboratam -missis nostris memoratis dare digneris. . . .

68. Classen, *op. cit.*, pp. 602-3, has rightly emphasized this parallelism.

69. *Ann. R. Franc.*, a°813, p. 137. The purpose of the Frankish mission is mentioned as follows: propter pacem cum Michahele imperatore confirmandam. *Ibid.*, a°814, p. 140: . . . Inter quas praecipua fuit legatio de Constantinopoli directa. Further the annalist reports the return of the Frankish ambassadors and the arrival of the Byzantine embassy and he concludes: et per eos descriptionem et confirmationem pacti ac foederis misit.

70. *Ann. R. Franc.*, a°814, p. 141; ob renovandam secum amicitiam et praedictum pactum confirmandum; a°815, p. 143: descriptionem pacti, quam Leo imperator eis dederat, retulerunt. Once again two different documents. *Ibid.*, a^is 824, 827, pp. 165, 174.

71. *Annales Bertiniani*, a°839, pp. 30-31.

72. For the treaties concluded with the local potentates of Moslem Spain, subordinated, at least in law, to the emirs, see above, n. 35.

73. This territory was later called *marca hispanica*; the legal accuracy of the expression has been questioned by R. d 'Abadal i de Vinyals, "Nota sobre la locucion Marca hispanica," in *Boletin de la Real Academia de Buenas Letras de Barcelona*, XXVII (1957-58).

74. *Ann. R. Franc.*, a°810, p. 133 (see above n. 49): Imperator Aquasgrani veniens mense Octimbrio . . . legationes audivit pacemque . . . cum Abulaz, rege Hispaniae fecit . . . Haimricum comitem olim a Sarracenis captum Abulaz

remittente recepit. . . . The restitution of a prisoner—a Frankish count—was a token of good will inspiring the confidence necessary for further negotiations.

75. *Ibid.*, a°812, p. 137: Pax cum Abulaz rege Sarracenorum facta; *Chronicon Moissiacense*, revised text (MG., SS. II), p. 259: Eodem anno Abulaz, rex Sarracenorum ex Espania . . . missus suos direxit, postulans pacem facere cum eo, quam . . . imperator denegare noluit; sed fecit pacem cum ipso per tres annos.

Arab sources also point out that "peace" or rather that truce, but in a very confused chronological frame; E. Levy-Provençal, *Histoire de l'Espagne musulmane* (2nd ed.; Paris & Leiden, 1950), I, 181-84.

76. *Ann. R. Franc.*, a°815, p. 143: Pax, quae cum Abulaz rege Sarracenorum facta et per triennium servata erat, velut inutilis rupta et contra eum iterum bellum susceptum est. We must note that *inutilis* does not mean "useless" but "harmful," "unfavorable.' On the raid by the Sarrasines, see Levy-Provençal, *op. cit.*, p. 185; same remark about the chronology as in n. 75.

77. *Ann. R. Franc.*, a°817, p. 145.

78. *Annales Bertiniani*, a°847, p. 53: Legati Abdirrahman regis Sarracenorum a Corduba Hispaniae ad Karolum pacis petendae foederisque firmandi gratia veniunt, quos apud Remorum Durocortorum decenter et suscepit et absolvit. Levy-Provençal, *op. cit.*, p. 212, n. 1 and p. 213, states wrongly that a truce was concluded: there was nothing of the kind.

79. *Ibid.*, a°863, p. 104: . . . legatum Mahomoth regis Sarracenorum cum magnis et multis muneribus ac litteris de pace et foedere amicali loquentibus solemni more suscepit, quem cum honore et debito salvamento ac subsidio necessario in Silvanectis civitate oportunum tempus, quo remitti honorifice ad regem suum opperiri disposuit. A°864, p. 114: Missum Mohometh regis Sarracenorum, qui ante hiemem ad se venerat, muneratum cum plurimis et maximis donis per suos missos ad eundem regem satis honorifice remittit.

80. The Arab sources mention the good relations between Muhammad I and Charles the Bald; this allows us to believe, like Levy-Provençal, pp. 282-83, that an agreement was concluded between them.

81. *Annales Bertiniani*, a°865, p. 124: Karolus missos suos, quos praecedenti anno Cordubam ad Mahomet direxerat, cum multis donis, camelis videlicet lecta et papiliones gestantibus, et cum diversi generis pannis et multis odoramentis in Compendio recipit.

82. Our study on *Les relations extérieures de la monarchie franque* (See above, n. 1), pp. 12-13 and n. 40 and 41, pp. 28-29 and n. 114-19.

83. I share the opinion of A. Kleinclausz, *La légende du protectorat de Charlemagne sur la Terre Sainte* (Syria, 1927) and *Charlemagne* (Paris, 1934), pp. 340-45. E. Joranson, "The alleged frankish protectorate in Palestine," *American Historical Review*, XXXII (1927), though extremely learned, seems to be slightly hypercritical in his conclusions.

84. Einhard, *Vita Karoli*, c. 16, p. 19: Ac proinde . . . cum legati eius . . . ad eum venissent et ei domini sui voluntatem indicassent, non solum quae petebantur fieri permisit, sed etiam sacrum illum et salutarem locum, ut illius potestati adscriberetur, concessit.

85. *Ibid.*, c. 27, p. 31. *Ann. R. Franc.*, a°801, p. 116.

86. Astronomer, c. 46, p. 634: In quo loco tres legati Sarracenorum a transmarinis venere partibus, quorum duo Sarraceni, unus christianus fuit, adferentes suae grandia munera patriae, odorum scilicet diversa genera et pannorum; qui pace petita et accepta remissi sunt. *Annales Bertiniani*, a°831, p. 4: ibique ad eum legati Almiralmumminin de Perside venientes pacem petiuerunt, qua mox impetrata reversi sunt. *Annales Xantenses*, a°831, p. 8: Legati Sar-

racenorum venerunt ad imperatorem pacem confirmandam et cum pace reversi sunt. See my article cited n. 82, p. 29.

87. Nithard, *Historiae* (see above, n. 3), III, c. 5, pp. 35-37.

88. These conferences have been the subject of studies among which some are comparatively old, but have kept their full value: E. Dümmler, *Geschichte des ostfränkischen Reiches*, 3 vols. (2nd ed.; Leipzig, 1887-88); R. Parisot, *Le royaume de Lorraine sous les Carolingiens* (Paris, 1899); J. Calmette, *La diplomatie carolingienne du traité de Verdun à la mort de Charles le Chauve* (Paris, 1901); F. Lot and L. Halphen, *Le règne de Charles le Chauve*, I (Paris, 1909); J. Calmette, *L'effondrement d'un empire et la naissance d'une Europe* (Paris, 1941); L. Halphen, *Charlemagne et l'empire carolingien* (2nd ed.; Paris, 1949). H. Mitteis, Politische Verträge im Mittelalter, *Zeitschrift der Savigny Stiftung für Rechtsgeschichte, Germanistische Abteilung* (1950), pp. 115-16 (and in *Die Rechtsidee in der Geschichte* [Weimar, 1957], p. 595).

89. In my opinion, the best study on the *fraternitas* is that of Halphen, *op. cit.*, pp. 323-51; see also Paradisi, *op. cit.*, pp. 232-39. The passage quoted in our text comes from Prudentius, bishop of Troyes, *Annales Bertiniani*, a°844, p. 48.

90. Here is a short account (BK = Boretius-Krause, *Capitularia*, II, n°000; AB = *Annales Bertiniani*, p. oo; AF = *Annales Fuldenses*, p. oo): 844, Thionville-Yütz, BK 227; AB 48 (3 brothers). 847, Meersen I, BK 204; AB 54 (id.). 851, Meersen II, BK 205; AB 60-63 (id.). 853, Valenciennes, BK 206 (Lothair I, Charles). 854, Liège, BK 207; AB 68 (id.). 857, Saint-Quentin, BK 268; AB 74 (Charles, Lothair II). 860 Koblenz, BK 242; AB 83; AF 54-55 (Louis, Charles, Lothair II). 862, Savonnières, BK 243; AB 94-95 (id.). 865, Tusey, BK 244; AB 116-17, AF (864) 62-63 (Louis, Charles). 867, Metz, BK 245; AB 135 (Louis, Charles). 867, Frankfurt, AB 136-37 (Louis, Lothair II). 870, Aachen, BK 250; AB 171-72 (envoys of Louis and of Charles). 870, Meersen III, BK 251; AB 171-74 (Louis and Charles). 878, Les Fourons, BK 246; AB 230-34, AF 92 (Louis the Stammerer, Louis the Younger). 879, Verdun; AB 236-38, AF 92-93 (Louis the Younger, envoys of Louis III and Carloman).

91. Boretius-Krause, *Capitularia*, II, nr. 205, pp. 72-74.

92. In two manuscripts (The Hague 1, f°24; Paris lat. 4638, f°165): Haec quae secuntur, capitula sunt anno DCCCLI incarnationis dominicae quando tres fratres reges, Hlotharius scilicet, Hludowicus et Karolus secus municipium Treiectum penes locum qui dicitur Marsna, iterum convenerunt et consultu episcoporum et ceterorum fidelium eadem capitula subscripserunt manibus propriis et inter se ac inter fideles suos perpetuo se conservaturos promiserunt. Quae capitula singulorum in populo adnuntiationes secuntur.

93. Prudentius, bishop of Troyes. A°851, p. 60: Hlotharius, Hludowicus et Karolus apud Marsnam palatium conveniunt. Vbi etiam fraterne paucis diebus morati, haec communi procerum suorum consilio atque consensu decernunt propriorumque nominum monogrammatibus confirmant.

94. Boretius-Krause, pp. 72-74, l. 11 and *Annales Bertiniani*, pp. 60-63.

95. Note the use, here and further, of this expression, called to a great future, as a definition of the obligations of vassals.

96. About these monograms of which the king was supposed to draw just one line: T. Schieffer, introduction to his edition of *Die Urkunden Lothars I und Lothars II* (Berlin and Zurich, 1966 [MG., in-4°, "Die Urkunden der Karolinger," III]), p. 42; G. Tessier, *Recueil des actes de Charles II le Chauve*, III (Paris, 1955), pp. 176-82, P. F. Kehr, in the introduction to his edition of

Die Urkunden Ludwigs des Deutschen (Berlin, 1934 [MG., in 4°, "Diplomata Regum Germaniae ex Stirpe Karolinorum," I]), pp. XXIX-XXX.

97. The *adnuntiationes* are to be found in three manuscripts out of four. Prudentius has found it unnecessary to reproduce them in the Annals of Saint-Bertin.

98. The reciprocal character of the obligations between the King and his *fideles*, which appeared in the capitulary of 843, at the end of the assembly at Coulaines (Boretius-Krause, II, nr. 254) will be found in several *adnuntiationes*. See the excellent pages of F. Lot, in Lot and Halphen, *op. cit.*, pp. 95-96.

99. *Conventus* of 844 (Thionville-Yütz), 863 (Savonnières), 870 (Meersen III), 879 (Verdun). See the short account in n. 90.

100. *Conventus* of Liège, Saint-Quentin, Koblenz, Metz, probably Aachen (see the short account in n. 90). No doubt this was also the case for other *conventus* about which our sources give us no clue as to this point.

101. Lengthy *adnuntiationes:* Meersen I and II, Liège, Saint-Quentin, Koblenz, Savonnières, Tusey. Vernacular: Koblenz. Omission of the word: Liège, Tusey. See n. 90.

102. Boretius-Krause, n°242, p. 154. In 870, the decision had been taken that the partition should be made with unanimous consent of the *fideles* of both kings. *Annales Bertiniani*, a°870, p. 170 (see below n. 106).

103. Verdun. *Annales Bertiniani*, a°843, pp. 44-45. *Annales Fuldenses*, a°843, p. 34; *Annales Xantenses*, a°843, p. 13. See my article "Zur Entstehungsgeschichte und Bedeutung des Vertrages von Verdun," *Deutsches Archiv für Erforschung des Mittelalters*, XII (1956). Meersen. *Annales Bertiniani*, a°870, pp. 171-75. See Parisot, *op. cit.*, pp. 368-78.

104. About *describere* and *descriptio: Annales Bertiniani*, a°842, p. 43; *Annales Fuldenses*, a°842, p. 33, a°843, p. 34; *Annales Xantenses*, a°843, p. 34. On the content of the *descriptiones*: Nithard, IV, 3, p. 44. See Ganshof, *Verdun*, pp. 320-25 and O. Clavadetscher, "Das Churrätische Reichsurbar als Quelle zur Geschichte des Vertrags von Verdun," *Zeitschrift der Savigny Stiftung für Rechtsgeschichte, Germanistische Abteilung* (1953).

105. Boretius-Krause, *Capitularia*, II, n°251; *Annales Bertiniani*, a°870, pp. 172-74.

106. Verdun. *Annales Bertiniani*, a°843, p. 45: Factisque sacramentis. . . . Meersen. AB, a°870, p. 170: . . . Quae divisio . . . ad hunc finem . . . pervenit ut in illud regnum quod inter eos secundum sacramenta prestita dividendum erat pacifice conuenirent et . . . cum consensu et unanimitate communium fidelium ipsorum inuenirent, secundum sacramenta inter eos praestita illud regnum dividerent.

107. The most important work is the one by E. Joranson, *Danegeld in France* (Rock Island, 1924). See also the article of F. Lot, "Le tribut aux Normands et l'Eglise de France au IXe siècle," *Bibliothèque de l'École des Chartes* (1924) and the classical work of W. Vogel, *Die Normannen und das fränkische Reich* (Heidelberg, 1906).

108. See above, pp. 26-29.

109. Charles the Bald. 845, *Annales Bertiniani* (= AB), p. 49. 866, AB, 125-26. 877, Boretius-Krause, n°280 (2 notices); AB, 213-14, *Annales Vedastini* (= AV), a¹ˢ 876-77, p. 41. Charles the Fat. 886, AV, 62; Abbon, *Le siège de Paris par les Normands*, ed. H. Waquet (Paris, 1942), II, v. 339, p. 90.

110. This is less certain because of the cautiousness of the annalists, but it seems likely.

111. Charles the Bald, 853, AB, 66. Louis III. 882, AB 247, AV 52.

112. 877. AB, 213-14. 884, AV, 55. In 884, the agreement was made in the name of King Carloman.

113. 860-61, AB, 82-83, 85-86. 873, AB, 194-95, Regino, *Chronicon*, ed. F. Kurze (Hanover, 1890), a°873, pp. 105-7.

114. 862, AB 89.

115. 864, AB 105. 882, AB, 247-48, AV, 51-52, *Annales Fuldenses* (pars III), 98-99 (continuatio Ratisbonensis), 108-9.

116. The text of AB 89 contains only the words *in sex milibus argenti*. One generally admits that *libris* must have been understood or have disappeared in consequence of a mistake in the copy. This is most likely but not absolutely certain: *denariis* should not be radically excluded.

117. The *Annales Fuldenses*, h. a° in the pars III (Mainz) estimate the amount paid to the Normans at 2,412 pounds, whereas the *Continuatio Ratisbonensis* give the figure of 2,080 pounds.

118. 882 (see n. 115).

119. 861 and 864 (see n. 113 and 115).

120. 882 (see n. 115), 886 (see n. 109).

121. 862 (see n. 114), 873 (see n. 113).

122. See above n. 99, treaties between Frankish emperors and kings. See also above n. 36, the treaty of 867 between Charles the Bald and Salomon, duke or king of Brittany and n. 112, the treaty of 884 between great men of the West-frankish realm acting in the name of King Carloman and the Normans.

123. See above as to what concerns the treaties with Byzantium, p. 33 and n. 68, and with Cordova, pp. 34-35. It is likely that the same happened with the treaties between Franklish emperors and kings, though we have no safe indication except for the treaty of the Fourons of 878, Boretius-Krause, II, n°246. The only existing copy is the one that was issued by Louis the Stammerer and designed for Louis the Young, as shown by the "prooemium" and by c. 3 (p. 169, ll. 7-15 and 26-32); see Krause, p. 168 and Parisot, *op. cit.*, p. 430.

III

French Attitudes Toward Literary Criticism

W. L. Wiley

The University of North Carolina at Chapel Hill

The French are, by their very natures and as a result of long practice, a nation of critics—and, more specifically, a nation of literary critics. Literary criticism in France has through the centuries become a high art, if not a fine art. Most French writers, therefore, whether they have been concerned with prose or poetry, have managed at the same time to indulge in some form of criticism. One thinks immediately of Du Bellay, Montaigne, Boileau, Voltaire, Victor Hugo, Sainte Beuve—or, more contemporarily, of Jean-Paul Sartre. Some observers, in looking at the French, have concluded that in France the secondary writers have laid down the critical laws which the primary writers rather subserviently obeyed. This is too easy a generalization, especially when one looks at the major figures listed above. And, in the nineteenth and twentieth centuries, there has been a great variety of critical opinion and a general objection to absolutism—for examples, the *l'art pour l'art* concept, the rejection of rhyme in poetry and the pastel shadings favored by Paul Verlaine and the symbolists, the *race,* the *milieu,* and the *moment* theory of Hippolyte Taine, the *faculté maîtresse* of Jules Lemaître, the cubism of Guillaume Apollinaire, the surrealism of André Breton, and the existentialism of Sartre and his followers. Nevertheless, there is some validity in the claim that, as far as the sixteenth and seventeenth centuries are concerned—which period will be the matter of consideration for this paper—the rigors of the critical boundaries were set in many cases by the less gifted composers. In any case, it was scarcely to be expected that poets like Ronsard and Racine would have also the critical preceptions of Aristotle or Horace. Therefore, the rules were laid down frequently by such pedantic law-givers as Jean Chapelain, whose reputation in his own day caused him to be known as the "oracle of Aristotle"; and by the pedestrian critic, the Abbé d'Aubignac, who spent a great deal of space in his treatise, *La Pratique du théâtre* of 1657, on the question of whether the Aristotelian "circuit of the sun" meant twelve hours or twenty-four hours. And the good tragedian, Pierre Corneille, suffered under the rigorous edicts of both Chapelain and D'Aubignac. As for D'Aubignac—who tried, occasionally, to write a play—the delightful *libertin,* Saint Evremond, said of him in 1672: "Je sais bon gré à M. d'Aubignac d'avoir si bien suivi les règles d'Aristote; mais je ne pardonne pas aux règles d'Aristote d'avoir fait faire une si méchante tragédie à M. d'Aubignac." It was at about this same time that Saint Evremond stated, with more cleverness than accuracy, "on n'a jamais vu tant de règles pour faire de belles tragédies"—and so few "belles tragédies."[1]

Literary criticism as it would be interpreted today scarcely began in France before the Renaissance—that is, before the sixteenth century. There had been during the Middle Ages, from the twelfth through the fifteenth centuries—and both in French and Provençal—various manuals destined to be of assistance to writers of prose or verse. These were for the most part mechanistic schedules dealing with figures of speech (the "couleurs de rhétorique"), verse forms, and complicated rhyme schemes; such programs probably had very little influence upon the good writers of prose and poetry like Alain Chartier, Charles d'Orléans, and François Villon. These treatises were most numerous toward the end of the fifteenth century and were by then called *rhétoriques.* A "first rhetoric" would be concerned with prose, while a "second rhetoric" would deal with poetry; a "full rhetoric," obviously, gave advice on the composition of both prose and poetry. The last of these rhetorics, *L'Art de pleine rhétorique* of Pierre Fabri, appeared in 1521. Another type of document supposed to be of assistance to the medieval rhymester was the *poétrie,* which was a compendium of stories, legends, and mythological characters that the versifier could weave into his writing.

The following of such codes of rules could hardly be expected to produce any great poets—nor did it. Modern literary historians have called the practitioners in verse of this period in French literature *rhétoriqueurs,* a term that fits them very well although it was not used in the fifteenth century. Terms that were used at the time to designate a versifier were *rimeur, orateur,* or *rhétoricien*—and the fourteenth century writer, Guillaume de Machaut, was called admiringly by his pupil, Eustache Deschamps, *le noble rhétorique.* Derogatory designations applied by sixteenth century critics to late-fifteenth century writers were *rimasseurs, rimailleurs,* and *versificateurs.* It is to be noted that none of these masters of intricate and convoluted rhyme schemes was called by himself, or in later Renaissance criticism, a *poète.*[2]

As the sixteenth century dawned, the French became conscious of the classical masters of criticism, Aristotle and Horace. The critical theories of Aristotle had been imperfectly known in the French Middle Ages except in the doctrinaire ideas of the *Rhetoric,* which led to Aristotle's being regarded as the protagonist of scholasticism and the model for techniques in argumentation. However, with the publication of the text of the *Poetics* in Venice in the early 1500's, the foundation for Aristotle's position as a literary critic was begun. His poetic doctrines first became known in Italy and gradually filtered into France after 1550. But the critical precepts of Aristotle were long obscured on French terrain by a preference for Plato, who was regarded in the first half of the sixteenth century as the prime defender of poetry. The fine scholar, Ramus (or Pierre de La Ramée), brought out in 1536 his *Animadversiones Aristotelicae* which urged an allegiance to Plato and a rejection of Aristotle. It was somewhat ironic that the ancient who had banished the poets from his ideal state was preferred in the early French Renaissance to the Greek philosopher who had first defended for the Western world the privilege of

artistic creativity. This situation was to some degree understandable in view of the fact that Plato had had a long and
varied interpretation through the centuries and, through
Plotinus and the Church Fathers, Platonism had blended
rather easily into Christianity and thus Plato was the one
ancient that was not completely pagan. And, the late fifteenth-
century Platonic Academies in Florence were not long in
making their imprint on the land across the Alps; the Ficino
Commentaries and the slightly later *Cortegiano* of Castiglione
took the straight road to France and found fertile soil among
the Platonists around Lyon.

From the Middle Ages on into the sixteenth and seventeenth centuries the French had a great respect for Cicero.
The famous definition of comedy as being a mirror of life and
an imitation of truth—attributed to Cicero and known through
Donatus—was quoted as Ciceronian gospel even by seventeenth-
century French critics. The Ciceronian (and Roman) five
parts of rhetoric—*inventio, dispositio* (skill in arrangement),
elocutio (enhancing words), *memoria,* and *actio* (dignified
delivery) were taken over by the French not only for oratory
but also for poetic manuals. And the dignified Bossuet, the
most famous French orator of his time and right-hand man of
Louis XIV, said that for the improvement of style it was
better to study the majestic periods of Cicero than the trivialities of poetry either in Latin or French.[3] Even dramatists
like Robert Garnier and Pierre Corneille (both of whom had
had an early training in law) showed the influence of Cicero,
along with a solid admixture of the *sententiae* and the rhe-
torical bombast of the younger Seneca. The French never
admitted a strong critical allegiance to Seneca during the sixteenth and seventeenth centuries; but his tragedies were more
easily available during the period than were those of Sophocles
or Euripides—and the long *récits* and pompous language in
many plays from Jodelle on down to Racine found their basis
in Seneca. A somewhat belated recognition of Seneca's effect
upon French tragedy was a colloquium in his honor held at
Royaumont in 1962. The two ancient writers most honored

by the French during the centuries of the Renaissance and the *grands classiques* were, for both epic and tragic foundations, Homer and Vergil. Homer was "le premier capitaine des Muses" and Vergil was his first lieutenant; Jodelle therefore wrote a tragedy on Dido and Racine drew strongly on the *Aeneid* for his *Andromaque*. Ironically, during this moment of great admiration for Homer and Vergil, there was no one in France who could write a good epic, even when all the rules and models were spread out in the market place. Ronsard never finished his dull *Franciade* and Boileau in his *Art poétique* of 1674 lambasted the poor French epics of the seventeenth century. Malézieux in the eighteenth century, with clear French logic and detachment, made the much-quoted statement, "les Français n'ont pas la tête épique"—and in confirmation of this opinion the eleventh-century *Chanson de Roland* remains the best epic in French literature.

That urbane Roman, Quintus Horatius Flaccus, was the ancient critic most admired by the French during the sixteenth century and he shared this position of admiration with Aristotle in the seventeenth century. Boileau almost deified Horace and for his art of poetry borrowed the essence of ideas and many of the phrases from the *Ad Pisones;* the *Satires* and *Epîtres* of Boileau, too, owed much of their substance and design to the similar forms of Horace. The critical concepts of Horace were given a good adaptation into French in 1544, in Jacques Peletier du Mans' *Art poétique d'Horace,* wherein Peletier seeks to apply the concepts of Horace to contemporary poetical composition. At that time, however, the ideas of Horace were blended with, and probably diminished by, the strong Platonic flavoring that was given to poetry.

In the 1530's when the French were becoming intoxicated with antiquity, a great deal of translation began to be done in France: first from Greek into Latin, and then from Greek or Latin into French. Several of Plato's dialogues were rendered before 1550, all of Terence, and many plays of Sophocles and Euripides. Translating at this time was held in such high regard that the fine scholar, Etienne Dolet, in 1540 wrote a treatise on the proper techniques, *La manière de bien traduire.* In it he showed the influence of Cicero and Seneca by suggesting that a translation, in addition to being accurate, should be full of resounding words so that it would be effective when read aloud. The peak of admiration for translation was reached by Thomas Sebillet in his *Art poétique* of 1548, wherein it was said that a translator was like a discoverer of a lost treasure who made it available again for the use of mankind. It was only a year later that Du Bellay maintained, in his *Défense et illustration de la langue française,* that translation had very limited value and that the *traducteur* was frequently a *traditeur,* or betrayer. Du Bellay and the Pléiade with its followers believed in pillaging the ancients, certainly, and bringing the spoils home; but it should be done in the manner of the bee's pillaging of the flowers with the resultant creation of a new substance, honey. The Pléiade's pillaging was often little more than plagiarizing: Du Bellay himself on one occasion borrowed forty-two lines from Ovid's *Tristia* without even a bare nod of acknowledgement of source.[4] In any event, after 1550 translation was little admired, despite the exception of Jacques Amyot's rendition into French of Plutarch, an effort much praised by Montaigne. Peletier thought that the translator should never be given "le nom d'auteur," but that he would enlarge the reading public.

The primary critical homage around 1550 was given to Plato. Sebillet said, in recognition of poetic inspiration, "le poête naît, l'orateur se fait." There was considerable mention of divine frenzy, of "divine afflation," in complete disregard of the fact that Plato had put the poet's frenzy on the same uncontrolled level as that of the soothsayer and the lover. Peletier du Mans in 1555 spoke of the divine origin of poetry and said that poets were the interpreters of the gods. Platonistic obscurity was to be seen in such poets as Maurice Scève and Antoine Héroët, and Du Bellay wrote a sonnet in which he described his soul as longing to put on its wings again in order to fly away in search of the perfect *Idée.* However, it was Du Bellay who added a note of balance to the concept of poetic frenzy. Every *poète,* said Du Bellay in the *Défense,* is possessed of an internal god-given talent that causes him to merit the name of poet; but the poets who will remain in the minds of later generations, unlike the *poètes courtisans,* will work late in their nocturnal vigils. It is thus that they will commune with the stars.[5]

If French criticism, in the sixteenth and seventeenth centuries, well-nigh deified Greek and Roman antiquity, it was quite derogatory of the literary efforts of other European nations and of the English across the Channel. Du Bellay was willing to call his language *barbare* in comparison with Latin, but not in relation to other tongues in Europe. French confidence in the superiority of their own language has never ceased to exist; and in the newspaper, *Le Figaro,* in 1963, the novelist and Academician, Georges Duhamel, dismissed English as a mere "langue commerciale." As early as 1521 Pierre Fabri stated in his *Rhétorique* that three basic languages came out of the Tower of Babel—Hebrew, Greek, and Latin—and that French had had the responsibility of carrying on this legacy of speech from the Biblical past. Both Du Bellay and Ronsard, a bit later in the sixteenth century, spoke of the trivialities of the Italian language, in marked lack of appreciation of the many borrowings the Pléiade made from the Italians. Du Bellay used the Petrarchan sonnet freely, and then criticized the "pétrarquistes" in France. And Ronsard said in his *Abrégé de l'art poétique* of 1565, in speaking of epithets, that they should have a Roman dignity, and not be strung along in trivial Italian fashion.

The Spaniards fared no better in French critical hands. Vauquelin de la Fresnaye in his *Art poétique* (begun in 1574) claimed that the famous Spanish romance of chivalry, the *Amadis de Gaula,* was originally rhymed in the dialect of Picardie and then the Spanish author "embellished his language" with the original. The tough old warrior and right-hand man of Henry IV, François de la Noue, particularly disliked the *Amadis* because he thought its farfetched imaginings would weaken any young warrior who read it. However, in the French translation of Des Essarts, La Noue thought the novel was much more acceptable than in the exaggerated Spanish original. Jules de la Mesnardière, in his *Poétique* of 1639, continued to attack the Spaniards—and, to some degree, the Italians. La Mesnardière found the great Spanish dramatist, Lope de Vega, an "esprit fort intelligent," but one who wasted his skills on the "multitude ignorante" (the French in the sixteenth and seventeenth centuries constantly attacked the *vulgaire*) even though Lope knew the rules and had written them down in his *Arte nuevo.* Boileau's remark in his *Art poétique* will be recalled: "beyond the Pyrenees" in a poorly regulated land a dramatist could break the rules "with impunity." La Mesnardière saw in France and her neighbors certain national characteristics that might have influenced critical attitudes. As for the French, he considered them "courteous, bold, inconstant, polite, fickle in love; the Spaniards were "presumptuous, tyrannical, politically astute, somber, ridiculous in love"; the English were "faithless, lazy, brave, cruel, property-conscious, hostile to strangers, arrogant, and self-interested." Though the French are not given a blanket coating of whitewash by La Mesnardière, they fare better in his hands than other nations close by.[6]

Since the sixteenth century the French have had few doubts about the superiority of their language over the other underdeveloped tongues of the world. The grammarian, Gilles Ménage, said in a letter of dedication of his *Observations sur la langue française* (1672) to the sophisticated chevalier de Méré: "Indeed, monsieur, since the establishment of the Académie Française (in 1635), our language is not only the most beautiful and most rich of all living languages, it is also the most restrained and most modest." At about the same time, le Père Bouhours, the Jesuit father whose critical opinions were so well-known in his day, wrote a series of imaginary conversations between one Eugène and his friend, Ariste, while they were walking along a beach in Belgium. Ariste remarks that it is wonderful to know languages, since they enable a person to go anywhere in the world without an interpreter.

Ariste concedes the truth of Eugène's statement but adds:
"All your arguments will not give me any desire to learn
Flemish." The reply to this reservation is: "Already French
is spoken in all the courts of Europe. Every foreigner who
has any wit at all prides himself on knowing French. Those
who hate us as a nation love our language."[7]

Bouhours has his interlocutors go on in further praise of
French, about which there is something *noble* and *auguste,*
lifting it *infiniment* above Spanish and Italian. Spanish lacks
real majesty, although there is nothing more "pompous than
Castilian," which gives "big names to little things." Man-
çanares, for example, is such a big word that one would think
that the Madrid river is "le plus grand fleuve du monde"
when in reality it is a "petit ruisseau qui est le plus souvent à
sec." Spanish is full of *pompe* and *ostentation* while French
has a "grandeur raisonnable." Italian, for its part, is too much
like burlesque and is frolicsome with its diminutives such as
bambino, bambinello, huometto, and similar forms. Spanish
is like an unbridled torrent, Italian is a gurgling brook, while
French is a splendid river (neither too slow nor too fast) en-
riching every area through which it passes, as its waters roll
along *majestueusement* with a current that is *toujours égal.*
French has in it a natural "order," is smooth, subtle, and capable of both clarity and tenderness; any awkwardness of phras-
ing in the language is the result of foreign importation, like,
said Bouhours, "the jargon of some German recently arrived
in Orléans."[8]

The English did not, during the classical period, escape
critical derogation on the part of the French. René Rapin, in
his *Réflexions sur la poétique d'Aristote* of 1674, attacked the
Italians, Spaniards, and the English for lacking measure and
restriction, and for not knowing how to "finish things where they
should be finished," something that Horace and Vergil understood. As for the English our neighbors, said Rapin, they are
rough and insular, and "separated from the rest of men"; therefore, "in their plays they are fond of blood, in keeping with the
nature of their temperament." The French, on the other hand,

are more "human" and a "sophisticated sentiment is legitimate for our tragedies." This feeling went on into the eighteenth century when, despite a growing critical *entente cordiale* between France and England, Voltaire in his famous letter on tragedy called Shakespeare's plays *farces monstrueuses*. A bit later the Abbé Raynal, in his *Nouvelles littéraires,* described the English theater for the duchesse de Saxe-Gotha: "You are acquainted, Madame, with the English theatre: it is without manners, without decency, without rules; these islanders are naturally so somber, so sad, so melancholy that the roughest, boldest, most exaggerated scenes are never too much to distract them and affect their emotions." Raynal then regretted that in recent years the French had had the bad taste to copy English tragedy and forget "Roman loftiness and grandeur."[9]

In the sixteenth and seventeenth centuries, then, the French in their critical attitude looked back to Greece and Rome. They sought to find rules for composition among the ancients, and were prone to find rigorous rules in what might be merely suggestions. Possibly more than any other nation in Europe, they respected order, ritual, measure, regularity, and form. Thus there was never in reality a "baroque movement" in the sixteenth and seventeenth centuries in France—despite latter-day efforts to discover one—since the mercurial elusiveness of the baroque could not appeal to the formalistic critical nature of the French. Yet many of France's own writers spoke out against pedantic expositions and lengthy interpretations. Rabelais criticized those who made compendia of compendia, and Montaigne attacked the pedants who tried to explain any given book, frequently in a wordy appendix longer than the book itself. Nevertheless, the French listened to a secondary critic like Jean Chapelain, the oracle of Aristotle; or to a primary critic like Boileau, who was called the legislator of Parnassus. It might be mentioned that the French during these centuries were very fond of Parnassus; for the formal entree of Louis XIV and Marie-Thérèse into Paris in 1660, a forty-foot Parnassus was constructed at a street intersection and on the "mountain" were nine Muses under the guidance of Apollo in a blonde wig.

And Jacques de la Taille had said in a little treatise of 1573, *La manière de faire des vers en français comme en grec et en latin,* that the best way to climb Parnassus was "on the road carved out by the Greeks and Romans."

French allegiance to the rigors of definition and to the rules might be noted in Antoine Fouquelin's *Rhétorique françoise* of 1555—a real study of rhetoric and not one of the medieval analyses of prose and poetry. Fouquelin hoped through his manual to recreate a few Demosthenes and Ciceros in France. The figures of speech—allegory, enigma, hyperbole, synecdoche, epanalepsis, and such things—should be studied early by the prospective orator. As a child his mouth should be "formed by a grammarian, so that he may pronounce all the sounds of the letters roundly and perfectly, and not vomit the words out of his stomach like a drunkard." The process of speaking was described in the sixteenth century by Barthélemy Aneau, who was a professor at a *collège* in Lyon. Aneau said, with attempted precision and exactitude, that correctly spoken French demanded *neuf instruments,* "nine instruments": the tongue, the palate, the gullet, two lips, and four teeth. The specific four teeth required were not indicated, but the theory as a whole was supposed to go back to some Latin treatise on the subject.[10]

The formalistic interpretation of ancient authority might be observed in the French attitude toward the unities. To Aristotle's unity of action and his suggested unity of time (or "circuit of the sun"), the French added in the sixteenth century a unity of place—with an assist from the Italian, Castelvetro. Even Ronsard in the 1587 edition of his works had some remarks to make on the unities. Tragedy and comedy, he said, are like mirrors to human life, but they must teach a lot of things in very few words, "since they are limited and compressed in a small space, that is to say one day." Ronsard then offered a prescription for easing the restrictions of the unity of time: "The most excellent masters of the profession of writing plays extend them from one midnight until the next, and not from daybreak to the setting of the sun, in order to have a greater extent and length of time." Vauquelin de la Fresnaye in his *Art poétique,* published in 1605, laid out specific unities of time for both tragedy and the epic: tragedy should be based on an "argument" of a whole day while an epic could deal with happenings that might take place in one year—another extension of Aristotle's poetic laws. Pierre de Laudun, in a rare opposing voice, said in his *Art poétique* of 1597 that if a tragedy had five acts, it was "completely impossible for all that to take place in one day." Chapelain, the critical spokesman for Richelieu and dispenser of the Cardinal's pensions, sought to put drama back on a regular course in 1630 with his *Lettre sur la règle des vingt-quatre heures.* Chapelain based his argument on *vraisemblance,* or verisimilitude, and maintained that nothing could be "less in keeping with *vraisemblance* than the poet's representation of the events of ten years in two or three hours." Chapelain argued further that ignoring the rules of antiquity brought confusion and little satisfaction from a play, "for there is nothing so certain as the fact that the production of pleasure, as with every thing else, is done through order and verisimilitude." Street entertainment and the farces, therefore, appeal only to the *vulgaire,* the "dregs of the people."[11]

The unity of place came to be accepted as a *vraisemblable* spot, one that was conceivably accessible to either the actors or spectators. Corneille, who had difficulty with the unity of time, conceded that it would be improper to set a play both in Rouen and Paris, although it might be possible to be in both cities within twenty-four hours. The Abbé d'Aubignac, however, was quite rigorous on the unity of place. In his *Pratique du théâtre* he refused to admit that a play could have its setting in two areas of Paris that were not contiguous. The same décor, for example, could not include both the Louvre and the cathedral of Notre Dame, since such juxtaposing was contrary to reality. A more confident critic like Boileau, in an era of the great tragedies of Racine, stated quite simply in 1674 the unities of tragedy: "one place, one day, one single action completed." The Reverend Père Le Bossu in 1675, in his lengthy *Traité du poème épique,* made some interesting comparisons between tragedy and the epic. He thought that the unities of time and place (nobody argued about the propriety of the unity of action) were proper to the theater, since a spectator would think it unnatural to sit in his seat and spend "days and nights without sleeping, without drinking, and without eating." Aristotle had put no time limit on the epic and it really was not necessary to do so, said Le Bossu, because a reader could stop any time for repose, good red wine, and some solid nourishment. Le Bossu could not resist, however, giving the epic a limit of a year in time, since he considered that the "winter is as little appropriate for the great work as the night is for tragedy."[12]

Le Bossu would find in the form of tragedy the mold in miniature for the epic; the longer narrative action of the epic would thus be an extension of the episode of tragedy. In an elaboration of this theory he made a rather amusingly precise analysis of the *Iliad,* which for him had an over-all duration of forty-seven days. And here is his method of measurement: Nine days might be omitted since they were concerned with the pestilence that struck the Greeks before Achilles' quarrel with Agamemnon, and eleven days of truce were given to Priam and the Trojans; twenty-seven days remained, eleven of which were needed for the convalescence of the Greeks, and eleven more were consigned to Achilles for the burial of Patroclus. The combats around Troy, therefore, began and ended within five days—and Achilles, the "premier héro du poème," fought only one day. The primary action of the *Iliad* was thus reduced in essence by Le Bossu to tragedy's twenty-four hour rule, though he readily conceded that there are other ways of "counting time" in an epic.

But French criticism in the sixteenth and seventeenth centuries was not concerned solely with the rigorous mechanics of fitting a tragedy into twenty-four hours or with how much limitation of material there should be in an epic. As early as 1565 Ronsard tried to define *invention:* he called it "the fine quality in the imagination for conceiving the ideas and forms of all things in order to represent, describe and imitate them"—but without creating "formes monstrueuses." *Disposition* was for him the "elegant and perfect arrangement and order of the things invented;" *élocution* was the "propriety and splendor of words well-chosen and ornamented with brief and sober *sentences*" so that verses might gleam like precious stones properly mounted on the fingers of some *grand seigneur*. To Ronsard's emphasis on *forme* and *ordre* the later period of French classicism added other critical universals—terms like *mesure, vérité, vraisemblance, bienséance, jugement,* and *bon goût*. These words were used with greater certainty by the school of 1660 than had been the case in earlier decades. Critics like Boileau, Racine, Bossuet, Bouhours, Rapin, Le Bossu, La Bruyère, and some others spoke with confidence of what was on their well-disciplined minds.[13]

By the middle of the seventeenth century the French language had become an instrument of precision and clarity, and there was little further need for tinkering with its structure. *Clarté,* which had been urged by such powerful figures as Malherbe and Vaugelas, was by 1650 accepted as a necessary attribute of both prose and poetry. The great critics, therefore, concerned themselves with larger concepts of the poet's art. *Vraisemblance,* for example, was not a question simply of portraying actions that would be accepted by the audience without proof —a definition of the Abbé d'Aubignac. Rapin lifted verisimilitude to a higher level and said that it was attached to the "universal principles of things." Factual truth could often be "defective," but verisimilitude, according to Rapin's more Aristotelian conclusion, molded "things as they should be." But he did think that a tragedy that disobeyed the unities would have no verisimilitude. Madame Dacier felt that the marvelous and verisimilar went along together, though the marvelous might be more appropriately used in the epic while a tragedy had to be very carefully based on verisimilitude.[14]

Another term that was given sober and formalized defining was *bienséance;* it could be used either in the singular or plural and meant the amenities or proprieties. The foundation for the ideological background of the word was laid by Horace in his art of poetry, and La Mesnardière stated that Horace "has left us an art of poetry where the greater part of the *bienséances* concerning the theatre have been touched upon." *Bienséance* would rule out any low words in tragedy as well as dismiss from it the crude pantomime of the farces. The very genteel chevalier de Méré described *bienséance* in personal behavior as the process of "doing the proper thing as though it were the natural thing." Rapin called *bienséance* the most universal of all the rules, since everything that was opposed to the rules of "time, customs, sentiments, and expression" was opposed to *bienséance*. One of the most intriguing terms of the period was *goût* or *bon goût,* taste or good taste. Taste had formalistic implication both for literature and society, and was a difficult term to pin down then even as it would be today. Méré made a pretty good effort at defining it; for him it was a "subtle discernment" that caused a person to choose "excellent things rather than mediocre ones." La Bruyère made a perceptive comment when he said that there is a "point of perfection" in art which only a person of "perfect taste" can recognize. Voltaire ruled Bayle out of his Temple of Taste because Bayle did not appreciate Racine's *Phèdre,* and Madame Dacier blamed what she considered the corruption of taste in the early eighteenth century on a lack of knowledge of Homer and too great an interest in the opera and novels.[15]

Other examples could be given of the rigorous standards of criticism in sixteenth- and seventeenth-century France, but these should be sufficient to show the nature of French allegiance to the rules in these decades. Later analysts, like Lessing in Germany and more recently René Wellek in our own country, have ridiculed French subservience to the rules during the Renaissance and the age of Classicism. However, any critical format that could nurture two lyric poets like Du Bellay and Ronsard, three dramatists like Corneille, Molière, and Racine, and a master of prose style like Bossuet can not be all bad.

And, as was said in the beginning, the French fundamentally like to be encased in a staunch and formalistic set of rules; it is natural to their well-cadenced and *de Gaulliste* souls.

NOTES

1. Saint Evremond, in his *De la tragédie ancienne et moderne* of 1672, states his opinions on the Abbé d'Aubignac—and on tragedy in general.

2. For a general treatment of this question, see W. L. Wiley, "Who Named Them *Rhétoriqueurs?" Medieval Studies in Honor of J. D. M. Ford* (Cambridge: Harvard University Press, 1948), pp. 335-49.

3. Bossuet's admiration for Cicero is to be noted in the great French orator's *Sur le style et la lecture . . . pour former un orateur,* which appeared in 1669 and 1670.

4. For an examination of this point, see W. L. Wiley, "Du Bellay and Ovid," *Romance Notes,* VIII (1966), 98-104.

5. Details in this paragraph are to be found in Thomas Sebillet, *Art poétique,* Book I, Chapter 3—on the differences between a poet and an orator; Peletier du Mans in his *Art poétique* of 1555, Book I, Chapter 2, makes the same distinctions between the poet and orator as does Sebillet; Du Bellay's sonnet on the soul's longing is in the *Olive,* and his comment on the necessity of hard work on the part of the poet is in his *Défense et illustration de la langue française,* Book II, Chapter 3.

6. For these opinions on the *Amadis,* see Vauquelin de la Fresnaye's *Art poétique,* Book II, vs. 1005-7. For the comments on Lope de Vega and various nationalities, see Jules de la Mesnardière's *Poétique,* sigs. T-V; Q_1v-Q_2 (pp. 122-23). This one-volume edition of 1639 has a strange pagination.

7. Gilles Ménage, *Obsérvations sur la langue française,* epistle of dedication, gave his opinions on the superiority of French: "En effet, Monsieur, depuis l'établissement de l'Académie Française, notre langue n'est pas seulement la plus belle et la plus riche de toutes les langues vivantes, elle est encore la plus sage et la plus modeste." Bouhours' conclusions are in his *Entretiens d'Ariste et d'Eugène* (Paris, 1671), pp. 37-40.

8. Bouhours, *op. cit., passim.*

9. See René Rapin, *Réflexions sur la poétique d'Aristote* (Paris, 1674), p. 35, for the Italians and the Spanish; and the Abbé Raynal in his *Nouvelles littéraires* of the *Correspondance littéraire* par Grimm, Diderot, Raynal *et al.* (16 vols.; Paris, 1877), I, 72, for criticism of the English theater. All translations of excerpts are my own.

10. Antoine Fouquelin, *La rhétorique françoise* (Paris, 1555), p. 51 verso, for the training of a child; and Barthélemy Aneau, *Quintil Horatian* (in E. Person's ed. of Du Bellay's *Défense*), p. 198, for the "nine instruments."

11. For many of these points, see Ronsard's preface to the third book of his *Franciade;* Vauquelin de la Fresnaye, *Art poétique,* Book II, vs. 253-60; Pierre de Laudun, *L'art poétique français,* Book V, Chapter 9; Jean Chapelain, *Lettre sur la règle des vingt-quatre heures, passim.*

12. Corneille takes up the unities of time and place in his *Discours des trois unités,* wherein he says that the journey from Paris to Rouen could be made "en poste" in twenty-four hours; Boileau's famous remarks on the unities are in his *Art poétique,* third *chant,* vs. 28 ff. Le Bossu, *Traité du poème épique* (Paris, 1675), II, 268 ff., discusses the duration of the *Iliad,* while his general opinions on epic and tragedy are to be found in his *Traité,* I, 11; II, 140, 265 ff.; III, 379.

13. These ideas of Ronsard come from his *Abrégé d'un art poétique.*

14. Rapin, *Réflexions,* pp. 27, 39 ff., 52—for ideas on *vraisemblance;* Madame

Dacier, *Des causes de la corruption du goust* (Paris, 1714), pp. 76-77, 98—for the marvelous and verisimilar.

15. For these points on *bienséance* and *bon goût,* see La Mesnardière, *La poétique,* sig. FF; the chevalier de Méré, *Oeuvres complètes* (3 vols.; Paris, 1930), II, pp. 10 ff., 128-29; Rapin, *Réflexions,* p. 108; Jean de la Bruyère, *Les caractères* (Lille, 1884), p. 7; Madame Dacier, *Des causes,* p. 26.

IV

1367: The Founding of the Spanish College at Bologna

Berthe M. Marti
The University of North Carolina at Chapel Hill

The subject of my talk today concerns one aspect of the history of medieval education. I have limited myself to a minor chapter of this history, that of the college because, although the rise and development of the medieval universities have been widely studied, and monographs have been published on the origins of most of the great European institutions of higher learning, the colleges have been neglected.[1]

The meaning of the words university and college has changed since the Middle Ages and I shall use them today in their medieval acceptation. *Universitas*, or university, which simply means a whole or a union, was, in academic circles, applied to the union of students and/or masters. The purpose of the university, or association, was to afford legal protection to students and masters residing in lands other than their own.[2] At Paris the majority of masters as well as students had come from other places and, soon realizing the helplessness of individuals isolated in foreign lands and the collective powers of guilds, they united into a well organized university under the leadership of the masters. This type of association was imitated by most of the northern institutions. At Bologna, where the professors were citizens of the town, the foreign students alone, who attended their lectures in vast numbers, needed this legal protection. The doctors of Bologna, therefore, as well as the students originating from the city, were excluded from the association or university. What we call university was then the *studium,* if it lacked some faculty, or *studium generale* if it offered training in all of them. Thus, other things being equal, The University of North Carolina, lacking the school of theology, would have been a *studium,* Duke, on the other hand would have been a *studium generale.*

Now a college, or *collegium,* was a very different thing. In Roman law, *collegium* meant a corporation and, in medieval scholastic centers, the word had come to be applied to an endowed residence for a body of generally impecunious scholars. Their need was obvious. The medieval student, like his modern successor, was faced with the necessity of finding board and lodging at reasonable prices. In towns famous for their *studium,* landlords were apt to make extortionate charges, in spite of constant efforts on the part of university officials, especially the rectors and councilors of the *universitas,* to control prices. Theological students could stay in monasteries. Students with sufficient means often got together in small groups, rented a house where they lived as a community and which they used as a sort of eating club. These voluntary associations are the prototypes of American fraternities.

But, unable to afford the expense of renting a house, buying furniture, and hiring servants, poor students often lived in squalid conditions. Wealthy patrons, therefore, began to establish endowed residences for them.[3] It is of this institution of the endowed residence for poor scholars, the college, that I shall speak briefly today. My talk will be focused mainly upon a college established for the benefit of needy students from Spain who had come to study in the famous *studium generale* of the city of Bologna; all of them were to be secular, no member of a religious order could be admitted. This Spanish college was set up by the last will and testament of Cardinal Egidio Albornoz in 1367, exactly six hundred years ago. It is as part of the celebration of its six hundredth anniversary this year that I have chosen to speak of this college, which has succeeded in surviving all the vicissitudes which beset the European continent during the six centuries of its existence.

I shall compare it briefly with a number of similar foundations endowed before the fifteenth century in Paris and Bologna. Though several survive today in the British Isles, the Spanish College alone on the Continent still functions in much the manner specified by the founder, and in the very buildings erected for it originally. In this, the Spanish College at Bologna is unique on the European continent, the sole survivor there of a medieval college.

I shall first discuss the origin of the earliest colleges, and the motives which prompted medieval men in general, and Cardinal Albornoz in particular, to found such institutions. I shall go on to examine some provisions in college charters, and in the Spanish College especially, with regard to the requirements for admission and the length of tenure of the scholarship. We shall glance at some of the statutes regulating the conduct of the students during their residence in the Spanish College. Finally, in view of the almost total disappearance of this type of institution, we shall consider some of the provisions made by the Cardinal and by other college founders to ensure the survival of their foundation.

The idea of founding what may be called the very first college came to an Englishman when, on his return from a pilgrimage to Jerusalem in 1180, he saw a room set aside in a Paris hospital for a few poor clerks. Let me quote the charter of this very simple foundation: "I Barbe d'Or, dean of the Church of Paris, and the entire chapter of the same church. We wish it made known to all present, or to come, that when Sir Jocius de Londoniis of London returned from Jerusalem and inspected with extreme zeal of devotion the administration of the hospice of the blessed Mary at Paris, for the poor and sick, he saw there a certain room in which, by an old custom, poor clerks were lodged. He acquired it, in perpetuity, from the proctors of the same house for the use of the said clerks at a cost of 52 pounds, by our advice and that of Master Hilduin, Chancellor of Paris, then a proctor of the same place, on this condition, that the proctors of the same house forever provide sufficient beds for eighteen scholars and clerks and each month twelve *nummi* from the alms collected in the hospital chest.

The said clerks should take turns at carrying the cross and holy water before the bodies of those who die in the same house, and each night celebrate the seven penitential psalms and the due prayers instituted of old. Moreover, that this remain firm and stable, the said Jocius ordered this charter of our constitution to be drawn up for the said clerks, and he demanded that it be confirmed by the mark of our seal. Done publicly at Paris in our chapter, the year of the Incarnation of the Lord 1180 . . . (the names of the members of the chapter follow).[4]

By 1231 this earliest college had moved to a house of its own, and was known as the Collège des Dix-Huit or College of the Eighteen. It lasted until the French revolution.

Though not so ancient, the most influential college on the Continent was the foundation of Robert de Sorbon, the *domus Sorbonica* or Sorbonne. Its history was outlined here in Chapel Hill by Professors René Hardré and A. Gabriel on the occasion of its septicentennial celebration in 1953—the Sorbonne antedates the Spanish College at Bologna by slightly over a century.[5]

This differs in various important points from other colleges, including the Spanish College. The main difference is the stress which Robert de Sorbon placed upon teaching in the house and the concentration upon the study of theology. The scholars, who already held the degree of Master of Arts, were all working toward the doctorate in theology. Resident masters were to provide lectures in this discipline to the bursars, whereas in most medieval colleges the students attended lectures given at the *studium* and were not taught in the college which, however, often had a resident-master who acted as a kind of *repetitor*. Thus Robert de Sorbon's college combined the functions of a house providing free board and lodging to poor scholars and residence to a community of secular priests who did not belong to the mendicant orders and who gave tuition-free lectures in theology to the scholars.

This determined the future course of the foundation which, as is well known, functions today in a manner totally different from that of a medieval college. Early additional gifts and the growing fame of its teachers made it possible for the Sorbonne to attract other distinguished theologians from the Paris *studium*. It soon was recognized as the center of the theological studies in Christendom and by the end of the fourteenth century was the seat of the most important of the Parisian faculties, that of theology, which it had absorbed. Henceforth it became a building, in which lectures were held, rather than a college. By that time colleges were found in most university towns. In Paris there were thirty before the end of the fourteenth century.

In Bologna, colleges were never as numerous as they were in Paris. One reason may be this: many men already through the liberal arts course, which was a prerequisite for admission to its famous faculties of medicine and law, came to Bologna for advanced training.[6] They were often men of substance, engaged in lucrative positions, who had no need of financial help.

Nevertheless, numerous youngsters in the arts and in the other faculties came from far away and had no means of livelihood. A Bolognese Bishop of Avignon, Zoen Tencarari (1242-61), made provision to take care at Bologna of eight youths from Avignon. Guglielmo Corvi of Brescia founded in 1326 the Collegio Bresciano, modeled on the Sorbonne. Again in 1362, the college of Reggio was established by a physician of Reggio, Guido Ferrarini, for students from the region of Reggio Emilia. Only a few years later the Spanish College was founded by Cardinal Albornoz (1367) while Pope Gregory XI established his *collegium gregorianum* in 1371, which in 1436-37 absorbed the colleges of Avignon and of Brescia.

There is no time even to sketch the life of this Spanish Cardinal, a brilliant diplomat and militant ecclesiastic, one of the greatest and most fascinating figures of the fourteenth century. An authoritative biography of him remains to be written and there is much unpublished material about him in the Bologna archives as well as in Spain. Born of noble parents, in youth he battled the Moors in his native Spain and spent the latter part of his life as Papal Legate in Italy, fighting military and diplomatic campaigns to regain the Papal State and restore the Pope to the throne of Saint Peter, after the long exile in Avignon.[7] That the struggle was successful is due in large part to his energetic and shrewd leadership. By an irony of fate, Pope Urban V had left Avignon and already reached Italy on his way back to Rome, when Cardinal Albornoz, who was so largely responsible for the Pope's return and was preparing to join him for the last stretch of the triumphal procession to Rome, fell ill and died near Viterbo on August 23, 1367. In his testament he left as his residuary legatee the college in Bologna, the buildings of which, still in use as a Spanish College today, were almost completed when he died.[8]

Colleges are among the most characteristic charitable foundations of the Middle Ages, and founders of such institutions were moved by the love of God, by the most devout intention to act according to the spirit of the Gospels, and by a sincere and humane concern for the welfare of poor scholars. But men's motives are seldom entirely pure and disinterested. From what we have seen so far, it is clear, first of all, that the privilege of admission to a college was in general restricted to students originating from the same land, diocese, or town as the founder. Guido of Reggio for instance had limited his benefaction to students from Reggio Emilia. The Collège des Douze Médecins, which Pope Urban V had founded in Montpellier with his brother Anglic, received only students from their own town and diocese.[9] Students at the Collège de Pélegry in Paris must be legitimate children and come if possible from lands owned by the founder's family, or at least from their immediate neighborhood. The Treasurer of the Church of Rouen wished that the scholars admitted to his college in Paris should be, if possible, either from Grand-Caux or from Petit-Caux, otherwise from the diocese of Rouen. In Montpellier, the Collège de Pézenas (March, 1338) was to take care of poor relatives of Bishop Trigard, the founder, and of boys from his town of Pézenas. Pope Gregory's foundation, the *collegium gregorianum* admitted twenty scholars from his city of origin, Limoges (or from the diocese of Limoges), and ten in addition from the Papal State in Italy. Unlike the majority of college founders, however, Cardinal Albornoz was not motivated by narrowly regional patriotism. His was a broader, if still national, vision.

[75]

He defined Spain as comprising, not only Castile and Aragon, but as the whole Iberian peninsula, including Portugal.

Some founders who restricted admission to candidates from their own town of origin also wished to express their gratitude by admitting to their foundation boys from the town or diocese which had honored them with high office. We saw that Zoen Tencarari, a citizen of Bologna, had made provision for boys from Avignon, because he was Bishop of that city. The French Pope Gregory XI, for instance, by admitting boys from the Papal State as well as from his native Limoges, stressed the fact that, as Pope and temporal ruler of the newly recovered Papal State in Italy, he had reached the highest position in Christendom. Thus, in their colleges, founders united their names with those of their own towns of origin and with the places where they had received honors. In so doing they built for themselves a living monument more eloquent by far than the dead stones on which ancient Roman officials had recorded their *cursus honorum*. For they believed that, in their college, generation after generation of scholars would, in perpetuity, remind posterity of themselves and of their careers.

None, to my knowledge, was ever more punctilious in this than was Cardinal Albornoz. He set up a detailed procedure whereby one scholar or more were to be selected and presented by each one of the places where he had at any time held office or received benefices. Thus of the twenty four scholars (by 1372 the number had been raised to thirty, so ample had the endowment been) four were to be presented by the city and diocese of Toledo where he had been archdeacon and archbishop, one to study theology, two canon law, and one medicine. From the city and diocese of Cuenca, where he had held his first ecclesiastical benefice and where he was still archdeacon when he died, four scholars also, of whom two were to study canon law, one theology, and the other medicine. And so on through every place with which he had ever been connected: Compostella, Saragossa, Daroca, Avila, Arevallo, Salamanca, Burgos, Leon, Palencia, Osma, Siguenza, Lisbon, Oviedo, Cordova. This list of patron churches reads like a summary of the cardinal's official biography, his *cursus honorum*.

Moreover, San Clemente in Rome had been his titular church, so the college chapel was to be named in honor of St. Clement. He was from Castile and had ended his career as Bishop of Sabina. So he placed the college, for all time, under the care of the incumbent Spanish Cardinal originating from Castile; or if, at any time, there were no such Spaniard in the college of cardinals, under that of the incumbent cardinal of Sabina.

Not only was the college to be the living monument of a great career, and the cardinal's expression of his gratitude to all the places which had supported and honored him, it must also perpetuate his own and his family's name. One way in which this was done was the specification that two scholars, who were to study canon law, were always to be elected by a member of the house of Albornoz. The cardinal added: ". . . But if, which God forbid, the house of Albornoz should be entirely extinct, the Church of Toledo shall act as its successor for the presentation of one student, and the Church of Cuenca for the other."[10]

Special privileges were decreed for the admission of poor members, and descendants of members, of the house. Careful provision was also made for the reception with due honor, and the entertainment by the college, of any member of the family who should at any time visit Bologna; and for special privileges, especially attendance at the meetings of the college corporation, to be granted any nonresident member of the family studying at Bologna.[11] Although the manner of selecting the scholars has altered drastically, the house of Albornoz and its descendants are still active today in the councils of the college and the Junta under which it operates.

But the main concern of college founders was the salvation of their souls. They trusted that, since they provided poor scholars with the means to study for many years with decorum, this meritorious act of charity would confer upon them some benefit after death. They hoped also that their next of kin would participate in these benefits.

Thus Cardinal Anglic Grimoard, who founded the Collège St. Ruf in Montpellier, in 1364, expressly states that he established it on behalf of his soul and that of his kin.[12] Such statements are found in practically all acts establishing a new college. More than this, however, founders provided for pious intercession within the college on behalf of their souls, and in perpetuity. Provision was always made for at least one chaplain (the Spanish College had four) to say Mass and prayers on their behalf and to celebrate daily the divine offices, attendance to which was compulsory for all students. Scholars had, for all time, the obligation to repay their debt of gratitude to the founder. I quote from the thirty-fifth statute of the Spanish College: ". . . Because the aforesaid scholars are under an obligation to show gratitude for the great benefits which they shall receive in the college, we urge and entreat them in the Lord always devoutly to commend to God, in their prayers, the souls of the said lord Cardinal of Sabina and of his kin. And in order that they may offer some repayment for the favors which they have received in the house of the said lord, we ordain and decree that on behalf of the aforesaid souls, each one from the said college shall, if he is a priest, celebrate Mass in reverence to the most Holy Trinity at least three times a month. . . . But all the others, who are not priests, shall be required to read through the seven penitential psalms every week, with the litanies and all the prayers. If anyone, suffering from the vice of ingratitude, should fail to observe this salutary statute, he shall be punished according to the judgment of the rector, and he shall absolutely be required to say the prayers which he had omitted. . . ." And from the sixteenth statute: "at the end of grace, both at the midday and the evening meals, all shall be required to stand up and pray, especially in commemoration, and on behalf of, the souls of the Lord Cardinal Egidio, our benefactor, and of his kin. They shall say a *Requiem Aeternam* with the psalm *De Profundis* and the prayer 'O God who wast pleased to raise thy servant to the dignity of the Episcopate' and also 'O God the

Creator and Redeemer of all the faithful. . . .' " In almost the same words, Pope Gregory provided, in the statutes of his own Gregorian College, for the intercession of his scholars, present and future, on behalf of his soul and those of his kin.[13] In the Collège des Douze-Médecins likewise, all residents were to say special prayers for the souls of the lord founder both at dinner and at supper.[14] Every Sunday, the scholars of the Collège de Rodez must hear Mass and pray on behalf of the founder's soul and of those of his family.[15] The Mass of the dead must be said in their college annually, *in perpetuo,* for Raymond de Pélegry and for his brother on the anniversary of their deaths; and the residents must also pray in the church of St. Andrew in Cahors, where the founder's parents were buried before the high altar.[16] The statutes of the Spanish College also provided for a commemorative service on the anniversary of the cardinal's death which is celebrated in the college chapel today.

Why did he select Bologna rather than some other *studium?* Spain was out of the question: It had been torn asunder by wars against the Moors; and its *studia* had declined. Much of his life had been spent in Italy where no *studium* could compare with that of Bologna, which still held the primacy in civil and canon law. Among the thousands of foreign students who flocked to Bologna there had always been numerous Spaniards. Though the cardinal himself had studied law at Toulouse,[17] his nephews, one of whom he made rector or governor of the city, had been trained in the Bologna *studium.* It was his intention that there an elite of distinguished Spaniards should be trained, who could fill administrative posts in Church and State with high competence, and supply with skilled men the depleted professions of medical doctors, jurists, teachers, and theologians.

Furthermore, Bologna was in many respects a key city in his plans for the rebirth of the Papal State. Geographically so situated on the Via Emilia, at the convergence of many roads, as to be of the greatest political significance, it had already received many benefactions from the cardinal. Moreover, its *studium* was beginning to show signs of decline, and it was imperative to retain there the population of foreign students which had contributed so much to making it a flourishing center of higher studies, first and supreme in law and, over-all, second only to Paris. A few years later Pope Gregory XI established there a college for poor students, for many of the same reasons which had prompted Albornoz to select Bologna.

Let me digress a moment in order to account in part for this decline which Pope and Cardinal were so anxious to arrest, by founding colleges for foreign students. Living expenses had risen to a point where masters as well as students found staying in Bologna almost intolerable. Moreover, although the town had declared itself a strong supporter of the Guelph party, there were factions and frequent dissensions, against which the church had to take strong measures. The Interdict in particular pronounced by Pope Benedict had so disrupted the *studium* that many students had left for those of Padua, Naples, and Pavia; and many others had gone home; the *studium* was in danger of losing its pre-eminence. In order further to appreciate the serious situation of the *studium,* we must briefly consider the position of the professors there, as it appears in the statutes of the municipality and of the university, various provisions of which are quoted by Rashdall. Held in the highest esteem, they were granted many privileges by the commune. They had organized themselves into a closed corporation, the college of doctors, which turned the profession almost into a caste. They had succeeded in making it practically impossible for a man who was not a graduate of the *studium* and a citizen of Bologna, to become a professor there. The position had, in addition, become almost the hereditary possession of a few Bolognese families. Yet though they were rich and respected, their lot was not enviable.

Since the economic prosperity of Bologna depended in large measure upon the vast population of foreign students attracted by the fame of the Bologna doctors, it was imperative that the city keep them there. They received lucrative offers from other *studia* and when anyone of them left, his students were apt to follow him. The terror of the Bologna Commune was the students' sudden departure from the city. It therefore passed decrees absolutely forbidding the professors to leave. Those who contravened were severely punished. We hear, for instance, of a certain professor of medicine who had moved to Pisa to teach. After recalling him in vain four times, it was decreed by the authorities that if he were ever captured, he would be beheaded as a traitor to the Commune.

Not only were the professors subject to this pressure from the commune. The students' university, entirely democratic as far as its own members were concerned, voted and enforced statutes to regulate the teaching and even the private lives of the professors, who were as we say excluded from the association. It had developed powerfully in spite of the joint opposition of the commune and of the regent doctors. The students had won the battle by the constant threat of secession and now played a very large part in the administration of the *studium*. They imposed their will in matters concerned with the curriculum and the professors' methods of teaching. Every year some students were charged by the rector of the university with spying upon the professors. They reported any failure to observe the statutes on the part of the teachers, who had been forced to swear allegiance to them, even though they had had no hand in framing them. Professors had to take an oath before the students' rectors that they would fulfill their teaching duties conscientiously. If a teacher arrived late to class, or if he kept his students after the bell had rung, he was fined. If in his lecture he failed to treat certain points at the precise date set for them, if he did not complete his program by the end of the term, or if he failed to use the prescribed method of disputation, he was likewise penalized. The students' rectors even at times sat in on the examinations. A professor must ask their permission to absent himself from Bologna, even for a short time. No wonder that when a political upheaval gave them the chance they were tempted to go elsewhere, and that at the time of the founding of the Spanish and of the Gregorian colleges, the schools and faculties were partly depleted. The new foundations helped to arrest for a time the decadence of the *studium*.

Let us now return to the colleges. I have several times

mentioned the statutes of the Spanish College. The earliest version of these has disappeared, but we know from various documents that it must have existed; and before any college could operate, it was necessary for such an instrument, however brief and simple, to be approved by the Pope, usually through a cardinal delegated by him to inspect the house and the provisions made for its organization. In the case of a college such as that founded by Raymond de Pélegry at Cahors, the Prince of Wales, as Duke of Aquitaine, also had had to approve the foundation in 1368.[18]

We do have a very early revision made less than ten years after the opening of the Spanish College, extant in one manuscript, now in the Gordan collection in New York, and an incunabulum at the British Museum. I shall now quote a few fragments from my edition and translation of it, in order that you may realize the provident care with which the cardinal and his executors attempted to anticipate and legislate about every contingency that might arise in the future. Although all statutes are based on the conventional formulae set down in the textbooks of the notaries, those of the Spanish College are more searching and detailed than most of the ones with which I am acquainted. I find in them an extraordinarily subtle combination of the excessively democratic organization of the Bologna university, and of the authoritarian and hierarchical dispositions, which regulated life in the religious houses. The scholars selected their rector, generally from their own ranks, by secret ballot, as well as their councilors. Like the student rectors of the university, the college rectors held great powers and heavy responsibilities, administrative, financial, and disciplinary. All important business, however, must be decided only after consultation with the whole college chapter whose members each had one vote. The college was a self-governing body, democratic in character since the authority was vested in the fellows and in the officers elected by them. They dealt with large sums of money and vast estates, as the heirs of the cardinal, during their residence.

But their authority was limited in various ways, specified by the statutes. A system of checks and counter checks, borrowed in part from monastic rules, ensured against the danger of laxity and abuse of power. The main difference between the college and the university was the fact that no member of the college, nor the whole college corporation, even if unanimous, had the power to introduce any new legislation or to make any exception to the rules. They did not make the statutes under which they lived and could not alter a word of the original constitution. This could only be done after an appeal to the Pope or the cardinal protector, who might order a revision made by a specially appointed Papal delegate.

Before admission, an examination into the candidate's qualifications (origin, poverty, character, and competence) was usually required,[19] to be taken in most cases orally before the whole college corporation. It covered the prerequisites, elementary grammar and reading in the case of young boys, as for instance at the Collège Rodez, where the scholars must be over nine years old and know their prayers and the psalter. Before they could be enrolled, more advanced students were examined in the subjects of the arts' course, grammar and rhetoric mainly. Cardinal Albornoz, aware of the difficulties that a youngster would encounter in Bologna if, after being presented by one of the patron churches and having come such a long way, he were refused admission, made humane provisions to help such candidates outside the college, until they could gain admittance.

The Seventh Statute of the Spanish College states: "Although, for those who wish to study well, a period of seven years is usually sufficient . . . because students are more remiss today than they used to be; and in order that they may make better progress, we ordain and decree that those studying in the aforesaid college may remain there for eight continuous years; for in such a long period they may well, if they so wish, rise to the honor of the master's degree."

The scholarship or *bursa* was generally held for seven or eight years. At the Collège des Douze-Médecins it was held for nine years, which included supervised practical training or *pratica*. At Pélegry they were entitled to all the scholars' privileges for seven years, but if they went on to study law they were granted an additional three years. At St. Ruf, students of canon law received an eight-year fellowship, but if they went on to study theology, they could hold it for twelve years. At Rodez, the length of tenure was no longer than five years.[20]

Upon admission to the Spanish College, each student was given a room which, unlike scholars in most other institutions, he shared with no one else. Statute 18 reads: "Each one of the above shall also have a room furnished at the expense of the college with one bed equipped with a mattress or a cover, a feather quilt, and sheets of coarse linen, a bench, a desk, and the straw necessary for the bed. And when these wear out they shall be replaced at the expense of the college, patched and repaired as the rector and the councilors shall see fit."[21]

They also received further supplies: According to the same statute ". . . every year the rector and each of the scholars and chaplains shall be given at the beginning of the school year one new academic gown adequately furred with sheepskin, such as the students at Bologna are normally accustomed to wear, and every year on the first of May, another unfurred gown of cloth of the statutory color, and a hood of the same color, or suitable cloth, worth twenty-five *solidi* (sous), at the expense of the college. They shall wear these clothes and no others, whenever they go to the schools or to the fee estates, this under the penalty of a fine of one *anconitanus* for each infraction, which they shall incur *ipso facto*.[22] Their clothes shall be decent, and they shall not wear unsuitable robes and garments or shoes with pointed toes, under the penalty of one *anconitanus* for each infraction. . . ."

The students were well fed: (Stat. 17): ". . . the rector as well as the scholars and chaplains, the manager and steward shall receive, every day on which the use of flesh meat is not forbidden, one pound of mutton or veal of ordinary quality, or other good meat, varying as the rector shall see fit, according to the requirements of the season. This shall be served along with some suitable dish, as the rector shall decide to ordain. The larger portion of the meat shall be served at the midday meal, the smaller at the evening meal. . . . They shall have wine mixed with water at the rector's discretion and as much bread and salt . . . as they may want and decorum permit. . . . But on feast days and on other days on which the use of flesh meat is not allowed, as much shall be spent on eggs and fish . . . as would otherwise have been spent on meat." (Stat. 16): "In the dining hall itself, the rector shall see to it that the food and other necessities are served to those who are seated in orderly and becoming fashion. . . . And during the meals, decorum, temperance and modesty shall be observed, and silence kept, during the second as well as the first course. For it is our will that, at that time, from the beginning of the blessing of the meal until all who have eaten rise from the table, a scholar or a chaplain shall read the Bible as is the custom of the religious orders . . . each one reading for a week, in turn, according to the seating order. He shall read in a loud voice and without haste, so that what he reads may be easily heard by all."

Sick students seem to have been well taken care of. They were visited daily by a doctor; servants looked after them and the cook was ordered to prepare special meals for them according to the regime ordered by the doctor; and a heated room was set aside in the college or outside to serve as an infirmary. During their illness they received in cash twice what would have been spent on their food if they had been in good health. But statute 19 warned: "the rector shall give careful and cautious attention to the possibility that some student might pretend illness when there is none." And a little later: "But because physical illness is often caused by sin, we ordain and decree that any sick person if he is strong enough and able, shall be required to confess within three days, at the most, from the time when he has taken to his sick bed. He shall confess all his sins purely and fully . . . otherwise, from that moment until he shall have obeyed our ordinance, he shall be suspended from all the aforesaid privileges."[23]

All sorts of precautions were taken to keep the boys out of harm's way. As in all colleges, the gates were locked every evening and a boy returning, after this was done, was put on bread and water.[24] If this occurred several times, he would first be suspended, then excluded from the college. Anyone who spent the night out was put on bread and water for three days, and, in addition, lost half of his year's scholarship. He was dismissed if he absented himself without permission for ten days. Statute 34 adds: "But if, after the gate has been locked, he should leave the house either through the window, or by some other machination, he shall forfeit all the rights which he has in the college and shall be expelled irrevocably."

Since lack of discipline had ruined many a college, penalties of all kinds were specified, from small fines to the stocks, an unusually harsh punishment, which is seldom found in college constitutions.[25] This was reserved for brawlers who had come to blows and were condemned to spend five days with at least one foot in a wooden stock, "and the day on which they shall be set free, they shall do penance by eating bread and water on the ground, in the sight of everyone" (Stat. 46). Playing dice was forbidden, and also playing instruments, though the statutes add: "with the exception of those who may wish to do so in their own rooms, for the sake of relaxation, without detriment or annoyance to their fellows" (Stat. 51). Bearing arms, even if worn in such a way as not to be visible, was severely punished (Stat. 43).[26] Receiving women was of course strictly forbidden (Stat. 29).

Soon after admission, the scholars must go on a tour of inspection of all the college holdings, farms, woods, lands, houses, shops, stalls, etc., both within and outside the walls of the city. This brings me to my last point, the preservation of college property and the survival of the Spanish College for which, as the joint inheritance of the scholars, they were singly and severally responsible. There is no time to go into the numerous ways in which the statutes attempt to safeguard the integrity of the college, the detailed accounts which the manager and the steward, the cook, and others must render daily or weekly. The bookkeeping was prescribed, and at the end of each year the books were audited and signed by the rector and councilors. Many of these dating from the very first years are still found in the archives of the college, which contain a great deal of interesting unpublished material. The monies, legal instruments, and other written acts of the college were to be carefully preserved in a chest which could only be opened by several persons together, each of whom held one of the necessary keys. One of the most interesting statutes deals with the care to be taken of the books left by the cardinal to the college. These are called the students' most precious treasure. They must be chained, a list of them established, to which is added every book newly acquired by the library, out of which they are never allowed to be taken.[27] We still have the list of the books willed by the cardinal, a fairly long one, which contains many legal and theological treatises. Many of these are still kept today in the rare book room of the college.

Yet it is less difficult to find reasons for the total disappearance of all colleges founded before the fifteenth century on the continent,[28] than to account for the survival of the Spanish College alone. Many declined because their revenues were inadequate and soon dwindled. Most of the remaining Parisian colleges were closed at the time of the Revolution. They were not reinstated later because, after the reform of the French University, their functions were performed by different types of institutions.

Several of the Bologna colleges were merged with the Gregorian College soon after its foundation. But Pope Gregory's college itself lasted barely a hundred years, being suppressed in 1472. Others disappeared about the same time. In Germany, Italy, and elsewhere, endowed foundations like colleges were always in danger, not only from wars and other upheavals, but from powerful neighbors. Archives in many cities contain documents, many of them unpublished, in which the officials of medieval colleges institute proceedings, or appeals, against governors or consuls of cities, bishops, monasteries, and others. Thus the Collège des Douze-Médecins in Paris was long in difficulties with the Abbot of Valmagne, and the dispute had to be settled by the Roman Curia.[29]

Some founders looked to persons in high positions to

guarantee the safety of their college. In 1384, King Charles VI placed the Collège Pélegry under his protection. And in 1393, the same King sent a *lettre de sauvegarde* placing under his protection the Collège des Douze-Médecins which had been established some ten years earlier.[30]

Cardinal Albornoz and his executors tried to leave nothing to chance. First, the college was placed under the protection of the authorities of Bologna. In the words of the sixtieth chapter "... since the said house, which shall perhaps have weak rulers, may in the course of time find itself in precarious circumstances, if it is not sustained by the favor of powerful and good men, we call upon the rectors, *podestà* and elders of the city of Bologna. Thanks to their justice, praiseworthy government, and the gracious favors which they have ever paternally bestowed upon the students, this holy *studium* has, from the distant past, ranked first among the schools of both branches of law. On account of all these reasons our aforesaid lord, the Lord Cardinal of Sabina, elected this city of Bologna for this, the work of his devotion. He trusted that, to show their reverence for God and their love of the said Lord Cardinal, the citizens of Bologna, who are much obligated to him, would protect this, his college, from the treachery, violence and oppression of evil men ... etc."

Yearly visitations of the college were next provided for and entrusted to the Bishop of Bologna and to the Prior of St. Michel de Busco who were given very broad powers of investigation, correction, and punishment. Stat. 39, however, gives this warning: "But since we have seen by experience that Bishops of Bologna then in office seized possession for themselves of the property of colleges similar to this one, if any bishop should attempt anything of the kind against the property of this college, not only such as is immovable, but also the movable goods, we command the rector, the councilors and each one in the college, under the penalty of perjury and of the privation of his rights in the college, which they shall incur *ipso facto,* to set aside all delay and straightway to bring an action before our Lord Pope and before the Lord Cardinal under whose protection we shall, in a later statute, place this college. Two of the most distinguished members of the whole college shall be in charge of this action, and they shall prosecute the affair to the end."

If the Bishop and the Prior failed to make the visitation, the Lord Archdeacon was to substitute for them; and he received for his trouble, "up to two ducats' worth of malmsey wine and sweetmeats (in maluasia et confectionibus usque ad duos ducatos)."

Most of all, the founder entrusted his college to future cardinals, the incumbent Spanish cardinal originating from Castile if, when problems arose, there should be one in the college of cardinals, or to the incumbent cardinal of Sabina. It is significant to note that through the centuries revision after revision of the statutes show these cardinals active in college affairs.

In the third statute it is stated that the Cardinal hoped, by founding his college "to obviate the ignorance of the Spaniards, for among them, because of the crises of wars and the innumerable other disasters which befell this province in his own time, the knowledge of letters and the number of trained men have been much reduced." In this the cardinal showed extraordinary foresight. For centuries, many alumni of the Spanish College have returned to the homeland, to make famous names for themselves, in law and the sciences, in the arts and theology. Outstanding contributions to the cultural life of Spain have been made, and continue to be made, by the *proles Egidii,* the foster sons of Cardinal Egidio Albornoz.

1. The most comprehensive study of the medieval colleges and universities is Hastings Rashdall, *The Universities of Europe in the Middle Ages*. eds. F. M. Powicke and A. B. Emden (Oxford, 1936) which will hereafter be referred to as Rashdall. For the history of medieval colleges and further bibliography, see: H. Denifle, *Die Entstehung der Universitäten des Mittelalters bis 1400* (Berlin, 1885); H. Denifle and E. Chatelain, *Chartularium Universitatis Parisiensis* (Paris, 1889-97); A. Germain, *Cartulaire de l'Université de Montpellier*, I (1890), II (1912); M. Fournier, *Les Statuts et Privilèges des Universités françaises*, I (Paris, 1890), which will hereafter be referred to as Fournier; James John, *The College of Prémontré in Mediaeval Paris* (Notre Dame, Indiana, 1953); A. Gabriel, *Student Life in Ave Marie College* (Notre Dame, Indiana, 1955); J. H. Beckmann, *Statuta Collegii Sapientiae* (Freiburg in Breisgau, 1957); F. Pegnes, "The Fourteenth Century College of Aubert de Guignicourt at Soissons," *Traditio*, 15 (1959) 428-43; Stephen D'Irsay, *Histoire des Universités françaises* I (Paris, 1933). Many of the documents concerning the founding of medieval colleges in France and Italy (I have limited myself in this paper to material relating to colleges in these two countries) are published in the various collections of papal bulls, privileges, etc., as for instance: Coquelines, *Bullarum Privilegiorum ac Diplomatum Romanorum Pontificum amplissima Collectio* (Rome, 1739); Lynn Thorndike, *University Records and Life in the Middle Ages* (New York, 1944).

2. On the *nations*, loosely organized companies of students coming from the same general area, see Pearl Kibre, *The Nations in the Mediaeval Universities* (Cambridge, Mass., 1948).

3. Although most medieval students were clerks, that is were tonsured and wore the clerical garb of those in minor orders, and were therefore entitled to ecclesiastical benefices, these benefices were hardly sufficient, in general, to provide poor youngsters with the bare essentials. College founders attempted to remedy this situation by providing for the students' sustenance as well as housing. For the Collège de Pélegry: pro eorum victu et sustentatione duo sextaria et una emina frumenti ad mensuram de Caturco [= Cahors] et duodecim barrilos sive sextaria vini . . . ; et pro coampanatgio et bursa pro quolibet pre dictorum, in qualibet septimana, unum crosatum argenti vel eius valorem, computando duodecim crosatos pro uno bono floreno. . . . Fournier I. For the Collège de Rodez: pueris illis dentur seu administrentur vite necessaria regulate et modeste, et pro vestibus et calceamentis cuilibet annuatim tres floreni cum dimidio. . . . If a student received substantial benefices, or inherited specified sums of money, he was in general required to leave the college. See Fournier I, 104ª (St. Ruf), 557ª (Pelegry) etc. See also Du Cange, *Glossarium*, *s.v.* portatum. Collegium Gregorianum, Stat. 17 (in *Bullarum . . . Collectio*, see n. 1 above), referred to hereafter as Coll. Greg.: "Statuimus quod si quemquam ex dicti collegii scholaribus contingat in antea beneficium seu beneficia ecclesiastica valoris annui quinquaginta librarum . . . aut in patrimonio tantum obtinere . . . de dicto collegio recedere et alteri cedere teneatur."

4. The Latin text of this document is published in the *Chartularium Universitatis Parisiensis* (n. 1 above) I, 49. I quote from the translation of Lynn Thorndike, *op. cit.* (n. 1 above) 22.

5. *The Septicentennial Celebration of the Founding of the Sorbonne College* ("Proceedings and Papers" [Chapel Hill, 1953]); A Gabriel, "Robert de Sorbonne," *Revue de l'Université d'Ottawa* 23 (1953), 475-514. See also Fournier, and H. Denifle and E. Chatelain, *op. cit.* (n. 1 above).

6. On the various colleges at Bologna see L. Frati, *Opere della Bibliografia Bolognese*, I (Bologna, 1888) nos. 6735-6907; C. Ghirardacci, *Historia di Bologna* (Bologna, 1669) II, 72, 302 f., 307 f., 603; M. Sarti and M. Fattorini, *De claris Archigymnasii Bononiensis Professoribus saeculo XI usque ad saeculum XIV* (Bologna, 1769, new ed. 1888-90), I, 414 ff.; G. Guidicini, *Cose Notabili della Città di Bologna*, (Bologna, 1873) V, 23-30; G. Zaoli, "Lo Studio Bolognese e Papa Martino V (anni 1416-1420)" *Studi e Mem. per la Storia dell' Università di Bologna* (Bibl. dell' Archiginnasio) ser. 1, III (1912) 107-88; A. Sorbelli, *Storia dell' Università di Bologna* (Bologna, 1940) I, 133 ff.; Rashdall, I, 197 ff.; P. Copeti, *De regali Almo Ancharano Collegio* (Bologna, 1763); A. Dallolio, *Il Collegio Comelli in Bologna* (Bologna, 1932); *Capitoli da osservarsi dalli Collegiali che pro tempore saranno aggregati al Collegio Comello* (Bologna, 1666); G. Buffito and Fr. Fracassetti, *Il Collegio San Luigi dei PP Barnabiti in Bologna* (Florence, 1925); *Constitutiones auctoritate S.D.N. Sixti Papae V confirmatae collegio Montis Alte in civitate Bononiae ab eo erecto praeseriptae* (Bologna, 1627); P. Guerrini, "Guglielmo da Brescia e il collegio Bresciano in Bologna. "*Studi e Mem. per la Storia dell' Univ. di Bologna*, VII (1922), 57-116. See also G. Zaccagnini, *La Vita dei Maestri e degli* Scolari a Bologna (Geneva, 1926). Many documents are published in the various volumes of the *Chartularium Studii Bononiensis* (Imola, 1907). See also Vicente de la Fuente, *Historia de las Universidades, Colegios y demás establicimientos de enseñanza in España* (Madrid, 1884).

7. For the biography of Cardinal Albornoz, and further bibliography, see H. J. Wurm, *Cardinal Albornoz, der zweite Bergründer des Kirchenstaates* (Paderborn, 1892); F. Filippini, "La riconquista dello Stato della chiesa per opera del Cardinale Egidio Albornoz," *Studi Storici*, ed. Amedeo Crivellucci, vols. V-VIII (1896-1900), and *Il Cardinale Egidio Albornoz* (Bologna, 1933); A. Jara, "Don Gil de Albornoz," *Rev. hist. y geneal. española*, II (1913); G. Mollat, "Albornoz," in Alfred Baudrillart, *Dictionnaire d'histoire et de géographie ecclésiastiques*, I (Paris, 1912) cols. 1717-1725, and *Les Papes d'Avignon* (1305-78), ed. 9 (Paris, 1949), 212-39, 248-58 *passim;* Figueroa y Torres, Conde de Romanones, *El Cardenal Albornoz* (Madrid, 1942); Juan Beneyto Perez, *El Cardenal Albornoz de Castilla y Caudillo de Italia* (Madrid, 1950); V. Fanelli, "Roma e il Cardinale Albornoz," *Studi Romani*, VI (1958) 413-21; "Il Cardinale Albornoz nel VI Centenario delle 'Constitutiones' " (1357-1957), *Studia Picena* 37 (1959); J. Glénisson and G. Mollat, *Gil Albornoz et Androin de la Roche, Correspondance des Légats et Vicaires-généraux, Biblioth. Ecoles françaises d'Athenes et Rome,* 203 (Paris, 1964).

8. On the Spanish College see: J. G. Sepulveda, *Brevis Bononiensis Collegii Hispanorum descriptio* in the edition of his collected works (Madrid, 1780) IV; G. Giordani, *Cenni Storici dell' almo Real Collegio Maggiore di San Clemente della Nazione Spagnola* (Bologna, 1855), Hermenegildo Giner de Los Rios and D. Pedro Borrao, *El Cardinal don Gil de Albornoz y su Colegio de los españoles en Bolonia* (Madrid, 1880). Miguel Angel Ortiz Milla, "El Colegio de España," *Bol. de la Real Acad. de la Historia*, 69 (1916) 426-36; Giorgio del Vecchio, "Il Collegio di Spagna a Bologna," *Annuario della cult. Ital.* (1923), and *Il Collegio di S. Clemente degli Spagnoli a Bologna* (Bologna, 1933); Edward Armstrong, "The Spanish College in the University of Bologna," *Italian Studies* (London, 1934), 273-94; V. Beltran de Heredia, "El Colegio de San Clemente de Bolonia y los Colegios Mayores de España," *An. Cult. Italo-Español*, I (1941); Berthe M. Marti, *The Spanish College at Bologna in the Fourteenth Century*, Edition and Translation of its Statutes, with Introduction and Notes (Phila-

delphia, 1966); J. R. Jones "The Six-Hundredth Anniversary of the Founding of the Spanish College at Bologna by Don Gil de Albornoz," *Hispania,* 50 (1967), 555-58.

9. At the Parisian College of Rodez bursars must come from Cahors, Fournier, II, 562: "de civitate seu diocesi Mimatensi de qua diocesi idem dominus fundator et nos originem duximus" (They must be legitimate children, and in addition have no physical defects). See Fournier, II, 139. Only students from the diocese of Rouen, and if possible, from either Grand-Caux or Petit-Caux were admitted to the college founded in Paris in 1268 by William of Saône. This was true of other colleges in Bologna. In his will, Zoen Tencarari, a Bolognese Bishop of Avignon, made provision for the care of eight youths from the diocese of Avignon, three to be selected from among the canons of the Cathedral, two from among the secular clergy of Avignon and one from within the diocese; Guido Bagnoli of Reggio established his college for students from the district of Reggio Emilia.

10. Stat. 3. All the quotations from the statutes are from my edition and translation (see n. 8 above).

11. Most college statutes contained similar provisions to honor members of the founders' families. See the statutes printed in Fournier. At Rodez, for instance: si aliqui habiles et docibiles pueri in genere nostro reperiantur ad discendum dictam scientiam seu scientias, undecumque sint oriundi, quod ipsi preponantur. . . .

12. Unde praefatus dominus Anglicus, episcopus Avinionensis, pro anima sua et parentum suorum et pro remissione suorum peccatorum, *ibid.* II, 106; II, 141.

13. Collegium Gregorianum (hereafter referred to as Coll. Greg.), Stat. 17 (*Bullarum* . . . *Collectio,* see n. 1) "Denique singuli scholares, quamdiu in praefato collegio moram traxerint, singulis diebus, quamdiu vixerimus, versum solum *salvum fac servum tuum* cum oratione *Deus omnium fidelium* etc., et post mortem nostram psalmum *De profundis clamavi ad te* etc., cum oratione *Deus qui inter apostolicos* etc., dicere teneantur. Item singuli non sacerdotes qualibet septimana septem psalmos poenitentiales cum laetaniis semel, sacerdotes autem quolibet mense unam specialem missam de *Sancto Spiritu* nobis viventibus vel de *Requiem aeternam* nobis vita functis, et psalterium quolibet anno, quamdiu ibi erunt, dicere sint astricti. Cf. also Stat. 12, 13.

14. Founded by Pope Urban V. For its statutes promulgated in 1380 by Cardinal Anglic, his brother, see Fournier, II, 137.

15. ". . . et pro animabus nostra et parentum ac consanguineorum nostrorum altissimum rogare, Fournier I 562b.

16. From the statutes revised in 1389: (Three resident priests) qui habeant specialiter rogare Deum in predicta missa pro animabus dictorum fundatorum et benefactorum suorum et dicti collegii et quod omnes scolares in dicta missa interesse debeant, *ibid.,* I, 354b; cf. 555a.

17. For bibliography about the university of Toulouse, see J. Puget, "L'université de Toulouse," *Annales du Midi* 42 (1930), 345-81.

18. On February 9, 1368, Fournier, II, 553.

19. From the statutes of the Collège de Pélegry revised in 1389: . . . si sufficientes et de legitimo matrimonio reperiantur . . . nec recipiatur . . . nisi adminus addiscat partes et bene competenter legat psalterium, et hoc ante receptionem videatur et probetur per magistrum et gubernatorem, Fournier II, 555b. For Rodez, *ibid.,* II, 561: habiles tamen ad discendum grammaticam et logicam in studio Caturcensi [Cahors].

20. Fournier, II, *passim.*

21. See for examples the statutes of Pélegry, revised in 1389: duo et duo dormiant in uno lecto qui sibi de linteaminibus habeant providere; in culcitra et pulvinari et cooperturis per administratorem et sumptibus collegii eiusdem provideatur. Que quidem linteamina, cum exibunt collegium, pro usu servitorum dimittere teneantur. *Coll greg.* 35: . . . camera fulcita ad modum scholasticum de tribus scannis, uno disco cum rota quatuor librorum et lettica cum culcitra, pulvinari et lodice consignetur, et ista perpetuo expensis collegii manuteneantur.

22. *Coll. greg.* 34: . . . Si quis autem praesumptuosus ita esset, quod pannum statuti in veste superiori alterius coloris quam alii deferre tentaret, ipso facto toto anno expellatur. On the proper clothing for college students see *Morale scolarium*, trans. R. F. Seybolt (Cambridge, Mass., 1921) p. 78; Rashdall, III, 386 ff.

23. *Coll. Greg.* 37: Mandantes etiam scolaribus universis, quatenus ante omnia advocent animae et salutis medicum, saepe et saepius confitendo . . . ut postquam fuerit eidem de spirituali salute provisum, ad corporalis medicinae remedium salubrius procedatur, et in debitam sanitatem velocius instaurentur.

24. The rector of the Collège des Douze-Médecins closed the gate "in prima noctis hora," Fournier, II. At Pélegry, the chaplain or rector himself must close and open the gate, cum clavi de sero et de mane et aliis temporibus opportunis, et claves portarum principalium singulis noctibus custodiat . . . ; *Coll. Greg.* 43: ulterius mandamus rectori, quod diligenter hora condecenti, videlicet in tertia campana noctis iubeat portam communem claudi, et de mane in campana diei et non ante aperiri, penes se continue claves de nocte retenturus. . . .

25. *Coll. Greg.* 30: punitio etiam cum ligneis compedibus singulorum famulorum. . . . According to Rashall, I, 202, punishment in the stocks is not mentioned in English or Parisian colleges till the sixteenth century. Expulsion at the Gregorian college was decreed against those who stayed six days away from the college. If they stayed away without permission one day and night, they were put on bread and water the next day; and for other offenses, see Stat. 41, 44, 45.

26. For further information on academic discipline, see H. Maack, "Grundlagen d. studentischen Disziplinarrechts," *Beitr. Freib. Wissenschafts und Univ. Gesch.,* 10 (1956). Many college statutes specify the punishments to inflict for each type of infraction. See for instance the Collège des Douze-Médecins (Fournier, II, 140b: (expulsion was decreed) si criminis qualitas hoc exegerit. The students were forbidden to own dogs (nisi unum canem communem si utilis videatur, pro custodia dicte domus), to play dice, carry weapons (portare ensem, gladium seu gladios ultra mensuram unius palmi), to introduce women into the house, etc. Expulsion was decreed at St. Ruf: Studentes, si non essent dociles et conversationis honeste . . . a dicta domo libere valeant amovere et amotorum loco seu locis alios honestos et dociles surrogare. . . . Expulsion from Pélegry, see Fournier, II, 568a.

27. In the Collège des Douze-Médecins there were as many keys to the library as there were resident students; the books, chained, were never allowed to be removed. For gifts of books to colleges, see Fournier, *passim.* A detailed list of such a gift of twenty-six books to Pélegry in 1395, for instance, *ibid.* II, 576a. *Coll. Greg.* 54: . . . statuimus et mandamus omnes libros in dicta libraria reponendos, cuiuscumque facultatis seu valoris existant, sub bonis clavibus perpetuis temporibus inchatenari. . . . See also Thorndike, *op. cit.* (n. 1) p. 168.

28. It has been suggested that colleges on the continent disappeared as a

result of the strongly centralized administration of the universities which gradually absorbed both the teaching staffs and the colleges. The opposite process of decentralization of the functions and life of the university in England served to preserve the colleges which almost entirely replaced the university.

29. Fournier, II, 158, 183ᵃ, 191ᵇ, 214, 235ᵇ, etc.

30. Texts in Fournier, II, 158ᵇ, 566ᵃ. After placing the college of Rodez under the protection of Jesus Christ (quem in eis facimus et constituimus principalem et defensorem) the founder of Collège Rodez called upon the consuls of the city of Cahors to look after its interests, *ibid.* 562ᵇ. *Coll Greg.* 56: . . . speciales protectores seu defensores, videlicet episcopum Ostiensem vice-cancellarium Romanum ac unum vel duos alios Cardinales, si qui sint de genere nostro vel de diocesi Lemovicensi, successive duximus ipsi collegio deputandos . . . ; Stat. 58: . . . nostros successores Romanos pontifices ac collegium cardinalium Romanae ecclesiae, praecipue legatos de latere in partibus illis vices Romani Pontificis gerentes, necnon omnes praelatos, barones, nobiles, et quoscumque officiales Ecclesiae, qui pro tempore erunt inibi degentes, ac etiam universitatem Studii Bononiensis . . . obsecramus, quatenus collegium . . . favoribus et praesidiis confovere.

V

The Alliterative Morte Arthure, *the Concept of Medieval Tragedy, and the Cardinal Virtue Fortitude*

Robert M. Lumiansky

University of Pennsylvania, Philadelphia, Pennsylvania

The alliterative *Morte Arthure,* among the most impressive Middle English poems, comes to us from around the end of the fourteenth century. It runs to 4346 lines, and exists in a single version as a part of the Thornton Manuscript, "a collection of poems and treatises on various subjects, some in English, some in Latin." This manuscript is in the Library of Lincoln Cathedral in England. A note at the end of *Morte Arthure* indicates that the hand is that of Robert Thornton, a Yorkshireman who was Archdeacon of Bedford in the diocese of Lincoln about the middle of the fifteenth century. We have, however, no shred of evidence concerning the authorship of the *Morte.*

The poem was five times edited between 1847 and 1915, and in late years notices have appeared of two new editions presently underway. Despite all of this editorial activity, however, surprisingly little analytical commentary concerning the poem—other than general praise—had appeared until recently. In 1960, William Matthews published a book-length work on *Morte Arthure,* called *The Tragedy of Arthur.* In a thorough new source-study Matthews showed that although the bulk of the poem comes from the chronicle tradition found in Geoffrey of Monmouth's *Historia Regum Brittaniae,* Wace's *Roman de Brut,* and Layamon's *Brut,* plus material from the French Arthurian tradition, important additions are from the widely popular medieval story of Alexander the Great, particularly

from *Les Voeux du Paon* and *Li Fuerres de Gades*. These
latter pieces belong to that branch of the medieval tradition of
Alexander which denounces him for pride in excessive conquest and killing, rather than to the other medieval Alexander-
tradition praising him as the ideal military leader and ruler.

On the basis of his source-study and of his reading of various
passages in the text, Matthews argued that the poet so shaped
his inherited materials as to present a highly original theme:
namely, that Arthur—like Alexander—was through pride guilty
of excessive killing, and that for this sin Fortune cast him down
at the height of his success. To Matthews, the poem is consequently a carefully structured kind of medieval tragedy, which
he calls "tragedy of Fortune." As he sees it, Arthur's dream of
the Nine Worthies and Fortune's wheel is the climactic passage
for any analysis of the meaning of the poem.

In 1966, Matthews' view was challenged by Larry D. Benson
in an article called "the Alliterative *Morte Arthure* and Medieval Tragedy," in the *Tennessee Studies in Literature*. Benson
does not accept Matthews' citation of certain passages in the
poem as evidence that the poet considered Arthur's extensive
killing a sin. Rather, he gives historical references to show that
Arthur's military severity is quite in accord with that expected
of and admired in a fourteenth-century leader. Benson also
points to the frequent instances of high praise of Arthur, as
indicating that the poet—in simple and straightforward fashion
—intended us to see Arthur as nothing other than a noble king.
To Benson, medieval tragedy is a far less complicated matter
than Matthews' conception of a neatly structured rise-and-fall
with emphasis upon personal guilt. Benson finds that in *Morte
Arthure* "The tension . . . is . . . not between good and evil,
between the 'excess' of earthly kingship and the virtue of renunciation; the tension is between two goods, between the
Christian detachment that is necessary for ultimate happiness
even on this earth and the complete engagement with an earthly
ideal that is necessary for heroism."

Neither of these two readings seems to me satisfactory. On
the one hand, Matthews has to play down the poet's obvious

intention of presenting Arthur as a glorious hero, despite the king's sinning. On the other hand, Benson chooses to skip over the poet's direct pointing to Arthur's faults within the theological context in which the poem exists. Therefore, to these two questionable and conflicting views of *Morte Arthure*—which any student of the poem now faces—I wish to add a third view. The core of my argument goes as follows: The poet is both widely read and deeply religious. In accord with his inherited narrative materials, he wishes to praise Arthur as the glorious British king successful in his war against the Roman emperor Lucius and noble in his last days of fighting against Mordred. But in so doing, he chooses—unlike previous tellers of this story—to present in some detail the religious implications of the latter part of Arthur's career. He arrives at a resolution of Arthur's failings and Arthur's glory by attention to two fundamental philosopsic concepts: medieval tragedy and the virtue Fortitude, both of which concern that ubiquitous medieval symbol, the goddess Fortuna.

Before examining the poem itself, we need to look at the two aspects of intellectual history which I believe furnish the background against which the poem is to be understood: the medieval concept of tragedy, and that of the cardinal virtue Fortitude. First, how are we to understand medieval tragedy? A favorite passage for all who have been interested in this matter is the definition given by Chaucer's Monk. He states:

> Tragedie is to seyn a certeyn storie,
> As olde bookes maken us memorie,
> Of hym that stood in greet prosperitee
> And is yfallen out of heigh degree
> Into myserie, and endeth wrecchedly (VII, 1973-77).

and,

> I wol biwaille, in manere of tragedie,
> The harm of hem that stoode in heigh degree,
> And fillen so that ther nas no remedie
> To brynge hem out of hir adversitee.
> For certein, whan that Fortune list to flee,
> Ther may no man the cours of hir withholde
>   (VII, 1991-96).[1]

Primarily on the basis of these remarks by the Monk, we have been told that the essence of tragedy in medieval literature is simply a fall from high place to low, from the top of Fortune's wheel to the bottom, without any necessity for an element of human fault, personal guilt, or tragic flaw. But what needs noting here is that the Monk's remarks are not Chaucer's effort to furnish a textbook definition of medieval tragedy; rather, they are the dramatic utterances of a character in a fiction called the *Canterbury Tales*. As such, they derive specifically from an individual whose interests are far from intellectual, as he tells us himself. His concerns are mainly with food, hunting, and other pleasures of this world. To look to him for help in understanding the real import of medieval tragedy would seem a trifle desperate. Actually, the fine irony in his statements lies in Chaucer's having a man of the Church—who should know better—deliver such a narrow definition of tragedy, a complex principle right at the heart of the Church's teaching.

A similar disregard of context has characterized discussions of another passage regularly cited in considerations of medieval tragedy: the lines in Book II, Prose 2 of Boethius' *Consolation of Philosophy,* the source for Chaucer's Monk's statements. We read in Chaucer's translation of the *Consolation,* roughly contemporary with the alliterative *Morte,* "What other thing bywaylen the cryinges of tragedyes but oonly the dedes of Fortune, that with unwar strook overturneth the realmes of greet nobleye?" On the basis of this statement, it has also been maintained that medieval tragedy is simply a fall from high place to low. But let us note that these words are not spoken by Lady Philosophy in her own right; she is here addressing the "I" of the *Consolation* "usynge the woordes of Fortune," as she says at the beginning of Book II, Prose 2. Certainly we should not expect a dramatic utterance by blind Fortune to provide us with anything but a limited definition of tragedy.

Where, then, should we look for a more adequate approach to an understanding of medieval tragedy than we can gain from Chaucer's Monk and Lady Philosophy's Fortune? Like others before me concerned with this matter, I turn to the full text of

Boethius' *Consolation,* that widely read and vastly influential handbook of medieval moral philosophy. I would find no difficulty in believing that the well-educated author of the alliterative *Morte* was familiar with the *Consolation.* Further, that Boethius' formulation was thoroughly acceptable in the teachings of the medieval Church has been well established.

To have a tragedy we of course must have a human being experiencing adversity. And if we are to understand that adversity as resulting from causes other than blind chance or inexplicable determinism, we must have a carefully worked out conception of the human being's relationship to the deity. It is just such a conception which Boethius synthesized for the Middle Ages in the *Consolation.* At the beginning we find the "I" of the book—Boethius, if you like—having experienced a fall from high place to prison, where he awaits execution. He is a "good" man, and he cannot understand why this "tragedy" has occurred. Then, step by step through the five books of the *Consolation,* Lady Philosophy leads him to an understanding and acceptance of a set of principles governing the individual's relationship to the deity. It is within this set of principles that the medieval writer and his audience understood a concept of tragedy.

The first of Boethius' principles is that God is beneficent, and that the right-thinking individual's highest aim should be to love God as the Supreme Good. Second is the insistence that man has free will: God's plan includes no place for chance or determinism. Third, God knows everything—past, present, and future—in a single stroke; but this omniscience does not determine the individual's actions or attitudes. Fourth, evil and adversity on earth, as part of God's plan, are to be understood as good rather than bad; they strengthen man's will by offering him the chance to choose good over evil and to withstand adversity. Fifth, the faculty of Reason is God in man, since through it he can control his animal passions and make choices which will lead him to eternal salvation.

A large part of the *Consolation* consists, of course, of Lady Philosophy's application of these principles to the practical affairs of mankind. And it is here that we learn of Fortune's role. All human beings aspire to happiness on earth. Real happiness—true felicity—can come only from love of God; but many men concentrate upon worldly goals such as riches, fame, or power. Thereby they attain only transitory earthly happiness —false felicity—and lose the chance of eternal salvation through their lack of proper understanding and love of God.

It should be noted that Lady Philosophy's applications do not immediately condemn a man because of riches, fame, or power. The important point is the individual's attitude toward such transitory earthly things. If he sets them above love of God, he is lost; if he sees them in proper perspective, he can attain true felicity. Concern with Fortune and her wheel, then, is an illusory creation of wrong-thinking men. To the man loving and imitating God, the loss of riches, power, and high place—the fall from the top of the wheel to the bottom—does not preclude attainment of true felicity. It is only the wrong-thinking man who is deeply concerned over the turn of Fortune's wheel, because he has set her earthly goods above love of God. The wise man does not rail against Fortune, for he knows that evil and adversity are a part of God's plan for man's good, even though the individual cannot completely comprehend this plan.

It is now apparent, I hope, that according to Boethius' very influential system the right-thinking man cannot be a tragic hero, even if he suffers a fall from high to low place. The right-thinking man is always well aware, however, of tragic possibilities. In no sense are we to consider the wrong-thinking man— sometimes called the tragic hero—a glorious example because he chooses to put major emphasis upon the goods of this world rather than upon the love of God. Rather, we are meant to realize the fundamental dilemma of the hero, facing earthly problems, who must keep those problems within the context of his own right-thinking. Indeed, we seem to state an impossibility when we speak of a tragic "hero" in a medieval context. Since whatever adversity the right-thinking man suffers is a part of God's beneficent plan, and since that man's concern is with the happiness that results from love of God, he simply cannot end "wretchedly." But—perhaps fortunately for the creators of literary works—we are not all at all times right-thinking men. Consequently the frequent possibility for medieval tragedy occurs when the hero chooses to seek temporal goals and does not keep them within the context of Reason as love of God. The "tragic flaw" in a medieval hero is therefore not so much in his immediate action as first in his mind. The narrowness of the Monk's and Fortuna's definitions of tragedy—cited earlier—thus lies in the assumption that Fortune, by depriving one of earthly prosperity, automatically reduces one to "wretchidnesse."

Against the background of Boethius' formulation, I find both Matthews and Benson less than convincing in the concepts of medieval tragedy which they apply to the alliterative *Morte*. Benson sees Arthur here as an Anglo-Saxon hero, and the thought of the poem as illustrating the "late Gothic ability to maintain contradicting attitudes and to derive aesthetic pleasure from the tension of unresolved conflicts."[2] Thus, in Benson's view, "The hero, like all men, will inevitably fall to death or wretchedness even though he be flawless, for the lesson of medieval tragedy is simply that man is not the master of his own destiny."[3] Such an explanation, in my reading, misses the fundamental Boethian point that to the right-thinking flawless hero, exercising his God-given free will, and to the right-thinking audience, tragedy cannot lie in loss of earthly goods or position, or even in death.

Matthews sets forth a much more complex explanation of medieval tragedy. For him, there exist two types of the tragedy of Fortune: the short account, simply of the fall from high place to low; and the complex account of rise and then fall, as in the alliterative *Morte*. In each, for Matthews, the tragic hero exhibits some personal guilt or excess in his deeds. Further, Matthews sees a type of "sentimental tragedy" in medieval literature, in which the hero or heroine suffers a wretched end, despite his or her unimpeachable virtue. In the light of Boethius' exposition, I would find it hard to believe that a medieval writer or his audience could have conceived of a "sentimental tragedy," or that the literary structure of an account—whether simple fall, or rise and then fall—could have been a crucial matter in a medieval writer's definition of tragedy. There is a vast difference in Boethian terms between the pathos of Virginia's noble death in Chaucer's "Physician's Tale," and the tragedy of an individual's dying without understanding his having placed earthly goals higher than love of God. As we shall see later, the Arthur of the alliterative *Morte* will know what to do when faced with the turning of Fortune's wheel. And his fate will not be to end "wrecchedly."

The second concept which I see as a part of the intellectual background necessary for an understanding of the alliterative *Morte* is that of the cardinal virtue Fortitude. It, like the concept of medieval tragedy, is closely connected with the idea of Fortune. Students of the Middle Ages and the Renaissance have long been aware of the systematized teachings in those periods under the rubric Virtues and Vices. That the latter have been studied in late years more frequently than the former is perhaps an observation irrelevant in this paper. In any event, I have found two recent studies in this area very helpful: the first, Rosemond Tuve's *Allegorical Imagery* (1966), gives marvelously comprehensive information concerning the topic; the second, William O. Harris' *Skelton's Magnyfycence and the Cardinal Virtue Tradition* (1965) concentrates upon the virtue Fortitude. Each of these books traces through the Middle Ages and beyond the transmission of the received view with which we are here concerned. The references there offered make clear that any educated man of the fourteenth century would have had Fortitude well up front in his thinking in any circumstance that involves a king, Fortune, prosperity, and adversity, as does Arthur's situation in the alliterative *Morte*. Here are some of the facts.

Cicero in *De Officiis* and *De Inventione* and Macrobius in his commentary upon *Somnium Scipionis* set the pattern for discussions of the Four Cardinal Virtues—Prudentia, Justicia, Fortitudo, and Temperantia—which became standard for the later Middle Ages, and which was used in part or as a whole by a vast number of medieval writers. Miss Tuve states that no author, "Latin or vernacular, writes a discourse on virtues that ignores these two founts of wisdom." Further, the discussions of the Cardinal Virtues came to be directly applied to the circumstances of kings or, as Macrobius called them, "protectors of commonwealths." Thus Hoccleve, as Harris pointed out, is thoroughly conventional when he structures his advice to Prince Hal in the *Regement of Princes* upon the four Virtues. The fundamental assumption is of course that the individual who exemplifies the Virtues is thinking and acting in accord with the dictates of God-given Reason.

From Cicero and Macrobius onward, a great deal of attention was devoted to the "parts" or aspects of the Virtues. Specifically in discussions of Fortitude, we find frequent emphasis upon certain qualities: magnificence, magnanimity, liberality, faith, steadfastness, patience, courage, constancy, perseverence, tolerance, and firmness. In early English the favorite translation of *Fortitudo* seems to have been "strength." For example, in the *Brodley Homilies* (90.30) we read, "Þæt feorðe mægen is Fortitudo, Þæt is strenðe oððe anrednesse"; and Chaucer's Parson speaks of "a vertu that is called fortitudo or strengthe, that is, an affecioun thurgh which a man despiseth anoyouse thynges" (728). But the most important point to be noted here in connection with Fortitude is that the numerous discussions of this Virtue down through the Middle Ages and the Renaissance regularly include a two-fold hortatory purpose: how the individual, usually a ruler, should behave in times of prosperity; and how he should behave in times of adversity. Cicero and Macrobius had treated both circumstances. In the latter's words, "one must bear manfully both adversity and prosperity." Centuries later, Lodowick Bryskett—in *A Discourse of Civvill Life* (1606)—wrote as follows:

> The mind must be so disposed and armed
> against fortune, be she froward or favorable,
> it may stand always invincible against all
> misfortunes and adversities, and yet not
> raise itself for prosperous successes. For it

> is as true a token of a base mind to be
> proud and insolent in prosperitie, as to be
> daunted and faint-hearted in adversitie
> and affliction.

And further:

> For who so is armed with true fortitude,
> outward things whatsoever they be, neither
> give nor take ought from them. But they
> that cannot temper themselves in
> prosperitie, nor beare adversitie stoutly,
> make it apparent that fortune mastreth them.[4]

This same two-fold function of Fortitude—as Harris and Miss Tuve showed—characterizes the discussions in the intervening centuries. As the fourteenth-century *Book of the Vices and Virtues* puts it, in speaking of the individual characterized by Fortitude, "adversite and prosperite he bereth and suffreth withoute bowynge on right half or on left half."

We are now in position to examine the alliterative *Morte* in relation to both the concepts of medieval tragedy and of the cardinal virtue Fortitude. Since Arthur is the center of the poet's attention, our main interest will be in the presentation of the king. It will be my contention that the learned and devout author of the poem intended his listeners to understand that Arthur first behaves in accord with this Virtue during most of his period of prosperity. Then he deserves and experiences adverse fortune, with the risk of a tragic end. In reaction to this adversity, however, he exhibits Fortitude and thus avoids ending wretchedly.

First, let us note that in his opening prayer the poet asks for the grace to "govern us here, In this wrechyde werlde thorowe *vertous lywynge,* That we may kayre to hys courte, the kyndome of hevyne, When oure saules schalle parte and sundyre ffra the body, Ewyre to belde and to byde in blysse wyth hyme selvene." Given such an opening, stressing "virtuous living," we are perhaps justified in expecting the accompanying narrative to have something to do with the Virtues, especially since the ending of the poem gives every indication that when Arthur's soul is "sundered" from his body it goes "to belde and to byde in blysse with hym selvene" in the kingdom of heaven. Indeed, near the end of the poem, after vanquishing Mordred, Arthur specifically says, "I thanke the, Gode, of thy grace, with a gud wylle; That gafe us *vertue* and witt to vencouws this beryns" (4297).

Second, we should observe that throughout his narrative the poet is deeply sympathetic with Arthur and the Round Table; he regularly bestows praise upon them and censure upon their enemies, and he allies himself with the British. It would seem doubtful that this author was so confused as to be saying to us, on the one hand, that Arthur and his knights were glorious heroes and, on the other, that they were great sinners who ended in tragic wretchedness. Granted, in the poem Arthur forgets moderation in the pride of conquest, Cador is guilty of rashness, and Gawain's impetuosity is heavily emphasized. But in the context of the whole work these failings do not condemn the heroes to tragic "wrechednesse"; that is, to eternal damnation.

Arthur's behavior early in the poem seems clear evidence of the poet's concern with aspects of the virtue Fortitude. From a fifty-one line passage (26-77) we learn of the king's conquest of numerous countries, of his establishing order in those countries, of his return home to rest and hunt and build the city Caerleon, and of his holding a grand feast for his chief followers at Christmas in Carlisle. He is called "ilke kyde conqueror," and never was there such "noblay" as his feast. Here certainly is a monarch at the height of prosperity exhibiting fully that part of the virtue Fortitude called magnificence and largess. But into the banquet scene come emissaries from the emperor Lucius to demand that Arthur appear in Rome to do homage and pay tribute to the emperor. Arthur's reaction to this demand is obvious and understandable anger, which frightens the emissaries; but the king controls his anger, and after charging the emissaries with cowardice, extends to them the fullest hospitality. Such control and magnanimity are of course in exact accord with the exercise of Fortitude by the ruler experiencing prosperity.

In a later passage (267-70) Arthur directly refers to his anger at Lucius' demand; but the point here is that his wrath did not lead him into "un-virtuous" behavior.

The king gives further evidence of restraint in the council-scene following the banquet for the Romans. Young Cador opens this discussion with jubilation at the imminent opportunity for fighting presented by Lucius's demands; as Cador sees it, the knights of the Round Table have become soft with lack of military exercise. But Arthur rebukes Cador for rashness:

> "Sir Cadour," quod the kynge, "thy concelle es noble
> But thou arte a mervailous mane with thi mery wordez!
> For thow countez no caas, ne castes no forthire,
> Bot hurles furthe appone hevede, as thi herte thynkes;"
> (259-62).

Here is the virtuous ruler, urging that a needed decision be based upon reason rather than passion. Accordingly, Arthur presents the legal circumstance: because his ancestors ruled Rome, he should collect tribute from Lucius, rather than do homage to the emperor. On this basis the other lords then make their vows to help Arthur overcome Lucius, and the king decides to go to war. Arthur's judicious and reasonable behavior in this council-scene can be directly applied to the last line of Cador's emotional speech: "And we shall wynne it agayne by wyghtnesse and strenghe" (258). While Cador doubtless understands "strenghe" as military prowess alone, for Arthur it seems to include the necessity of meeting Lucius' demands with the reason and courage that are aspects of Fortitude in the behavior of a ruler.

The views of Arthur given in his answer to the emperor's ambassador, in the latter's description of the king to Lucius, and in Arthur's charge to Mordred as regent, accord fully with the requirements for a virtuous ruler. Such traits are further illustrated in the king's victory over the giant of Mont St. Michel. In this fight Arthur—as the philosophers say—is God's champion (827), fighting to right the wrongs done to his people (888,

1053). As such, he not only exhibits the courage and strength demanded of the virtuous ruler, but by distributing the captured treasure to the "comouns of the contre" (1211) he specifically illustrates the "part" of Fortitude called liberality in time of prosperity.

Meanwhile Lucius and his army have been plundering France. Arthur, again acting in accord with reason, sends a delegation under Boice to demand that Lucius withdraw or meet Arthur in a single combat. But Gawain impetuously slays Lucius' uncle, and the war has begun. The British are successful in this first engagement, and send Arthur news of the victory. He immediately gives thanks to Christ and Mary, because "Alle is demyd and delte at Dryghtynez wille!" (1564). Then he thanks his knights (1596). The second engagement comes as Cador and his men convey the prisoners to Paris; Arthur is again absent from the fighting. Lucius' men ambush the convoy. Again the British are successful, but when Cador returns to tell Arthur of the victory, he must report that fourteen British knights were killed in the fighting. The king is deeply saddened by the loss of these knights, and immediately he is angry with Cador for rashly losing them. His second rebuke of Cador is much sterner than was his teasing tone in the council-scene. Arthur's point is that a wise leader does not risk the lives of his men except in planned battle (1924). Cador answers that, since he won a great victory, he resents this rebuke. Arthur at once restrains his anger, praises Cador, and assures the latter that as the king's nephew and heir-apparent he has Arthur's full support. It would seem that both rebukes of Cador are motivated by Arthur's desire to instruct him as heir-apparent in the judicious restraint necessary for virtuous leadership. The banquet which Arthur serves in his own tent to honor the knights who won the second engagement is a fine example of princely magnificence and magnanimity.

We move next to the main battle in the war against Lucius, and here we see Arthur as active participant in the military action. "Owre wyese kyng," as the poet calls him, learns that the emperor has decided to go to Sexon; by a brilliant ruse and a forced march he has his troops in position before Lucius arrives. Lucius, faced with this situation, decides that a pitched battle is unavoidable. In the fighting Arthur performs marvelously: "with the helpe of my Lorde" (2128) he destroys the giants who are getting the best of the Britons; he avenges Sir Cayous' death with heroic slaughter; and, just as it seems that the Romans will be victorious, he kills the emperor Lucius. One would look far for a clearer example of outstanding military leadership. Then, in his moment of victory, he exhibits the magnanimity and liberality called for by the treatises on Fortitude. Two senators, who have escaped death by hiding, ask the king's mercy in the name of Christ:

> Grante us lyffe and lyme *with leberalle herte,*
> For his luffe that the lente this lordchipe in erthe! (2318-19).

The "gude kynge" liberally grants the request, treats the bodies of the emperor and his chief followers with respect, sends them back to Rome in the care of the two senators, buries the fallen British knights with honor, and takes his troops into Germany to rest.

In his first message to Lucius (419) Arthur had vowed to cleanse Lorraine, Lombardy, and Tuscany of the emperor's supporters. Now, therefore, he calls a council of his leaders to ask their help in overcoming the Duke of Lorraine, who "rebelle has been unto my Rounde Table" (2402) and who has helped Lucius. After Lorraine is stabilized, he says, he will turn into Lombardy and Tuscany. (*Turkanyne* of line 2408 seems clearly a scribal error for *Tuskayne*). But in this projected campaign he will not molest the Pope's holdings; he will "spare the spirituelle" and go forth again as God's champion (2415).

The British travel to Lorraine and prepare to attack Metz, the capital city, with the aid of French troops. Arthur's confidence that he deserves and has God's help in this campaign is made clear in his retort to Sir Ferrere, who cautions him not to expose himself to the arrows of the defending bowmen (2446). The first assault upon the city fails and Arthur makes preparations for a long siege. Since his allies, the French, seem underfed, wise leadership requires his sending out a small group, led by Florent and Gawain, to forage for cattle. As in the first two engagements against Lucius' troops, the small detachment encounters the enemy and, in this instance, wins a great victory over the Duke of Lorraine, who is captured. Arthur, encamped before Metz, with his usual liberality receives the herald who brings this joyful news; he awards him one hundred pounds (3031).

Metz is then conquered and ransacked. When the Duchess of Lorraine, with the Countess of Crasyne and her maidens, begs for mercy "for sake of youre Criste," we find the following passage describing Arthur (3054):

> He weres his vesere with a vowt noble;
> With vesage *vertuous*, this valyante bierne
> Mels to hir myldly with ful meke words,—

The king assures the Duchess that no further harm shall befall her and her people, and he stops the assault. Further, he issues orders that his troops should not molest the women of the city nor mistreat the men; and he arranges for stable government in Lorraine. Once again the poet has shown us Arthur as a victorious leader exhibiting the magnanimity required as a part of Fortitude, this time with direct reference to the king's "virtuous visage."

Arthur now takes his troops to Lucerne for a rest-period, after which they cross into Italy by St. Gothard's pass, where they defeat the defending garrison. Then the king sends five hundred Frenchmen, under Florent and Floridas, to capture the city of Combe in Lombardy. The detachment wins the city. Arthur "with knyghtly wordez" gains the support of the "comouns" and establishes order. Such an exhibition of magnanimity in a conqueror means that "alle the contre and he full sone ware accordide" (3133). The lord of Milan, hearing of the British capture of Combe, sends emissaries and gifts, and offers to be Arthur's subject. Arthur, on advice from his council, gives a safe-conduct to this lord, who arrives to swear fealty (3150).

To this point in the narrative, as I read it, the poet has shown Arthur as a ruler and leader regularly exhibiting the kind of severity in war which Benson documented as contemporaneously expected and admired; but—more importantly —we have also regularly seen Arthur exhibiting the magnanimity expected and admired in a virtuous hero. He becomes angry, but he restrains his anger. He fights viciously, but he is magnanimous toward his conquered enemies. He views himself as God's champion, and he works to bring law and order to the conquered territories. Thus he has so far conducted himself according to the principles of Fortitude as they apply to a ruler in time of prosperity.

Now, however, a sharp change occurs in Arthur's thinking and action, as he turns into Tuscany. This change is crucially important to an understanding of the poet's presentation of Arthur, and to an interpretation of *Morte Arthure*. No longer is the king concerned with anything except conquest, and no longer do we find any indication that the poet would have us consider Arthur as God's champion. Let us look at a part of the first pertinent passage:

> [Arthur] Takes townes fulle tyte with towrres fulle heghe;
> Walles he welte downe, wondyd knyghtez
> Towrres he turnes, and turmentez the pople,
> Wroghte wedewes full wlonke, wrotherayle synges,
> Ofte wery and wepe, and wryngene theire handes;
> And alle he wastys with werre, thare he awaye rydez,
> Thaire welthes and theire wonnynges, wandreth he wroghte!
> (3150-58).

Here indeed is a difference from the Arthur whom we have come to know in the preceding 3000 lines of the poem. Now he is not called, by himself or by the poet, an agent of God, Christ, or Mary, as he earlier regularly was; now he is not magnanimous to widows and all women, as he was in Lorraine; now he does not stabilize the conquered areas—rather he leaves them in chaos and devastation. The poet specifically tells us here that Arthur causes "wandreth" or evil destruction, the same vice with which Lucius was earlier charged (323, 2370), and to which Mordred later admits (3889). Here is no leader acting in accord with the Fortitude expected in time of prosperity; here indeed is a sinner. The remainder of this crucial passage clinches the point: Arthur's army now "spoylles dispetuouslye," destroying the vineyards of the conquered; Arthur now expends great sums, though he was for a long time sparing of expense. His extreme behavior becomes widely known and he is generally hated: "disspite es fulle hugge!" (3163). Perhaps the most damning comment in the passage is that, after conquering Tuscany, he "turmentez the pople" (3153). And even the harsh sound of the verses in this passage seems to suggest his loss of virtue.

The next section of the poem reinforces the negative view of Arthur established by the passage we have just examined. He leads his troops to Viterbo, conquers it, destroys its vineyards, and waits to hear from the authorities in Rome. Meanwhile, he and his knights riotously drink and make merry. A week later a cardinal comes to beg Arthur to "hafe pite of the pope" (3180). The cardinal makes clear that the religious authorities wish within a week to crown Arthur emperor in Rome. To seal this promise Arthur accepts hostages (3190). His suspicion here is indeed sharply different from his earlier declaration that he would not molest the Pope's holdings (2412). Once more there is a formal banquet; but the brief description of the banquet, in contrast to those earlier described, does not contribute to a view of Arthur as magnificent ruler. Actually, when the banquet is over, we are shown the least admirable view of Arthur in the whole poem (3207). He boasts of his successes; he gives no credit to God or to his knights for his victorious situation, as he did earlier (400, 1209, 1559); he simply exults in his own power and prosperity. On this note he goes to sleep.

At this point, quite understandably, comes Arthur's disturbing dream of Fortune and the Nine Worthies. It of course calls up recollection of his earlier dream as he sailed to France; in both instances we are given the dream and its interpretation by the philosophers. But the import of the second dream is markedly different from that of the first. That we are in the midst of a turning in the course of the poem is made clear when the poet tells us that during Arthur's second dream "alle his mode changede" (3222). The upshot of his dream and of his philosopher's interpretation of the dream is that his "fortune es passede" (3394). When the Duchess—i.e., the Goddess Fortuna—whirls her wheel to cast Arthur down, she tells him—in Christ's name—that he shall lose his prosperity and his life because he has lived long enough with delight in lordship (3387). The interpretation of the king's dream is even more specific. The philosopher tells him that Fortune is his foe because he in his pride has killed innocent people (3399), and that he shall die within five years (3402).

It is a major part of my argument that Arthur's dream of Fortune and the Nine Worthies, and the direful interpretation of that dream, are to be understood in direct relation to the sharp shift in his behavior as he turns into Tuscany. At that point, he relinquished his reasonable actions as magnanimous conqueror and gave himself over to conquest purely for self-aggrandizement. Consequently, hard upon that change in thinking and action, we find Arthur facing the prospect of adversity in the turn of Fortune's wheel. The Duchess in the dream for a time accords him all courtesy, seemingly as reward for his behavior until he reaches Tuscany. But then she changes —as he had changed—and predicts adversity for him (3386). The philosopher says that Arthur should build abbeys in France as penance (3403); but he promises the king that Fortune shall include him among the nine noblest on earth (3438), and that he shall be forever renowned for his conquests (3445). Nevertheless, says the philosopher, the king will receive tidings within ten days of wicked men oppressing his people in Britain (3448). The philosopher concludes his interpretation with the following advice:

> I rede thow rekkyne and reherse unreasonable dedis,
> Ore the repenttes fulle rathe all thi rewthe werkes!
> Mane, amende thy mode, or thow myshappene,
> And mekely aske mercy for mede of thy saule! (3452-55).

The "unreasonable deeds" and the "rewthe werkes" are those committed by Arthur in the various parts of Tuscany, when he gave up his magnanimous behavior in accord with the teaching concerning that kind of Fortitude required of a ruler in time of prosperity. As Chaucer puts it in his balade *Lak of Sted-fastnesse,* addressed to King Richard, "Vertu hath now no dominacioun."

The next passage in the poem, which describes Arthur's reaction to the prospect of adversity signalled by his dream and the philosopher's interpretation of the dream, warrants quotation in full:

> Thane rysez the riche kynge, and rawghte one his wedys,
> A redde actone of rosse, the richeste of floures,
> A pesane, and a paunsone, and a pris girdille;
> And one he hentiis a hode of scharlette fulle riche,
> A pauys pillione hatt, that pighte was fulle faire
> With perry of the Oryent, and precyous stones;
> His gloues gayliche gilte, and grauene by the hemmys,
> With graynes of rubyes fulle gracious to schewe;
> His bede grehownde, and his bronde, ande no byerne elles,
> And bownnes over a brode mede, with brethe at his herte;
> Furth he stalkis a stye by tha stille enys,
> Stotays at a hey strette, studyande hyme one;   (3456-67).

Here we see Arthur, faced with imminent adversity through a deserved turn of Fortune's wheel, dressing himself in full kingly regalia and solitarily studying his circumstance. I would not think that we strain this passage beyond its capacity if we see in it the poet's desire to show us Arthur regaining—after his lapse in the conquest of Tuscany—the magnificence and courage that are parts of the virtue Fortitude. But now his display of that virtue must be in relation to adversity—the turn of Fortune's wheel from high to low—rather than, as formerly, to prosperity. In the fighting in Tuscany he turned to ruthless conquest for personal glory, without thought of God or of the people's good. Thus he earned widespread "disspite" (3163) and made himself subject to Fortune. Now, seeming to realize his error, and in magnificent array symbolic of kingly Fortitude in adversity, he studies his circumstance in solitude. As in earlier times, he is angry at the turn of events (3465); but he controls his anger.

The predicted adversity is not long in coming upon him. Craddock, encountered by chance as he penitentially travels to Rome, tells the king that Mordred has usurped the kingdom, given parts of it to foreign supporters, assembled a fleet to oppose Arthur's return, married Guenivere, and got her with child (3552). The king's immediate reaction is to call upon the Cross as he vows revenge against Mordred (3559). Then he assembles his council, tells them what has happened, and says that he will return to Britain with his best knights to defeat Mordred. But, as a wise leader, he first arranges for the proper governance of the conquered lands: Howelle and Hardolfe are appointed to rule; and Arthur's instructions to them even include dealing "tendirly" with Tuscany (3586). Certainly, he here illustrates a return to thinking and action in accord with the principles of Fortitude. Now he and his knights quickly journey through Tuscany, Lombardy, Germany, and into Flanders. There in fifteen days he gathers his fleet and sails for England. Fortune has turned her wheel and he has experienced the fall from high to low place through Mordred's betrayal in Britain. But in the face of this adversity he is doing all he can to punish the traitor and restore the kingdom. It is as if he is saying, with the Pleintif in Chaucer's Boethian balade, "For, fynally, Fortune, I thee defye!" Thus I find it quite appropriate that, as Arthur leads his ships against Mordred's fleet, the poet makes mention of the king's banner, which displays "a chalke-whitte maydene, And a childe in hir arme, that chef es of hevynne" (3649). Once again, Arthur is Christ's knight.

Although Arthur defeats and captures Mordred's fleet, the latter still has 60,000 men on the shore. While waiting to land, Arthur—as provident leader—looks to his wounded men and horses (3723). But the impetuous Gawain wades ashore with a small troop and foolishly attacks Mordred's army. It is soon clear that the attackers will be annihilated (3792). From this point on to its end the poem is full of religious passages. Thus Gawain, for 18 lines, comforts his men with the prospect of heaven as their reward for dying in battle against Mordred's Saracens: they shall sup with "prophetes, and patriarkes, and apostlys fulle nobille" (3807), in the presence of Christ. In the fighting Gawain is killed by Mordred, and we see the latter lamenting the "wandreth" he has caused (3889).

Arthur now rushes into the battle and kills many of Mordred's men; but then he comes upon the slain Gawain. The lengthy following scene, depicting Arthur's reaction to Gawain's death, is important to our consideration of Fortitude as a thematic concern in the poem. The loss of his beloved Gawain makes real for the king the essence of the adversity predicted for him by the Duchess with her wheel and by the philosopher: the poet says, "Was never oure semliche kynge so sorrowfulle in herte" (3947). Arthur's grief is so great that he wishes to die, and he actually faints with sorrow and despair. Here, according to the manuals treating the Virtues, is improper behavior for a leader expected to exhibit Fortitude in adversity. Thus it is that Sir Ewayne immediately admonishes the king in stern words:

> "Blyne," sais thies bolde mene, "thow blonders thi selfene,
> This es botles bale, for bettir bees it never!
> It is no wirchipe i-wysse to wryng thyne hondes,
> To wepe als a womane it es no witt holdene!
> Be knyghtly of contenaunce, als a kyng scholde,
> And leve siche clamoure for Cristes lufe of hevene!" (3974-80).

Even this brusque lecture does not at once recall Arthur to steadfastness in adversity. He states that Gawain has innocently died because of his, the king's, sin (3986); he collects Gawain's blood in a helmet; and he lifts the corpse to be transported to Winchester.

Arthur's emphasis here upon his "syne" takes us directly back, of course, to the king's dream of Fortune and the Nine Worthies, to the philosopher's interpretation of that dream, and to Arthur's having failed during the conquest of Tuscany to behave in accord with the principles of Fortitude in prosperity. We have also just seen the king forget the principles of

Fortitude in adversity, when grief over Gawain's death brought him to complete despair. Here he is very close to ending in tragic "wretchedness" because of the turn of Fortune's wheel. But now Ewayne's admonition has its effect, and the king vows twice by Christ and Mary (3998, 4040) never to take pleasure or rest until Gawain is avenged and Mordred, who "my pople distroyede," is dead (4045). The despair into which the king fell when he found Gawain dead is "wanhope," an aspect of the mortal sin of Sloth which Chaucer's Parson and many of his contemporaries lecture against; it is also the negation of the principle of Fortitude in adversity which the manuals on the Virtues prescribe. Consequently the poet included the stern speech by Ewayne; from this point to his death near the end of the poem Arthur will exhibit no weakness born of despair in the face of adversity. His steadfast determination becomes so strong that no one of his followers dares dispute his decision to pursue Mordred, despite his outnumbered circumstance (4050).

The king follows Mordred into Cornwall. Although Arthur has only 1800 men against 60,000, he attacks; and we are told that this would have been an unequal struggle except that the "myght of Criste" was with Arthur (4070). The king twice encourages his men for the sake of "our Lord" (4084, 4089); and he confidently expects to enter heaven when killed in the battle (4091). His words to his troops show almost joyful acceptance of the situation:

> I gyffe yow alle my blyssyng with a blithe wille,
> And alle Bretowns bolde, blythe mote ye worthe! (4103-04).

In the battle Arthur's followers fight so well that no earthly king on his deathbed "bot Arthure hyme selvene" ever received such honor (4170). Mordred is killed and his army dispersed; but Arthur is mortally wounded. In a lengthy final scene he grieves over the loss of his knights, thanks God for giving him the "vertue" to win the victory (4297), asks for a priest, appoints Constantine his successor—since Cador is dead—, orders Mordred's children to be slain, forgives Guenivere, and dies with "In manus" upon his lips. He is then buried at Glastonbury by the "baronage of Bretayne" with great worship and mourning. The poem ends with reference to Arthur's noble descent from the Trojan heroes, "as the Bruytte tellys." That the poet's intent through the last 400 lines of the poem, as earlier, is to glorify Arthur seems beyond dispute.

In conclusion, my contention has been that the alliterative *Morte* is to be read neither as an example of medieval tragedy nor as an illustration of tension between earthly power and spiritual renunication. In my view, we most closely approach the meaning of the poem when we observe that Arthur, after exhibiting virtuous magnificence and magnanimity in prosperity, risks tragic consequences by concern with self-glorification in Tuscany, rapidly shifts to steadfastness in adversity as he returns to Britain, approaches a wretched end through despair in reaction to Gawain's death, and then courageously rallies to a noble death and departing. In each of his two lapses from proper kingly behavior—one in time of prosperity and one in the face of adversity—he receives direct admonition: (1) through the dream of the Duchess and the philosopher's interpretation of that dream, and (2) through Ewayne's lecture against despair. Thus I read the work of this learned and devout poet as an *exemplum* setting forth aspects of the virtue known as Fortitude, as they apply both in prosperity and in adversity. The literary consequence of this exemplary purpose is an outstanding poem which at the same time presents a glorification of Arthur and a theological explanation of his catastrophic end as a result of Mordred's betrayal.[5]

NOTES

1. F. N. Robinson (ed.), *The Works of Geoffrey Chaucer* (Boston, 1957) p. 189.

2. Larry D. Benson, "The Alliterative *Morte Arthure* and Medieval Tragedy," *Tennessee Studies in Literature*, XI (1966), p. 75.

3. *Ibid.*, p. 79.

4. Lodowick Bryskett, *A Discourse of Civvill Life* (1606), pp. 216-17.

5. After this paper was prepared the following item appeared: John Finlayson (ed.) *Morte Arthure* (Northwestern University Press, 1967). See also the same author's *"Morte Arthure:* The Date and a Source for the Contemporary References," *Speculum*, XLII (1967), 624-38.

VI

Medieval Landscape Painting: An Introduction[1]

François Bucher
Princeton University, Princeton, New Jersey

Medieval landscape painting has never been analyzed as an entity in spite of its paramount importance for the understanding of the outlook of medieval man. For the fashion in which man represents himself and his surroundings in the visual arts is the most immediately telling index of his changing totality. The examples listed here could be considered self-portraits of successive ages of European humanity. I would hope that this study, which can be no more than an initial blueprint for the treatment of the subject, could be projected toward an analysis of more recent developments in the visual arts, for which we find prefigurations in the developments characterizing medieval painting.

A complete study of landscape painting in the Middle Ages, ranging from its beginnings in the catacombs to the fourteenth century in southern Europe and to about 1450 in the North, would of course have to encompass not only descriptions of nature in literature and the other arts, but also major changes in the social fabric. This would specifically include the increase in travel through pilgrimages, the Crusades, and later the wanderings of clerks and scholars. It should deal with the hunt as a cultural and social institution and would also have to touch upon developments in philosophy, theology, and, above all, in the history of science, including specifically geography, botany, zoology, and astronomy.

All we can do here is to touch upon some of the characteristics of medieval poetry, using viable published translations which are not necessarily literal. Our purpose in doing so is

[119]

*to show the contrast between poetry which usually consists in
an immediate personal response to an event or a series of emotions and the visual arts whose function was usually public and
subservient to a style which reflects the* preferred *vision of the
world at a given moment, and therefore—I submit—transmits
a more valid and more generalized analysis of the basic tenets
of an historical era.*

The basis of human experience rests on two sensations: touch
and vision. Touch is an earlier and more immediate sensation.
One pinches oneself to make certain that one is awake. But the
ultimate corroboration of earthly existence is the perception of
a third dimension either through vision or motion. The nether
world in antiquity was an almost two-dimensional gray world.
According to the Tibetan Book of the Dead, the first stage of
death is sheer whiteness. The infinity of a Byzantine gold-
ground is as two dimensional as the blue haze over distant hills,
or of a cloudless sky which poets alternately call a bodiless cover
spanning the horizons, or an avenue into timeless infinity. The
earth is still flat for many of us and the sun still rises and sets
because we have not yet expanded our experience of space to
universal dimensions.

It is my thesis that if no recorded history existed except for
visual documents, it still would be possible to reconstruct the
basic tenor of humanity's mood in any chosen period of time
and geographical space through an analysis of the representation
of human figures and of the surroundings through which they
move or in which they are fixed. The visual record of man and
his environment ranges from an introspective mode indicating
a loss of control over the visible world to extroverted, dynamic
representations standing for man's expanding consciousness
and pleasure in the universe. The images studied here therefore range from spiritual ideograms to tangible re-presentations.
This polarity between the spiritual (*spiritus*-breath) and the
tangible (*tangere*-touch) habitations of the human mind seems
to be the *Psychomachia* of Western culture. Nietzsche called it
the Dionisiac-Apollonian conflict, but it had already found its

most telling expression in medieval representations of the battle between virtues and vices as outlined by Prudentius, and more subtly in the imagery showing man in relationship to his environment, spiritual or natural.

The subject has never solicited great interest mainly because our image of medieval man is still strongly influenced by prejudices dating back to the sixteenth-century and romantic constructions of the last hundred years. Medieval man appears still as a fragmented somewhat disjointed fabrication of clearly defined types, resembling thus the composite flatness of the *Imago Hominis* introducing Matthew in the Gospel Book of Echternach (Paris, Bibl. Nat. Lat. 9389; Ill. 1). Critical poems, ruthless characteristics of personalities, a tongue in cheek disrespect for God's creation, and sharp observation are neglected elements found frequently in medieval literature.[2] These poems may even contain a destructively jocular arrogance. Thus Cecco Angiolieri da Siena (*ca.* 1260-1312) demanded a near destruction of the earth so that he might have the pick of the loveliest remaining girls.[3] Medieval descriptions of nature, jokes, minstrel's songs, the *Carmina* of wandering scholars seem even today highly contemporary and have never been studied in context.[4]

One could mention among the many still widely held misconceptions Gothic architectural planning which was based not on instinct but on a web of geometric progression which had been tested in practice by the architects in charge of the lodges. The fifteenth-century plan for the never completed north tower of St. Stephen in Vienna (Akad. der bild. Künste, Nr. 16872) attests to the precision of thousands of similar designs (Ill. 2).

But the contact of medieval man with nature is perhaps the major area in which our concepts need correction. It is true that the treatment of figures in their surroundings went through major visual changes in medieval painting. These changes have almost automatically been projected into interpretations of medieval man's emotional reactions toward his immediate environment. This reaction in fact seems to have changed little.

A comparison of the mosaic in the apse of San Vitale in Ravenna (dated before A.D. 547) representing the Empress Theodora about to enter the sanctuary in which she will offer a chalice, with the Falling of the Stars in the Beatus of St. Séver (Paris, B.N. lat. 8878, fol. 116r, Rev. 6:12-16) painted a few decades after the year 1000 shows striking and fundamental differences (Ill. 3, 4). It is true that Theodora's presence is fixed in space through the use of frontality and a row of interlocking figures which must be almost weightless since two of the dignitaries tread on each other's feet. It is also true that the location of the fountain in relationship to the door, or of the royal conch placed behind—or is it above—Theodora are not clear, and that the well documented minute stature of the Empress is considerably enlarged stressing her social importance. But if the group approaching the building seems as fixed before a backdrop as in an early family daguerreotype, it nevertheless remains a courtly procession arranged in an intimate and elegant garden atmosphere. The Beatus of St. Séver strikes a different note altogether, quite apart from the content. The stage on which the figures moved has now been tilted up. Foreground and background have become interchangeable almost as in a work of Op-art. The stars, which fall from the rolled up dark blue firmament like daisies, are before Christ's *mandorla* but disappear behind the disintegrating mountains. The sky is blood red and topped by a brown compartment of nothingness. Below, two-dimensional mountain props move toward each other but not with sufficient violence to explain the people's frantic escape toward oval, light yellow cave openings. Instead of a moment of the highest dynamic drama we are given the impression that amidst a carefully staged ballet of destruction time has been stopped. The events of a short moment are designed to stare at us with unblinking force which slowly percolates into our brains where they remain fixed (See also Ill. 30, 36).

Let us now turn to two poems, each of which is contemporary with one of these illustrations:

If lilies now had come to candid birth
or roses, soft with crimson, met the eye,
grown wild or plucked from my small plot of earth,
I'd send them, lowly things, to one so high.
But lacking these, with humbler herbs I'll try.
Love makes a vetch a rose; and as you'll see
amid these fragrant herbs of mine there lie
the purple violets for [your] nobility.
For they both breathe a royal murex-dye
and tinge with grace and scent the greenery:
two qualities that we may know you by.
Their beauty is a scent eternally.[5]

Let us juxtapose this charming poem with the closing lines of another, no less florid piece:

No lily for me, violet or rose,
Lilies for purity, roses for passion are denied,
Nor violets van, to show with what pure fire
The bride does for the bridegroom burn.
I know not how to gild my marigolds,
Proud poppies and narcissus not for me,
Nor flowers written with the names of kings.
All that this blockhead zeal of mine could find
Was privet blossom, falling as I touched it,
That never boy or girl would stoop to gather,
And of it, badly woven, ill contrived,
I twisted these poor crowns.
Will you but deign to wear them,
Hide neath the victor's laurel this poor wreath—
Clumsy the work, a silly weight to carry,
And yet revile it not, for it is love.[6]

At least at first glance these two flower offerings would seem not only related in time but also in spirit and might best be fitted into late antiquity. The first poem was dedicated to Queen Radegund (d. 587) by the poet and bishop Venantius Honorius Clementianus Fortunatus (*ca.* 530-609). The second seems more consciously naïve. But the laurel under which the clumsy wreath is to be hidden and the elegant Latin direct one's attention toward Rome rather than the North where Sigebert of Liége (*ca.* 1030-1112) wrote it in conclusion to his Triumph of the Theban Legion five centuries later.[7]

This is not the place to compare the stylistic nuances setting these two poems apart. The fact remains that in both cases we deal with related personal moods, while the two illustrations can be set apart in time and space at a glance. Antiquity lingered on as witnessed by a few lines quoted from *Dum Diana Vitrea* sometimes attributed to Abélard (1079-1142):

> When Morpheus has passed
> To drowsy fancy sending
> A light wind blowing,
> Ripe corn bending,
> Rippling waters flowing
> Over pure sands,
> Millwheels turning,
> while still the mill stands,
> Then robbed of all discerning
> The eyes close at last. . . .
> Then under pleasant boughs,
> While grieving Philomel descants,
> Sweet it is to drowse,
> Or still more sweet perchance
> To woo some pretty creature on the lawn:
> Spicy garden odors breathing,
> Roses round our couch enwreathing
> To snatch delight in slumber's sustenance. . . .

A more existential atmosphere typical for the close of a sophisticated age colors the often sadly humorous cynicism guiding the thoughts of William of Poitiers, ninth Duke of Aquitaine (1071-1127) when he exclaims:

> I'll make some verses just for fun,
> Not about me nor anyone,
> Nor deeds that noble knights have done,
> Nor love's ado
> I made them riding in the sun,
> My horse helped too.

When I was born I cannot say
I am not sad I am not gay
I am not stiff nor dégagé
What can I do?
Long since enchanted by a fay
Star touched I grew.
Dreaming for living I mistake,
Unless I'm told when I am awake
My heart is sad and nigh to break
With bitter rue
And I don't care three crumbs of cake
Or even two. . . .
I've made this verse if you allow
I think I'll send it off right now
To one who'll pass it on somehow
Up in Anjou,
He'd tell me what it means I vow,
If he but knew.

The first stanza is a textbook example demonstrating a poet's ability and freedom to discard conventions, which were re-introduced as a joke in the second but last stanza (not given here). Such liberty is the poet's but not the painter's prerogative, including the present. The wide ranging freedom of poetic thought could be discussed at great length and is almost symbolically enhanced by the Chevalier de Ribérac who declared:

I am Arnault catching the wind
I hunt the hare with a big ox. . . .
And swim against the rising tide.

In contrast to the literature of the eleventh and twelfth centuries, it seems to me that Romanesque art shows a barely contained urgency toward an expansion into the Christian universe of the Gothic age (Ill. 37-39). It does not matter that one of the Carmina Burana around 1200 exorcizing fauns, nymphs, sirens, hamadryads and satyrs is followed by the festive pagan outcry:

"Estivantur Dryades, Colle sub umbroso."[8]

The cathedrals stood and others were under construction. But the poetic and pastoral literature continued alongside the public statements of the age giving us insights into man's most intimate and personal reactions to nature in contrast to the visual arts in which these feelings were subordinated to a larger and more rigidly controlled view. In literature the same may be true for the great public monuments, the epics, in which nature is often tainted according to the prevalent outlook of the period. We must therefore proceed with a system of checks and balances, avoiding mistakes based on the visual arts of interpreting the absence of identifiable objects in nature during certain periods as a disregard for the natural environment. It does not really matter that the twelfth century was not interested in the representation of identifiable plants as long as we simultaneously acknowledge the existence of the Irishman Crazy Sweeney. In one of the most beautifully descriptive poems of the Middle Ages, he becomes an antlered being, homesick for the woods, their herbs, bushy, leaf laden oak trees, hazel bushes with their sweet nuts, little blackthorn, watercress green crested on the brink of blackbird springs, tiny thyme, green strawberry patches, apple trees, briary bramble, yew trees, ivy, holly shrubs, ash, birch, and aspen trees, mountain chains and glens, flocks of larks, wood pigeons, woodcocks, foxes gnawing at bones, little foxes full of fraud, herons with their croaking cries and so on.[9]

Let us remember that the poet had at least theoretically an infinite supply of parchment, or could usually take up more or less time of his audience, while the artist was (and still is) bound to the surface which limited him to the representation of essential elements of his outlook which had been shaped by society and defined by the patronage paying him to create a definition of the contemporary scene and almost never to present his personal ideas.

Since the scope of this essay does not allow for more than the briefest analysis of the views on nature in the Middle Ages we are using an abbreviated method juxtaposing poetry with painting in an attempt to demonstrate or on occasion to bridge the chasm between the personal and public spheres of creation.

If poetry inspired by nature evolves from an intimate and almost always emotional basis after the initial choice of form, type of meter, rhyme, and the introduction of one or two conventionalized *topoi*, medieval landscape representations are much more rigidly defined both from the point of view of style and content. We should remember however that certain types suited for circumscribed subjects evolved here also, much as the *topoi* in literature.

Very roughly we can discern the following distinct approaches which could be combined and were prevalent at different times:

1. The *calendar landscape*. Invented in Roman art, it illustrated the labors of the months. It was frequently used in painting, mosaics, and reliefs and provided a platform from which Italian and French fourteenth- and fifteenth-century landscape painting evolved.

2. The *botanical sketches*. Among them is the famous collection by Dioscorides of Anazarba compiled in the first century A.D. from which many later compendia were derived. Primarily they served medical purposes. From the fourteenth century onward the often very beautiful sketches were once more based on actual nature studies which frequently included landscape elements. Extensive studies of flowers were of course the basis for landscapes made up almost exclusively of floral elements. (Mille Fleur Tapestry.)

3. *Zoological and pseudo zoological drawings*. They were used for the innumerable bestiaries which often show animals in an abbreviated and mostly conventionalized natural environment.

4. *Cosmological schemes*. They may include landscapes chosen to complement symbolic figures or personifications.

5. *Geographical treatises*. They provided an opportunity for the presentation of strange humanoids and monsters in natural or fantastic surroundings. The Roman text book of surveyors, the *Agrimensores*, is preserved in medieval copies containing landscape-elements. Maps as the Tabula Peutingeriana or the Hereford Mappa Mundi, a world map of the

late thirteenth century, and furthermore, highly interesting astronomical maps often show landscapes or are related to landscape painting.

6. *City scapes.* St. George in Saloniki, Visigothic churches, and Carolingian manuscripts contain rigidly codified cityscapes or representations of courtyards which were eventually abbreviated into "ideograms" leaving nothing more than a crenelated gate. All these examples have antecedents in the Greco-Roman world. Christianity contributed a new iconography and a revised view of the world, which at first was still rooted in the classical pictorial narrative.

7. The *narrative representations* of subjects from the Old and New Testament were essential for the eventual creation of new experiments in landscape illustration.

8. One of the expressions of a new outlook are *highly conventionalized landscapes* composed of interchangeable props used throughout much of the Romanesque period for abbreviated landscapes.

9. The *visionary, unearthly landscape* can be considered a truly medieval invention. It includes representations of the Heavenly Jerusalem as a garden and can be taken over almost completely by the gold-ground before which figures or props emerge. The so-called second Golden Age in Byzantium and the Ottonian period produced the most important examples of these pictorial environments which often aim at an anagogical experience.

10. The use of *floral elements* in the finials and the window tracery often achieved something approaching a mathematical landscape, to which an organic terminology was given. (Krabbe, Kreuzblume, Riese).

11. The *true landscape* may either describe a historical event in great detail, as in the Bayeux embroidery, stressing figures action before conventionalized backdrops. It may have romantic overtones as in the frescoes in the Palace of the Popes in Avignon, or in the representation of the good shepherd in early Christian art. It may consist in the depiction of an ornamental forest, of birds in flight over hills, of hunting scenes, and even-

1. Gospels from Echternach, Matthew (Paris, B.N. Lat. 9389)

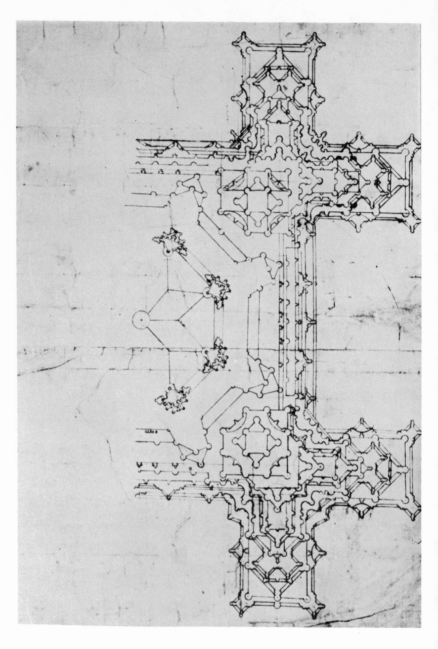

2. Plan for the north tower of St. Stephen, Vienna (Ak. d. bild.
Künste, Vienna, Nr. 16872)

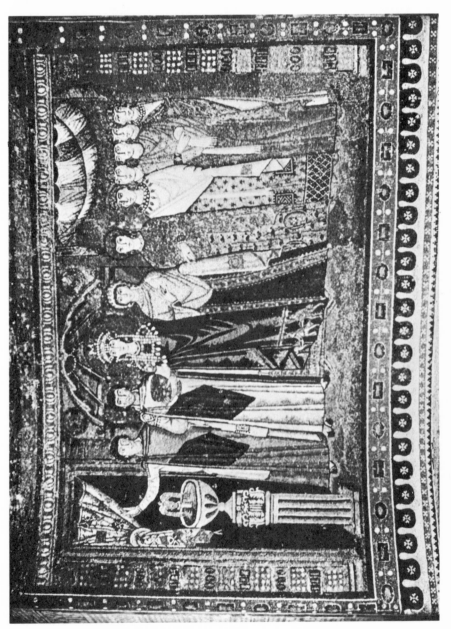

3. Theodora and courtiers (Ravenna, San Vitale, Apse)

4. Falling stars (Beatus of St. Séver, Paris, B.N. Lat. 8878, fol. 116r)

5. Death of Penteus (Pompeii [now Naples, Nat. Mus.] House of the Vettii, Dining Room)

6. Sacred landscape with figure of Cybele (Pompeii [now Naples,
Nat. Mus.])

7. Warships entering harbor (Pompeii, House of the Vettii)

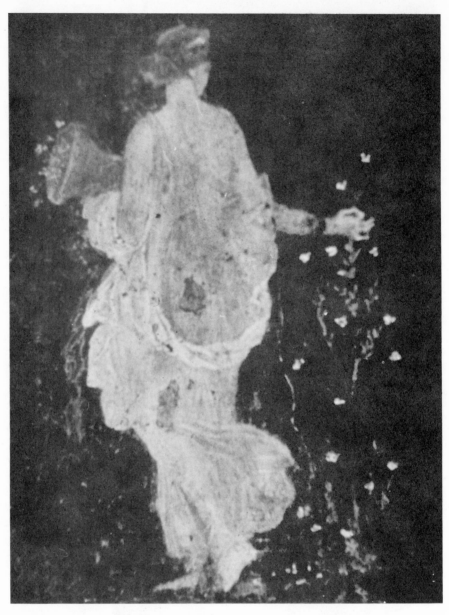

8. Flora (?) (Baths of Stabiae [now Naples, Nat. Mus.])

9. Amor and Psyche (Rome, Catacomb of Domitilla)

10. Good shepherd Jonah and Orantes (Rome, Catacomb SS. Peter and Marcellinus)

11. Hunting scene (Piazza Armerina, Villa of Maxentius [?])

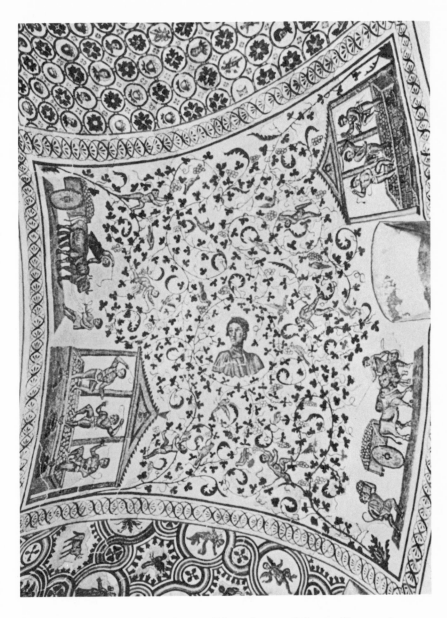

12. Vault mosaic (Rome, Mausoleum of Santa Costanza)

13. Good shepherd (Ravenna, Mausoleum of Galla Placidia)

14. Crossing of the Red Sea (Rome, S. Maria
Maggiore, Mosaic)

15. Saints and martyrs (Ravenna, S. Apollinare Nuovo, Mosaic)

16. Apse with transfiguration (Ravenna, S. Apollinare in Classe)

17. Mosaic vault in the apse (Ravenna, San Vitale)

18. Landscape (Damascus, Court of the Umayyad Mosque)

19. Finding of Moses (Dura Europos, Synagogue)

20. Genesis scenes (Ashburnham Pentateuch, Paris, B.N. N. acq. Lat. 2334)

21. Flight into Egypt (Castelseprio)

22. David and allegorical figures (Paris Psalter, B.N. Gr. 139)

23. Ezekiel's vision (Paris, B.N. Gr. 510, Homilies of Gregory of Nazianzus)

24. Genesis scenes (Homilies of Jacobus Kokkinobaphos, Paris, B.N. Gr. 1208)

26. Coronation Gospels, Matthew (Vienna, Schatzkammer)

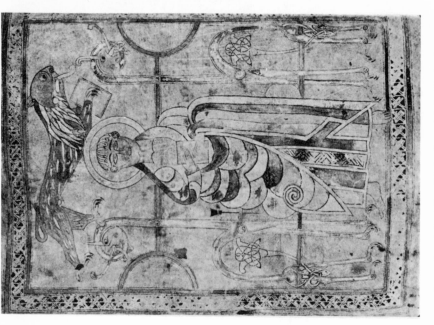

25. Gospels of St. Chad, Mark (Lichfield Cathedral)

27. Gospelbook of St. Médard, Fountain of Life (Paris, B.N. Lat. 8850)

28. Psalm 51 (Utrecht Psalter, Univ. Libr. MS 32)

29. Moses and Joshua (Moutier Grandval Bible, London, Br. Mus. MS 10546)

30. Satan releases the locusts (Beatus of St. Séver, Paris, B.N. Lat. 8878)

31. Battle of Hastings (Bayeux Cathedral, Embroidery)

32. Visitation in fol. 10v and Nativity in fol. 13v
(Book of Pericopes, Trier, Stadtbibl. MS 24)

34. Otto III enthroned (Munich, Staatsbibl. Lat. 4453)

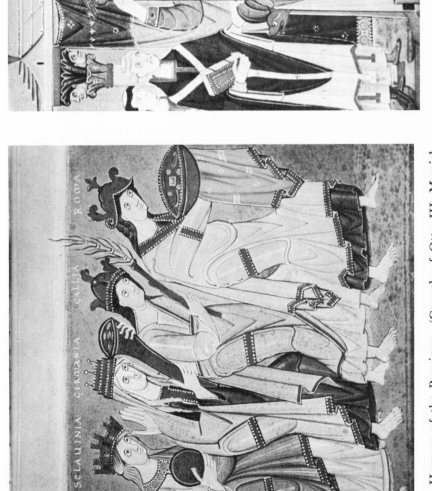

33. Homage of the Provinces (Gospels of Otto III, Munich, Staatsbibl. Lat. 4453)

36. Storm in the Sea of Galilee (Hidta Gospels, Hessische Landesbibl. Darmstadt, MS 1640)

35. Luke (Gospels of Otto III, Munich Staatsbibl. Lat. 4453)

37. Luxury (Tavant, St. Nicolas, Crypt)

38. Original sin (Maderuelo [now Prado], Church of the Holy Cross)

39. The Tower of Babel (St. Savin-s-Gartempe)

40a. The Creation of Eve (Ferentillo, S. Pietro)

40b. Adam names the animals (Ferentillo, S. Pietro)

41. Adoration of the Magi (Berthold Missal, New York, Morgan Libr. M 710)

42. Carmina Burana (Munich, Staatsbibl. Lat. 4660)

doſes qui ſont eſ maiſons   remorant pour eſtier et de

43. Falcons (Frederick II De Arte Venandi, Paris, B.N. fr. 12400)

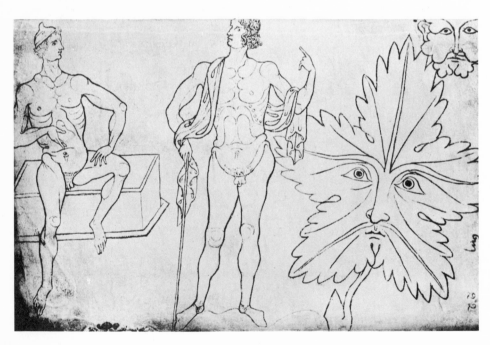

44. Statues and foliated faces (Sketchbook of Villard de Honnecourt, Paris, B.N. fr. 19093)

45. Flight into Egypt (Giotto, Padua, Arena Chapel)

46. Flight into Egypt (Kariye Camii, Istanbul)

tually on the brink of the Renaissance of actual identifiable views of Mont St. Michel (Brothers Limbourg) or the Lake of Geneva (Konrad Witz). The first pure landscape known to me after the period of migration represents a forest populated by birds and must be dated shortly after 1219 (see Ill. 42).

The vision of the world of a wealthy Roman citizen was so far ranging that it covered European art and whetted the appetite of the connoisseur, many of whom became collectors, mostly of Greek art including works of famous painters and occasional forgeries. Once prices had risen and the supply was running low, copies and imitations of earlier works were commissioned often to include painted frames. Many patrons allowed themselves the added, sophisticated luxury of a seeming intrusion into their privacy by having artists paint vistas breaking through the walls and opening up views into peaceful formal gardens.

In the dining room of the House of the Vettii in Pompeii, decorated around the middle of the first century B.C., the painters recreated a classicizing Death of Penteus, based almost certainly on a Greek original, and at the same time opened up prospects into a courtyard by using the unpopular but effective single point perspective (Ill. 5). A most sophisticated informal composition now in the National Museum in Naples provides us with a quick glimpse out into the street where a slave is about to pass a statute of Cybele seated in the early morning sun (Ill. 6). The quickness of this view, the careful observation of the effect of light and air on the receding cityscape invites comparisons with the secure views on nature of the nineteenth century. In the Roman paintings as well as in those of the nineteenth century impressionists the portents of an imminent and fundamental change are often evident. The House of the Vettii contains a view of warships entering a harbor at slow speed (Ill. 7). The virtuosity of the painter whose quick brush strokes never missed moves us into the realm of an appreciation of a splendid technician, hired perhaps on the basis of his reputation for speed and his ability to add a surprising *trompe l'oeil* settled above the painted frame. The important change lies in our inability to fix either a time of day or night, or to plot the location of the colonnade in the background. Increasingly in Roman art moments were being lengthened, the concept of time and with it the view of the world began to change imperceptibly. Eastern Mystery Cults became fashionable, the problem of the draft was discussed with increasing frequency, rumors of new sects in the Middle East reached the capital while Augustus reigned peacefully and supreme. By the end of the first century the political situation had become less stable, the Barbarians and their customs were viewed with benevolent apprehension. Discussions on the symbolic nature of the gods were no longer considered as heretical. The representation of Flora in the Baths of Stabiae (Naples, National Museum) datable in the late first century A.D. presents us with a most startling and fundamental change (Ill. 8). Here one of the loveliest maidens of antiquity picks a flower with a precious, studied gesture. She floats before a green plain, comes from nowhere and goes nowhere. The light emanates from above left, but the body has lost its substance and throws no shadow.

The world of the Eclogues and Georgics had become a conventionalized backdrop. The slow contraction or neutralization of the background, seem for instance in the mosaics of the works of the months in St. Romain en Gal datable in the third century, gives us a step by step account of a complete recrystallization of the human psyche which was to determine the character of the eastern Empire, but could no longer organizationally handle riot torn Rome. The archetypal fear of the loss of our shadow described in many stories, and most frequently connected with a sale of one's soul to the devil characterizes one fundamental change in the evaluation of the human body whose central position is as essential for the defense of an anthropocentric system as an assertion of the intellect. ("Mens sana in corpore sano" was thus in Greek and Roman terms never a platitude.)

Amor and Psyche, presumably as symbols of Christian love painted around A.D. 250 in the Catacomb of Domitilla in Rome, stand on a receding strip of land and project brown blotches painted in as an afterthought (Ill. 9). But in a ceiling decoration in the Catacomb of SS. Peter and Marcellinus which must be dated at about the same time, the inconclusive indication of a light source illuminating the Good Shepherd and the narrative of Jonas is one of the few indications of material existence (Ill. 10). The figures of the four *orantes* begin to recede into a light and shadowless environment, and the tangibility of the body has become a questionable aim for painters. Eastern frontality and linear fixation and Eastern beliefs in a human existence as an infinitesimal moment suspended between non-being and eternal salvation or damnation have almost obliterated the interest in the senses carried by the body through an environment which could be enjoyed and controlled. The immense eyes of the Constantinian portraits stare into infinity. Painted backgrounds become unicolored, even white and later gold. The mid-third-century frescoes of Dura Europos, which will be discussed below, are an important milestone in this direction (Ill. 19).

There are of course nostalgic and pathetic flash backs making use as it were of cutouts taken from an earlier period. The hunting mosaics in the villa of Emperor Maxentius (?) in Piazza Armerina in Sicily are only one of hundreds of examples in which spirited figures, inspired by earlier art, perform a staccato activity in an aseptic environment (Ill. 11). Shadows have become snake or sticklike streaks on a two-dimensional surface. The straight ground-lines over which the figural groups evolve in almost weightless abandon are at least still parallel to each other in contrast to other contemporary examples. If points of reference in depth have disappeared, one would assume that gravity would be next to vanishing. Pan now has lost his hiding places.

In the Christian Mausoleum of Santa Costanza decorated toward the middle of the fourth century the cutouts, showing putti gathering and making wine in an allusion to the Last Supper, are now part of independent visual systems (Ill. 12). The portrait bust appearing framed by the supremely elegant linear system of four wine tendrils does no longer need to be related to any of the surrounding elements. And looking at the disparate elements of bygone country pleasures one is reminded of John of Garland's (*ca.* 1180-1252) lament on ancient poetry:

> . . . Now withers the Latin tongue,
> The springtime fields of ancient poets are bare.
> Across the flowering meadows the North wind blows,
> And they are winter starved.[10]

But a contemporary, Ausonius (*ca.* 310-95), watching the roses in his formal garden puts it even more succinctly in saying:

> Quam longa una dies, aetas tam longa rosarum.[11]

The contact with the Greco-Roman tradition was now becoming more and more tenuous. Scenes in which a figure is still integrated into a landscape become romantic reminiscences of a past which still survived in the court circles of the Eastern empire and were fostered by aristocrats or by Roman patrons who commissioned illustrated editions of Vergil, Terence, and other authors. The mid-fifth-century Good Shepherd above the entrance of the Imperial mausoleum of Galla Placidia in Ravenna shows Christ, young and beardless and touched by the imperial purple, a Roman Prince aware of the recent events in Rome only insofar as he turns away from the world to contemplate the peaceful simplicity of the country (Ill. 13). The times were harsh. Galla Placidia, daughter of Theodosius I, Roman Empress of the West, hostage of Alaric I, wife of Ataulf murdered after a year of marriage in 415, married to the Byzantine General Constantius who having become co-emperor died shortly thereafter, refugee at the court of Theodosius II, regent for her son Valentinian III who became emperor, can be said to have had a life befitting the times. But Christ is shown as the untroubled shepherd of the Eclogues. Could there be a more fitting description of this nostalgic scene or a more moving testament of the resignation of the Roman citizen than the poem of Claudius Claudianus (died *ca.* 408) written a few years before the Gothic invasion of Rome while he watched an old farmer near Verona:

Happy the man, who his whole time is bound
Within the hedges of his little ground,
Happy the man whom the same humble place,
The family cottage of his race,
From his first rising infancy has known,
And by degrees sees gently bending down,
With natural propension, to that earth,
Which both preserved his life and gave him birth.
Him no false distant lights, by fortune set,
Could ever into foolish wanderings get.
. . . .
. . . .
About the spacious world let others roam,
The voyage, life, is longest made at home.[12]

The mosaics in the nave of Santa Maria Maggiore in Rome
dated between A.D. 432-40 cross the threshold into another
world whose roots lie in the East, and whose formal vocabulary
had already deeply affected catacomb painting (Ill. 14). The
landscape begins to be tilted toward the pictorial plane, the
horizon is pushed up higher and higher. Ideograms or formal
shorthand which will conventionalize, abbreviate, and finally
reduce images as that of the city, the forest, the palace, to the
most minimal still graspable demominators, are introduced. The
superimposition of heads indicating a large crowd is one of
these conventions, as is the regulation of size based on the social
station. It had already defined the stature of emperors in public
Constantinian and Theodosian reliefs and is seen here in the
increased size of Moses touching the Red Sea with his rod,
and the superhuman measurements of the pharaoh drowning
in the upper plane. These conventions were about to become
standardized visual vehicles. The seemingly floating diminutive
rider in the upper reaches of the city gate demonstrates how
older ideas, such as the decreasing size of figures shown in a
distance, had become unimportant and perhaps even misunderstood.

In the Codex Vergilius Romanus (Vatican Libr. Lat. 3867,
fol. 44v, Georgics III), the shepherds and animals are almost

parallel with the picture plane; shadows and the horizon have vanished. This second-rate work, dated probably in the first half of the fifth century, provides nevertheless an index of a changed visual attitude.[13]

The double conflict of Christian art at this time, namely the introduction of an Eastern formal vocabulary into official commissions and the increasing reasons for a justification of art which was soon to be questioned in the iconoclastic controversies, was to a large extent resolved in a series of sixth-century mosaics in Ravenna which are among the most moving preserved witnesses of a truly Christian monumental statement.

The saints carrying their crowns of martyrdom while advancing in an imperial procession toward the apse of S. Apollinare Nuovo are devoid of weight and individuality (Ill. 15). Perhaps because of this and because of their innocently vacant faces they successfully transmit to us the simple pleasures of paradise arranged for them in an abstracted and formal spring landscape. This joy springs from the same spirit which filled Prudentius (A.D. 348-405) who four or five decades earlier could have inspired this very procession singing of eternal spring:

> Illic purpureis tecta rosariis
> omnis fragrat humus, calthaque pinguia,
> et molles violas, et tenues crocos
> fundit fonticulis uda fugacibus.
> Felices animae prata per herbida
> concentu parili suave sonatibus
> hymnorum modulis dulce canunt melos,
> calcant et pedibus lilia candidis.[14]

But there is an even more exact description of this scene, illustrating the mysterious and stable workings of the poetic mind discussed briefly above. Or could Sigebert of Liége (1030-1112) simply be echoing the text of Prudentius when seven centuries later he names:

> Hinc virginalis sancta frequentia
> Gertrudis, Agnes, Prisca, Cecilia,

Lucia, Petronilla, Tecla,
Agatha, Barbara, Juliana. . . .

He pervagantes prata recentia,
pro velle querunt serta decentia,
rosas legentes passionis,
lilia vel violas amoris.[15]

In contrast to this conscious visual naïveté, the apse of S.
Apollinare in Classe, dedicated to the patron saint of the church
is a highly sophisticated union of opposites (Ill. 16). Flanked
by the twelve apostles, Apollinaris stands in a formal and unearthly garden, whose horizon almost imperceptibly melts into
the gold-ground sky from which the hand of God has released
the *Crux Gemmata* which is surrounded by the star-studded
universe reflected also in the chasuble of the praying saint.
Appollinaris, thus a witness to the transfiguration, seems ready
to intone the Hymn to the Holy Cross of Venantius Fortunatus
(*ca.* 530-610):

The royal banners forward go;
The cross shines forth in mystic glow,
Where He in flesh, our flesh who made,
Upon the tree of pain is laid.
. . . .
O tree of beauty! Tree of light!
O Tree with royal purple dight!
Elect on whose triumphal breast
Those holy limbs should find their rest!
. . . .
. . . .
Decked with the fruit of peace and praise,
And glorious with triumphal lays.
Hail, Altar! Hail, O Victim, thee.[16]

This febrile and high-strung poem, quoted only partially, makes
one take a second look at the almost total symmetry and almost
rigid order, which gives the effect of an awesome peace rarely
repeated in Christian art. The same sentiment is echoed above
in a less inspired and restored representation of the Holy Je-

rusalem. And one wonders if this stillness may not also tell us of a regimented stability of an age in which the very idea of abstraction in art reflects the final, reluctant transition to a Christian interpretation of tangible things and at worst gives alienated viewers a possibility to escape. Maximian, who gave us a ruthlessly honest autobiography around A.D. 625, describes his encounter with a girl in Constantinople. After his unsuccessful attempt to consummate their liaison, she breaks down and he tries to console her with the prospect of more potent lovers. This may be a standard literary situation, but her reasons for crying are not, for she says: "It is not that! It is the general chaos of the world." Here in a passing remark an abyss opens, showing perhaps more poignantly than any other statement of the period an awareness of a disjointed epoch.[17]

In sixth-century Byzantine art perfect simplicity had reached a sophistication which allowed for the convincing creation of heavenly gardens as they could only be imagined in the rapturous ascent toward an anagogical experience. The apse vault of San Vitale in Ravenna, completed *ca.* A.D. 547 celebrates the appearance of the Lamb of God (Ill. 17). Supported by four archangels pointing to the four cardinal directions and standing on blue spheres, surrounded by trellised, rigid floral patterns on gold ground, and furthermore buttressed by peacocks and flowers in eternal bloom, the lamb emerges from the indifferent neutrality of the universe. The glass cubes of all these mosaics were set at slightly differing angles, so that they catch the light in successive moments, imbuing the decoration with a mysterious life of its own. We can judge the psychological, or should one say the psychedelic impact of this technique in a description of the even more abstract decoration of Hagia Sophia in Constantinople (532-37). If Sir John Mandeville who saw it *ca.* 1360 describes it only as the "fairest and noblest church in the world," his reaction can be excused because of his knowledge of Gothic cathedrals. For Procopius, who praised the structure shortly before the earthquake of 558, it is a universe. Looking at the columns and marbles he says that "one would think that one had come upon a meadow full of flowers in bloom." The piers are "like perpendicular cliffs." In an ode by Paulus Silentiarius recited perhaps at the opening of the church on 24 December 563, the terminology becomes more personal: "Yet, who even in the measures of Homer, shall praise the marble pastures, gathered on the lofty walls and spreading pavements of the church (will fail). . . . The many colored marble shines with flowers of deep red and silver." He goes on to describe the geographical origin of these minerals imported from Egypt, Sparta, Lydian creeks, from under the Lybian sun, from Celtic crags and states: "the marble that the land of Atrax yields, not from some upland glen, but from level plains, (are) in parts freshly green as the sea . . . or again like cornflowers in the grass, with here and there a drift of fallen snow."[18] Made up of these parts the church becomes a model of the cosmos: "Whoever raises his eyes to the beautiful firmament of the roof, barely dares to gaze on its rounded expanse sprinkled with the stars of heaven, but turns to the fresh, green marble below, thinking as it were, to observe the flower bordered streams of Thessaly, and budding corn, and woods thick with trees, leaping flocks too and twining olive trees, and the vine with green tendrils, or the deep blue peace of the summer sea." Only men who have forcibly and recently lost touch with the reality of nature were able to project such a variety of landscapes upon the abstract patterns of decoration preserved in large part to this day in Hagia Sophia.

With the iconoclastic edict of Leo III proclaimed in 726 and enforced until 842-43, one of the major breaks in the continuity of European art occurs. Religious pictorial production came to a standstill in the East, except for outlying provinces of the Empire where it was slowed down to the extreme. If the fall of Rome can be considered as the end of an era in world history, the year 726 represents an equally incisive break in the development of the visual arts. It most probably affected the Latin West much more deeply than has hitherto been ascertained. The connections between Islamic iconoclasm, especially the edict of Caliph Yazid II of 721 and the Byzantine destruction of works of art have as yet also been insufficiently related.[19]

The Mohammedan attitude certainly affected the thinking on religious art at the Byzantine court.

It is therefore ironic that the last and perhaps most extensive Roman landscape should be found in the Umayyad Great Mosque (Djami el Oumawi) in Damascus, at that time the capital of an Empire which stretched from the Indus to the Pyrenees (Ill. 18). The mosaics cover an immense expanse of the walls and arcades and are usually dated *ca.* 715. One wonders if the program was not at least completed by a group of Constantinopolitan artists, recently out of work. The decoration consists of two interlocked schemes. Above the capitals we find representations of palaces reminiscent of the complex and elegant cityscapes decorating the base of the dome of St. George in Saloniki. The inner wall is given to a landscape of delights, which is isolated from the world by a windswept stream and guarded by a row of immense trees which merge with the pictorial plane. Villas near the water, colonnaded courtyards, castles and mountain lodges strung before a brilliant gold ground are elements which lead us back to formal conventions found in Pompeii. Were it not for the absence of any living thing this landscape would give us an accurate impression of idealized East Roman country living. Above all it transmits a reflection of the landscape friezes in Byzantine palaces and country villas which may have triggered the descriptions of Procopius and Paulus Silentiarius of the interior of Hagia Sophia.[20]

The disciplined informality of the Damascus landscape was not repeated in preserved monumental examples of the Middle Ages until the frescoes in the Palace of the Popes in Avignon. The mosaic floor of the bath in the Palace of Khirbat al-Mafjah dated *ca.* 743 is dominated by reasonably realistic cut out elements consisting of an immense central tree over two antelopes at the left of the trunk and a lion attacking an antelope at the right. The landscape as an ambiance was here replaced by particles of a landscape intended as pure decoration.[21]

The East continues to surprise us with delightful, forcibly resurrected landscapes, which ring true only when they are highly spiritualized, and when the marriage between the two-dimensional world of the East and the exploratory quick style of the long gone Roman West is successfully consummated.

The frescoes in the Synagogue of Dura Europos dated before A.D. 256 may serve as a reminder of the Eastern formal vocabulary (Ill. 19). In spite of the unavoidable Hellenistic influences in this trade city where Greek was the official language, and in spite of the early date, the Finding of Moses confronts us with an archaic treatment of the landscape. Reeds are strung along a flat band of the Nile in which the nude and flat Thermutis stands, having rescued Moses from his box. In a simultaneous representation he is handed from one attendant to another. The sequence of events bypasses three frontally arranged servant girls, and is driven on by the two attendants who introduce Jochebed the mother of Moses to the Pharaoh who is flanked by two attendants and faces not Jochebed, but the viewer. A fortified flat city gate closes the composition at the right. The background is uniformly red-brown, there is neither a horizon nor any indication of aerial perspective. The figures exist in an airless, pictorial space and are almost completely fixed in time. Putting the question in its simplest and most generalized context, one could state that it is surprising and of the highest interest that a vision of the world formulated by the hieratic vocabulary of the nomads, steppe and desert people wins out over the Hellenistic world. We shall note a similar development as soon as figural and narrative art emerges again in the barbarian West.

One of the most telling examples of the conversion of classical means of illustration and the Eastern disinterest in illusionary pictorial space is found in the Genesis scenes on fol. 6r of the Ashburnham Pentateuch (Paris, Bibl. Nat. Nouv. Acq. Lat. 2334) which may be North African or Spanish and is most probably datable in the seventh century (Ill. 20).[22] The picture page is a two-dimensional unit divided into three superimposed solidly colored bands. The uppermost of them is crimson, the center strip is green, and the lower "landscape" is tinged mauve-brown. The figures move freely before these color curtains and the memory of illusionistic space to which they could be related is preserved in the hazy outlines of rocks and freely placed vegetation. If formal perception can sometimes help to analyze the total context of the social fabric, one could extrapolate that the outlook on life by both painter and viewer has been reduced and that his freedom of movement has been impaired. The manuscript could in fact be the first reflection of the shrinking of the Mediterranean environment due to the onslaught of Islam.

Looking forward for a moment and touching upon an extremely complex subject which would deserve a separate treatment, we must briefly consider the character of the continuing representations of the Greco-Roman landscape through the end of the thirteenth century as intellectual and often completely self-conscious re-creations.

After the end of Iconoclasm the art of the Eastern Empire began to adjust to the changed political and spiritual atmosphere. Beginning with the Macedonian Dynasty in 867 and ending with the Comnene Imperial House reaching into the Latin conquest of Constantinople in 1204, there were bursts of artistic activity on two fronts. Church decoration had by now become codified and left little to the iconographic inventiveness of the artists who were therefore able to concentrate on formal refinements. In the more private sphere of manuscript painting, however, experimentation with all the inventions of a millennium took place, ranging from eclectic, consciously antiquarian compositions to almost abstract anagogical creations.

Castelseprio in northern Italy is a public work which shows an early stage in the increasing refinement of standardized themes (Ill. 21). Joseph and Mary on their journey to Bethlehem (or Flight to Egypt) have emerged from an arch which offered them a tight but believable passage.[23] The quick immediacy of the scene, the brilliant use of highlights and of the usual classical perspective of experience attaches the Castelseprio frescoes to a misunderstood but boldly used Roman spatial device. The stability of iconographically fixed subjects becomes evident in the connections of this scene with the representation of the same subject in the Kariye Djamii in Constantinople dated in the first decade of the fourteenth century (Ill. 46). By that time the seemingly improvised composition was codified. The highlights are more regularly patterned, and the difference of media may account for some other superficial changes. The major difference lies in the relationship of the figures to the surrounding space, which had become conventionalized.

One of the most elegant re-creations of the bucolic genre of Roman antiquity is found in the frontispiece of the Paris Psalter (Paris, Bibl. Nat. Gr. 139 fol. 1v.) dated most probably in the tenth century (Ill. 22). The allegorical level of this classicizing composition is represented by melody, echo, and Bethlehem who surround David in a carefully staged still-picture which is deeply moving in its self-consciousness. Most of the text book commandments governing Hellenistic depictions of Orpheus are used, as aerial perspective, sheep and goats in "typical" views, mountains rocks, and trees arranged in successive planes, the self-contained mood of the figures shown if possible in contrapposto and the country villa which suggests sophisticated outdoor living. But the sum total of the impression is artificial and brings to mind the aristocratic country games performed at the courts of Burgundy and of eighteenth century Versailles. By the eleventh century the Latin West had created a more varied formal and iconographic vocabulary, and left us nothing of the kind, with the exception of the poems and memories of the literati, who were still much more closely in contact with the classical tradition. A ninth century Irish gloss in a Priscian manuscript in St. Gall (MS. 904) demonstrates this:

> A hedge of trees surrounds me,
> A blackbird's lay sings to me,
> Praise which I cannot hide.
> Above my lined booklet,
> The trilling birds chant to me.
> From the top of the bushes
> In a grey cloak the cuckoo sings.

May the Lord shield me from doom!
I write well under the greenwood.[24]

This may be taken as a naïve exclamation of a scribe sitting
in the spring sun of the Carolingian age. But eventually, and
more closely related to the atmosphere in the more urbane East,
a series of writers began to cultivate the high art of nostalgia.
One of them, Baudry Abbot of Bourgeuil (1046-1130), would
write only on tablets coated with green wax and was most
critical of the colors used for the large initials painted for him
by Gerardus who after all had mastered the "Arabic art." He
liked to have poems read to him before he began to write,
accompanied by a nightingale. He also liked to watch the
maidens bathing in the Loire, for their bodies shone whiter in
the silvery water:

> Unda quidem Ligeris teneris infusa puellis
> Corpora lotarum candidiora facit.

He corresponded with nuns, was distraught that his Ovid was
not returned, and somewhat sad that after having become archbishop of Dol in Brittany, he could not take his roses with him:
"But roses like the roses of Bourgeuil, I have not found here
. . . and I begin to sigh. . . . Not that I would go back, but I
would fain see flowers fairer than are here."[25] While thoughts
like these were transferred to the pictorial world in the East,
there is no reflection of them in Romanesque painting, and we
may conclude that the Western painters had a considerably
more exciting creative life than their counterparts in the East
and the Literati.

This is not completely true however for one type of landscape which was developed to perfection in the East: the spiritual or visionary landscapes. They vary in style, but become
very often formally and iconographically indestructible entities.
Above all they demonstrate more clearly than anything else
the deep chasm which now separated the Byzantine world from
antiquity.

In spite of the fantastic and surrealistic scene describing

the vision of Ezekiel in the Homilies of Gregory of Nazianzus offered to Emperor Basil I (867-86; Bibl. Nat. Paris Gr. 510) there is no artificiality in the tale playing in a landscape which is oblivious of the size of the figures, and flames out into one of the most visionary skies painted in Eastern art (Ill. 23). Questions of weight, of the presentation of a model of the immediately visible natural environment, and time have lost their importance in a rarified atmosphere which seems to exist between the realities of salvation or damnation, death and resurrection as commanded by the will of God. The Homilies of Jacobus Monachus of Kokkinobaphos (Paris, Bibl. Nat. Gr. 1208, fol. 47r.) dated in the early twelfth century thus transform nature into an image of an image of reality in which all the rules of the tangible world have ceased to exist, and have been replaced by faith (Ill. 24). In spite of its great sophistication and strict artistic discipline, this is an "image pieuse" offered as pious gift to God. Sophisticated naïveté in an urban civilization is perhaps the ultimate achievement in the visual creative cycle of a civilization. It is of the highest interest to observe that here Byzantine culture has reached a statement comparable to the less elegant but much more potent Ottonian pictorial inventions, which were certainly influenced by pictures leading up to our present example.

Turning to the West we run into a situation whose complexity is such that many of the most important questions have yet to be answered.

In centuries of migration the nations from the north which were to become heirs to the Roman civilization touched upon most great centers of civilization be it through conquest or embassies. The Goths, Franks, Lombards, and Burgundians settled among the still functioning nuclei of Roman civilization. Theoderic the Great, King of the Ostro-Goths (*ca.* 454-526) had been held hostage in Constantinople, and was used by the emporor Zeno to lead the campaign against Odoacer. He conquered Ravenna in 493 and became Governor of the Romans shortly thereafter. Shuttling back and forth between Rome and Ravenna he could not avoid seeing some of the works discussed above in situ or in the making. He almost certainly commissioned two mosaic panels representing his palace and the harbor in S. Apollinare in Classe. In spite of this his tomb is a work which still betrays memories of a neolithic world. Reminiscences of a northern past can to a lesser degree still be found also in the Carolingian structures as in Germigny des Près or Lorsch where proportions or decoration echo the vocabulary of steep wooden structures whose basic characteristics survived in the northern European stav-churches and in some of the early medieval Spanish stone halls and chapels. It is of course possible that the tiredness of the Western Empire which —paralleling its history—had seen a slow disintegration of the Greco-Roman forms, but had been unable at the same time to create a truly new artistic vision either in painting or in architecture, welcomed and perhaps even encouraged an imported approach to the arts. To the conquered it would seem fresh, while to the conquerors even seemingly archaic departures from their ingrained traditions would have become a challenging experiment. Venantius Fortunatus (*ca.* 530-600) who visited the Rhineland in 560 gave vent to these feelings when seeing the wooden structures of the Germans—he exclaimed: "Hence with you, walls, piles of stone! Much prouder seems to me the masterful works joined from timber. . . . Normally we are protected by stone . . . but here the friendly and neighbouring woods offer protection." The description of the mighty mead-hall of Hrodgar in the Beowulf poem certainly corroborates the pride of the Barbarians in their architectural achievements.

The stubbornness with which the two-dimensional and often extremely complex and at first glance ornamental world of migratory art survived is nevertheless one of the most interesting questions in the history of taste. Like no other societies these nomadic people knew the third dimension, the shape of lands, animals, and vegetation as well as the threat of natural forces. To them as to all the Nomads the visual catharsis necessarily lay in the negation of a chancy nature. Images were thus invented in which the battling forces of the cosmos, the infinite succession of ever changing horizons, and the nonpermanence

[144]

of every living thing were rigidly telescoped into one single plane in which the monstruous conflict of creation and destruction could be submitted to the most disciplined systems of symmetry ever devised and thus controlled. The last organized group to be more or less forcibly settled in Normandy before striking out for England, the Normans, quickly understood and experimented with the principles of Romanesque architecture. But even they, after having conquered the horizons with their ships, were never truly interested in conquering the third dimension in the visual arts. And when this same nation, now comfortably settled in England, continued to look beyond the horizons of their Island, it was once more the world which provided the necessary experience of space. It may be for this reason that England did not significantly contribute to the history of painting and even less so of sculpture until relatively recently.

St. Mark in the late eighth (?) century Gospels of Saint Chad in the Library of Lichfield cathedral (fol. 142v) or St. Matthew in the Echternach Gospels discussed earlier (Ills. 1, 25) are hieroglyphic renderings of the human shape and would have to be read intellectually by anyone steeped in the tradition of a vicarious experience of reality through naturalistic renderings. Both figures are seated. In fact the sophisticated ornamentation surrounding St. Mark is nothing but a forcibly flattened chair with a back and armrests formed by two dragons neutralizing themselves by biting their own necks. The cushion on which the Evangelist is seated appears as two hemicycles. There are indications of a total disregard or perhaps an inability of the artist to project three-dimensionally. The hindquarters of the lion are in front of the chair, his foreparts are however behind the halo. The ink-stand which should have been attached to the armrest is placed "behind" Mark. The seat and the top of the chair's back are extended to merge with the frame, reinforcing the artist's intention to remain within the second dimension. A dark mauve-brown seems the only color the painter wanted to use. The painter of the Echternach Gospels was more adventuresome; he added a second tone: yellow. And looking at picture after picture in the Books of Kells and Lindisfarne, or at another St. Mark in a Gospelbook now in St. Gall (Stiftsbibl. MS 51), one asks oneself if indeed these could have been the same men who could describe nature in its various moods with an accuracy for which it is difficult to find parallels. An anonymous, perhaps eleventh-century poem based on an earlier song tells of a storm:

> When the northern wind comes flying,
> All the press of dark waves crying
> Southward surge and clamour, driven
> To the shining southern heaven,
> Wave to wave in song replying.
> . . . .
> And the waves go eastward, thronging
> Far to find the sun-tree growing.
> . . . .
> Waves round Skiddy isle go pouring,
> On Caladnet's beaches roaring,
> In gray Shannon's mouth complaining.
>
> Full the sea and fierce the surges,
> Lovely are the ocean verges.
> On the showery waters whirling
> Sandy winds are swiftly swirling,
> Rudders cleave the surge that urges.
> At the mouth of each dark river,
> Breaking waters surge and shiver,
> Wind and winter meet together. . . .[26]

It is perhaps this awareness of cosmic forces entangled in a never ending battle, which governs the febrile and fixed fight of intertwined beasts and lets man recede or even disappear from an environment which he feels unable to control permanently. There are in the Hyberno-Saxon and Norse literature poems praising life and the sun. Ezra Pound and others felt inspired to translate ninth and tenth century Anglo-Saxon poems in which poets took a ruthlessly honest look at the reality of man and of nature.[27]

Many of these poems are full of existential discontent and

reflect the unstable political background during the end of the first millennium. Constant raids and invasions over land and sea seem to have affected large segments of the population to such an extent that agriculture suffered. Disease and hunger were rampant and the population decreased.

It is in this context that one must judge the emergence and the importance of Charlemagne. As far as painting is concerned we can safely say that the rules for artistic production with which Charlemagne was familiar had been valid since the second Iron Age or in the case of the St. Gall representation of Mark for a Millennium, reaching back to the second La Tène culture. It is a credit to Charlemagne, perhaps the greatest mind of medieval history, and to his choice of a first-rate entourage that (instead of being called Stupor Mundi as later Frederick II) he was praised among others by Modoin of Autun who rhapsodized his achievements in the following hexameter:

Rursus in antiquos mutataque saecula mores,
Aurea Roma iterum, renovata renascitur orbi.

These two lines introduce the term Renaissance to the West.

I would assume that the majority of scholars, should they have stumbled by chance on one of the author portraits in the Schatzkammer Gospels (Vienna Hofburg) somewhere near Rome, would have attributed the image of St. Matthew to a Roman painter turned Christian (Ill. 26). Emerging from the Palace School, commissioned perhaps by the emperor himself this book which traditionally is said to have been found in the tomb of Charlemagne by Otto III during the recognition ceremony of the year 1000 became the Coronation Gospels of the Holy Roman Empire. It is therefore by no means hypothetical to assume that the style used for one of the most elegant representations of a Greco-Roman philosopher at work was the style which Charlemagne wanted to launch, even if Constantinopolitan artists had to be hired as Beckwith assumes.[28] Had his successors been of equal stature two or three generations of enlightened rulers might well have been able to break the boundaries of a two-dimensional world view which surfaced even in Charlemagne's immediate surroundings. Thus the Fountain of Life in the Gospelbook of St. Médard of Soissons (Paris Bibl. Nat. Lat. 8850) does on one hand betray a familiarity with architectural prospects from Roman antiquity perpetrated in the mosaics of St. George in Saloniki, of Damascus, and in Spanish Visigothic fragments published by H. Schlunk (Ill. 27). But the arrangement of the bases of the columns, the steeply ascending landscape and the flat use of color and other details betray an artistic temperament used to a positioning of objects on a two-dimensional grid. And here, perhaps more than in other examples, the freedom of the word as compared with the visual conditioning of an age becomes evident. Walafrid Strabo (809-49) describes how he tends his garden and the flowers therein, gladioli, poppies, radishes, lilies and German roses. Or he contemplates the moon's splendor shining in "naked heaven" and asks that the "radiance from her lamp" become a token between himself and an absent friend.[29] Alcuin's death in 804 is lamented by Fredegis in a moving description of the little house around which stand the trees "with their sighing branches," "a little flowering wood for ever fair, Small streams about thee."[30] Even the months were renamed to characterize them more aptly. February became Mudmonth and May Joymonth. And the great curiosity of Charlemagne's court—the elephant Abu-Lubabah (Father of Intelligence) given him by Haroun al Rashid—is integrated into this world and accorded a hero's death in the expedition against the Danes of 810.[31] Carolingian writing and poetry even in a more serious vein is either perfectly matter of fact as Einhard's Vita Caroli Magni (817-36) or still in touch with nature even while it decays

> Violets whiten, lilies darken,
> Even while we speak, the grass
> Springs up ripens withereth

says Hrabanus Maurus in one of his more somber moods.[32] The formal undercurrent in the representation of the Fountain of Life begins to be echoed in an eleventh-century poem of Peter

Damianus (1007-72) who talks about man's parched mind, "cramped within its carnal prison" which is "cleansed from all its dregs" and in peace after partaking in the Font of Life.[33]

The enthusiasm brought about by the liberation of artistic vision through the Carolingian revival gripped a few artists who were ready to explore the human figure in space in a more unorthodox fashion. Their paintings are bold, sometimes undisciplined and as in the case of the master of the Ebbo Gospels (Epernay, Bibl. de la Ville, MS 1 dated before 823) filled with an almost febrile and highly expressive vigor.[34] One of the most inspiring series of sketches in Western art is found in the Utrecht Psalter which originated in Hautvillers or Reims about A.D. 820 (Ill. 28). The vivacity compressed into the small drawings showing figures inspired by the complex imagery in the Psalms is so overpowering and of such high quality that almost any of the groups can be greatly enlarged without losing their impact. Our example depicts *Psalm 51* (50) describing Nathan's visiting David to berate him for the murder of Urias. David faces Nathan, Bathsheba flees into the villa, Urias lies dead on a hillock. The right half refers to II Samuel 12 in which the rich man (here as a shepherd) orders his servant to take the ewe lamb away from the pauper. A lingering inspiration from the preceding Psalm's tenth verse: "For every beast of the forest is mine and the cattle upon a thousand hills" may have helped to shape the quickly sketched ascending landscape which is so suggestive and airy in most of the other illustrations as well that they have been compared with Chinese art. Even if—and this is likely—these motifs are based on an early Christian manuscript, the liberation of the artist from the rigid patternization of nature whose seemingly chaotic freedom he understands as well as the human body's motion through space, remains one of the phenomena of art history. This immediate and personal style is the first western medieval image to come close to the freedom of poetic imagination which we discussed in previous ninth-century examples.

Charlemagne's dream of a united world which—for a moment —included even troup movements against the East Roman

Empire as demonstrated by F. L. Ganshof (see p. 30) collapsed with the Treaty of Verdun in 843. Already the sequence of Moses receiving the law in the Moutier-Grandval Bible (London, Brit. Mus. 10546, fol. 25v) executed in Tours under Abbot Adalhard between 834-43 shows a readjustment of nature to a more restricted intellectual ambient (Ill. 29). Perhaps based on a preiconoclastic Byzantine prototype, the two scenes have now been interconnected formally so that they exist in the same plane. The five arches of the building entered by Joshua and Moses are echoed by the base of a banner-like Mount Sinai which is surrounded by dark blue interrupted only by a white strip through which grow two symmetrically arranged trees. The curtain of clouds splits to release the hand of God, to which Moses seems attached while floating above the sharply receding parapet of vaults sheltering the *filii Israel*. One could say that here we visually witness the reduction of the early ninth-century humanistic programs in the arts. Inching toward the Millennium, the idea of the possible end of the world is only one factor in the restrictive atmosphere of the tenth and eleventh centuries which encompass the height of feudalism. Man, now bound to the soil, plagued by frequent war games among the lords, by dangers of invasion from many sides seems to have become more passive in his outlook. The construction of new churches was lagging and the exclamation from one of the Carmina Sangallensis:

> Ecce tubae crepitant
> Quae mortis iura resignant
> Crux micat in coelis
> Nubes praecedit et ignis,

is pictorially recorded in the terror of the apocalyptic plagues in the Beatus of St. Séver (Paris, Bibl. Nat. Lat. 8878, fol. 145v) dated before 1050 (Ill. 30). The locusts to whom "was given power, as the scorpions on earth have power" and to torment men for five months (Rev. 9:3-11) inspired the artist who follows the text with the exception of the renaming of Abaddon-Apollyon who appears as Satan. With Picasso's "Guernica" this leaf is one of the most poignant representations of the despair of humanity confronted with destruction. The red green and yellow checkerboard pattern itself on which the figures are caught in a cosmic chess game of horror and the surrounding frame render an escape from the monstruous onslaught impossible. Only a society of people who felt that their fate was largely predestined could have produced such a ruthlessly clear vision of the inescapable and preordained. It is not surprising that twentieth-century painting has begun to move once more in this direction.

A strange mixture of fear and hope pervades even poetry. An anonymous tenth-century writer expresses this strange mixture by saying:

> Ego fui sola in sylva,
> Et dilexi loca secreta,
> Frequenter effugi tumultum
> Et vitavi populum multum.
> Iam nix glaciesque liquescit,
> Folium et herba virescit,
> Philomena iam cantat in alto,
> Ardet amor cordis in antro.[35]

The year 1000, which was as H. Focillon demonstrated by no means a fixed event, came and went, and Raoul Glaber sang the praise of Europe being covered by the white robe of new churches.[36] Hymns to spring are galore, some of them including detailed descriptions of plants and animals such as:

> Scant of breadth the burdened bees
> Carry home the flower spoil,
> To the mountain go the cows,
> The ant is glutted with its meal. . . .[37]

The Norman question was about to be solved in the expedition to England which is prefigured in many northern poems dealing with the sea and the fun of battle. There is sadness in the Saxon country and an anonymous poet's fascination with the grave described in every gruesome detail:

low the side-walls
(low) the roof is built
in that lodging of mold,
the den decays. . . .[38]

Typically enough man looks to nature whose beauty in
many cases seems to serve as a medicine for hopelessness as in
this eleventh-century anonymous Irish poem:

What folly for a man on earth
His praise of God to end,
When birds don't stop that have no soul.
No spirit but the wind.[39]

There is a wealth of poetic modes in the tenth- and early
eleventh-century literature and often a realism which has rarely
been surpassed especially in the Norse battle poetry. The clang
of metal upon metal has seldom been described more dramatic-
ally than in the famous Death Song of Haakon the Good by
Eyvindr Finsson which tells of spearheads shivered, shields
shattered, crushed breastplates, skulls and sword fire blazing in
the bleeding wounds. And even here nature is immediately at
hand when "on blades gushed blood surf like breakers on
rocks."[40]

Turning to the visual equivalent of these descriptions, the
Bayeux Embroidery is an anticlimax. Commissioned most
probably by Odo Bishop of Bayeux and half brother of William for display at the consecration of the cathedral in 1077,
this immense political *pièce justificative* (230 x 19 ¾ feet)
shows the mustachioed Saxons in desperate straits defending a
Hastings hill (Ill. 31). Historical accuracy is preserved in the
lower band showing the Norman dead and the penchant for
decoration is freely explored in the thematically strange borders
which seem to follow the action on an allegorical level and
includes birds and other animals as well as little men displaying
sexual prowess. The extremely narrow spatial planes recede
toward the top. In this respect the landscape is logically organized; in others it introduces ideograms on, in, or before
which the lively, uncouth figures perform the conquest of

England which in the eleventh century must have appeared as a continent.

The total outlook of society upon the man-made model of the world cannot be rapidly changed, which is the strength and tragedy of historical dynamics including of course the present. It is very moving to watch the slowly expanding pictorial notion of man's natural environment through the eleventh and twelfth centuries. A book of Pericopes, presented to Archbishop Egbert of Trier (Trier, Stabtbibl. MS 24) by the monks of Reichenau, Keraldus, and Heribertus between A.D. 977 and 993, gives a tentative reinterpretation of aerial perspective (Ill. 32). The visitation (fol. 10v) shows Mary and Elizabeth meeting before the gate of "a city of Juda" (Luke 1:40) which stands as a solid ideogram at the right. The "ground" is yellow, changes to a dark pink in the middle ground above which stretches a band of blue sky. How tenuous and experimental this treatment of space was, becomes clear from the Nativity scene on fol. 13v. A light green ground before which the shepherds stand gradually changes into blue, curving forward to merge with another green area receding toward a light blue which is intensified at the top. Into this landscape consisting of colored vapor the turret and the castle of Bethlehem are placed with a total disregard for visual support.[41]

The portrait of Otto III in his (?) Gospels (Munich, Staatsbibl. Lat. 4453 fols. 23v-24r) proves how experimental the Ottonian landscape still was (Ill. 33-34). Originating from Bamberg or Reichenau around 997-1000, the portrait reflects the concept of the Holy Roman Empire as expressed by Gerbert of Aurillac who wrote to the emperor on 26 December 997: "Ours, ours is the Roman Empire. Italy fertile in fruits, Lorraine and Germany fertile in men, offer their resources and even the strong kingdoms of the Slavs are not lacking to us. Our august Emperor of the Romans art thou, Caesar, who, sprung from the noblest blood of the Greeks, surpass the Greeks in Empire and govern the Romans by hereditary right, but both you surpass in genius and eloquence."[42]

The emperor is approached by Rome, Gaul, Germany, and

"Sclavinia." The green, blue, white, and pink bands indicate the outdoors while representatives of the clergy and of the army in the form of two bodyguards flank the autokrator, who governs the *orbis terrarum* by divine right. His fixed frontality and the columns of the aedicula, which in fact are in front of the dignitaries but switch behind them to merge with the bottom frame thus preserving the integrity of the figures and the second dimension, are conventions which still emerge from the arts of the period of Migration.

It is in the ecstatic spiritual landscape that the Ottonian artist succeeded most fully in uniting his formal vocabulary with the pictorial content. In the same Gospels (Fol. 139v) St. Luke carries above him the portraits of five Old Testament figures including David, Habakkuk, and Sophonias as memory images in a mysterious process of materialization emanating from their works poised in his lap (Ill. 35). In this visionary world which transmits an anagogical experience, size, weight, and spatial relationships are no longer of any concern. The hypnotic stare of Luke determines the hypnotic message. The figure is removed from the tangible world and seems to float toward the viewer, decreasing its size, and then again away from him, assuming thus gigantic proportions. The same undefined spatial quality already characterized the floating cross of the Transfiguration in the apse of S. Apollinare in Classe in Ravenna. But here we have the totally abstract heavenly landscape in which earthly matters have ceased to exist.

The same could be said for many other Ottonian manuscripts as for instance the Bamberg Apocalypse (Bamberg, Staatsbibl. A. II 42, esp. fol. 57r) where angels may actually use the gold ground as a foil behind which they sit in a never-never land. It is this sense for vistas into infinity which in the last analysis makes these works two dimensional. This effect is most clearly seen in the most dramatic representation of a storm at sea known to me in Western art. On fol. 117 in the Gospels for the Abbess Hidta of Meschede (978-1048) made in Cologne, the Norse ship in which Christ sleeps pitches toward some maelstrom in the bottomless sea (Ill. 36). Those who have experienced the sudden silence surrounding a ship adrift in a valley of water, or have guided a glider through a thunderhead will understand the poignant impact of this silent and opaque moment in which human beings seem suspended before the impersonal threat of nature. Only men whose emotional radius was still strictly limited and circumscribed by a closed society could create this realm of Ottonian pictures evolving in an airless world. A Goliard's song dated in the first half of the eleventh century sums up this feeling in its closing lines: "I hold my peace, for when will come my spring?"[43]

But slowly the *orbis terrarum* is redefined. Romanesque frescoes are too well known to be discussed at length. From the late eleventh through the mid-twelfth century and beyond, the representation of landscapes ranges from a completely abstract two-dimensional approach to scenes staged on a narrow plane by oversized figures. In Master Hugo's pictures in the Bury St. Edmunds Bible, the background may become a green rectangle inscribed in a blue rectangle. Only additional props give an indication of the outdoors or provide a shorthand note on the location of the scene.[44] Sometimes a background is altogether lacking as in the dramatic representation of vices and virtues in the crypt of St. Nicolas in Tavant (Ill. 37). Luxury, a sizeless figure designed with a supreme sense of abstract realism, kills herself in despair. These images begin to detach themselves from the Carolingian eclecticism and the restraining spatial grid of the Ottonian age. Man to be in conflict with the world needs an aim outside himself. In spite of the lack of any spatial references the figure seems about to tumble forward in a nightmarish combination of unbridled emotions carried in a body which has the reality of a ghost. Viewed by candle or torch light the Psychomachia of Tavant still produces the impact on twentieth-century viewers which Prudentius (*ca.* 348-405) intended his readers to receive when he wrote:

> Venerat occiduis mundi de finibus hostis
> Luxuria, extinctae iamdumdum prodiga famae,
> delibuta comas, oculis vaga, languida voce,
> perdita deliciis. . . .

lapsanti per vina et balsama gressu,
ebria calcatis ad bellum floribus ibat.[45]

The contact with the immediately visible reality is a long time in the making. In the frescoes of Maderuelo (West wall, lunette) the background is now painfully lacking. The trees of paradise seem to serve mainly as a two-dimensional compositional device. In spite of the floating aspect of the geometrized figures the relationship between their size and the size of the trees has become rational (Ill. 38).

In St. Savin sur Gartempe, which is the most breathtaking preserved ensemble of Romanesque church decoration, a series of experimental elements are pulled together (Ill. 39). In the fresco showing the construction of the Tower of Babel, the stage of one man depth and one man height provides the minimum cubic footage for human action.[46] The figures are grouped in dynamic rhythms and forcibly adapted to the cramped quarters, as if the artist wanted to make the viewer aware that the early twelfth century stood before an imminent expansion. Significantly enough it is among the few and as yet sparsely explored Romanesque paintings of Italy that we find an early *summa* of the successive steps taken by Romanesque artists in examples such as S. Pietro Ferentillo at the confines of Umbria. The creation scenes, datable in the mid-twelfth century, are related to the Italian Giant Bibles. But the larger surface allowed for experimentation. The creation of Eve is still shown in a conventional mode with surfaces tilted up to meet the viewer and the four rivers of Paradise emerging incongruously from the rock on which Adam sleeps in a relaxed pose (Ill. 40a). In the Naming of the Animals, however, Adam stands on a hillock containing the source of the rivers. Behind him stretches a narrow brown plain cut off from a steeply rising dark green hill above which spreads the dark blue sky. At the left a brown mountain rises and a stag and an ox *behind it* peer into the scene. This successive development of landscape plains may seem like a small step in the rediscovery of the spatial continuum. But let us not forget that the horizon—a long lost device—indicating infinity makes its appearance here and that Adam stands in the *foreground* and is provided with a body which is put into action by still conventionalized but already functioning muscles which are no longer subjected to abstract geometrization (Ill. 40b). Some of the animals such as the unicorn and the griffin are apocryphal, others look like cutouts placed into the frescoe at random. The total composition nevertheless adds up to one of the earliest tangible views of man's environment in Western postclassical art. These scenes are based on sixth-century or even earlier Western examples, most conveniently grouped around the now almost totally destroyed Cotton Genesis.[47] The same recension also inspired the mosaic cycle in the narthex of S. Marco in Venice and other monuments which played an important role in the development of German and English art.

It is true that many examples of Western medieval art hark back to late antiquity as do many works of the Carolingian and Comnenian-Macedonian revivals in the East.[48] But the Romanesque return to the representation of a more immediately experienced view of the landscape cannot be called a revival. We deal here with a slow almost independent pictorial rediscovery of the visible world into which any useful examples of the past were integrated.[49] And a few decades later the Western creative genus was going to strike out on its own. For in St. Denis, on June 11, 1144, a new architecture, sometimes to be called the *opus francigenum* was presented to a large assembly of dignitaries and prelates. Its successors, the city cathedrals, were to become the matrix and monumental educational tool of the artistic world of the thirteenth and fourteenth centuries.

In the second decade of the thirteenth century a major stylistic breakthrough in regard to an objective description and pictorial as well as sculptural representation of man and of his environment occurs. The details of these fundamental developments are reserved for a later and more extensive study which must include important steps taken by the humanities and sciences within a restructured educational system. The more dynamic and rational observations and more rapid interchange of ideas provided the basis for the second stage of medieval man's public acknowledgement of his position regarding nature. The suggestions which follow can be nothing more than hints touching upon general trends and a few important figures.

The most striking result of a more anthropocentric view of man is found in the fully three-dimensional figure of Roland (formerly Mauritius, etc.) in the left jamb of the South portal of Chartres cathedral. This statue whose feet are firmly implanted on a base revives the classical *contrapposto*. The same is true for the classicizing sculptures of Reims which seem to be based on Flavian statuary. Similar steps were taken in "public" literature which begins to range wider through many spheres of human experience. The Song-Play of *Aucassin et Nicolette* and other pieces not only contain relaxed and realistic descriptions of man's motion through nature, but also several levels of highly personal fantasies.[50] Pictures of machinery, construction methods, and even increased representations of artisans and scientists at work attests to a new awareness of Homo Faber in almost any realm of activity. Thus a picture of an astronomer with an astrolabe, accompanied by a scribe and computist on fol. 1v. of the so-called Psalter of St. Louis and Blanche of Castile, dated after 1225, introduces the growing concern leading toward a tabulation of the universe.[51] New concepts of distance go hand in hand with occasionally charming experiments toward a forcible expansion of space as in the Berthold Missal (New York, Morgan Libr. M 710.) dated 1200-1232. Here the artist goes through great pains and almost mechanical gyrations to create an illusion of depth through the introduction of a frontal and dorsal view of blue horses (Ill. 41).

The forest in the Benediktbeuren *Carmina Burana* (Munich, State Libr., Lat. 4660) which is populated by birds and other creatures borrowed partially from bestiaries is among the first pure landscape representations in postclassical Europe, if the manuscript can indeed be dated shortly after 1219 as suggested by Hilka and Schumann.[52] The trees are still abstractions but the conventionalized animals moving before and behind them introduce a forced and unconvincing spatial comment (Ill. 42). The lively treatment of the "cut-out" birds may be connected with zoological studies of which *De Arte Venandi cum Avibus* by the Emperor Frederick II is the most impressive. The first preserved copy of the original manuscript is dated before 1266.[53] It contains 915 studies of birds and thus presents a feat of observation which was not to be repeated until modern times. A French copy of *ca.* 1300 (Paris Bibl. Nat. Fr. 12400) which seems closely allied to the lost original shows highly sophisticated pictures of birds in flight and at rest. In spite of this the landscape usually remains nothing but a prop to set up the figures or animals (Ill. 43). Flowers and trees are sometimes botanically identifiable but more usually stereotyped.

No example could highlight this brief discussion of the transitional phase of observation of nature from the end of the twelfth century into the first decades after 1300 better than the notebook of the architect Villard de Honnecourt dated *ca.* 1220-30 (Paris Bibl. Nat. Fr. 19093). On fol. 22 an intensive preoccupation with nature finds a whimsical and even almost symbolic expression (Ill. 44). The two figures at the left are most likely based on Roman statuary and show Villard's somewhat dubious attempt at the creation of anatomical design and the classical *contrapposto*. The leaf which becomes a face and the face turning into a leaf at the right were drawn after the figures and reveal a relaxed familiarity and even a close identification with nature. The same idea was formalized on another page showing two heads fringed with symmetrical foliage and a realistic study of two plants. Similar capitals can be found in France, England, and later in Germany and Italy. The literal humanization of identifiable forms of nature in public art attests to the increasing familiarity of medieval man with his environment which was now explored through picnics and simple zoos which earlier had been the prerogative of the aristocratic class.

The step by step shift from an ideogrammatic view of the world to a tangible approach reflecting man's growing interest in a control over his environment and thus an increasingly anthropocentric point of view of the world is clearly demonstrated by the visual arts of the thirteenth and fourteenth centuries. No other artist gives us a clearer sense of the excitement which accompanied the rediscovery of man's central position in the scheme of things than the Florentine painter, sculptor, architect, and city planner Giotto. The creation of his cycle on the Life of Christ in the Scrovegni or Arena Chapel in Padua parallels in time and in importance Dante's composition of the Divine Comedy. With Grosseteste (*ca.* 1175-1253), Roger Bacon (*ca.* 1214-94), Dante, and Giotto we enter an era leading to the Renaissance and beyond. It is not surprising that the vision of Giotto contains pictorial precepts which were to achieve fruition a century later in the work of Masaccio. A comparison of the Flight into Egypt in the Arena Chapel with the contemporary treatment of the same subject in the Kariye Camii or Church of the Saviour in Chora in Istanbul demonstrates the force and discipline of Giotto's perception (Ill. 45, 46). The pictorial surface which was in each case defined by a predetermined iconographic scheme was fully used by Giotto to increase the proximity of the group and thus the immediacy of the scene. The effect is heightened by the fact that the frame cuts half an attendant off while Joseph is about to step behind it, a device already used in a more sophisticated manner in Castelseprio (Ill. 21). But while Castelseprio presents us with somewhat misunderstood echoes of classical pictorial inventions, Giotto's discoveries are fresh and based on a keen observation of nature. The realistic treatment of the donkey for instance can only have been based on studies from nature, a procedure which was to become a specialty in Upper Italy as O. Pächt has shown.[54] While in Castelseprio the ground ascends quickly toward a vista of turrets inside the city, and while in the Chora church the elements of the city and the slab-like mountain have been separated from the foreground strip, Giotto integrates his figures in a tight space grid whose only remaining element of abstraction is the carefully camouflaged middle ground. Instead of the fantastic rocks whose forward movement increases the speed of the fleeing family, Giotto's background mountain reverses the group motion. The measured movement of the figures are thus almost halted, and the moment remains fixed forever in pictorial time.

This new, still somewhat formal realism and Giotto's ability to catch a moment and to hold it is also one of the characteristics of fourteenth-century poetry. It is found in Petrarch (d. 1374) especially in a *Canzone* in which he tells of the evening hour, "the rapid sky bends westward; and the hasty daylight flees to some new land, some strange expectant race . . . night pursues rolling its deepest black, from highest peaks into the sheltered plain, the sober woodsman slings upon his back his tools, and sings his artless mountain song, . . . the shepherd finds a cave recessed in crags, . . . and there he sleeps untroubled solitary . . . sailors on their bark throw down their limbs on the hard boards to sleep. . . ."[55] An even rougher realism characterizes English poems as for instance a servant's girl description of her encounter with her lover Jack:

> Then he'll take me by the hand
> And lay me down upon the land
> And make my buttocks feel like sand
> Upon this high holiday. . . .[56]

With Giotto we have in fact reached the moment in Western art in which the private and poetic vision of nature and the public and official representation of man's environment begin to merge. After the frequent tensions and contradictions between the almost unchanging emotional reaction to man's natural environment and his intellectual view of the world, it would come as a fitting conclusion to reminisce on the ascent of Mont Ventoux undertaken by Petrarch and his brother on April 26, 1336, and to compare his statements with the delightful frescoes of forested parks with a fish pond and other scenes of nature in total harmony with man in the Palace of the Popes in Avignon. To meander through these, and representations of French closed gardens and parks of the fourteenth and fifteenth centuries, to watch a *condottiere* riding between cities, or the citizens at play and at work in the frescoes of Simone

Martini and the brothers Lorenzetti in Siena would indeed provide a fitting connection with our starting point.

I thus anticipate the future task of writing the second part of this introduction to be as pleasurable as Folgore da San Gimigniano's (1270-1330) view of June:

> Di giugno dovi una montagnetta,
> Coverta di bellissimi arboscelli,
> Con trenta ville e dodici castelli,
> Che siano entorno ad un cittadetta,
> Ch'abbia nel mezzo una sua fontanetta
> E faccia mille rami e fiumicelli,
> Ferendo per giardini e praticelli
> E rinfrescando la minuta erbetta.
> Aranci, cedri, dattili e lumie
> E tutte l'al tre frutte savorose
> Empergolate siano per le vie;
> E le gente vi sian tutte amorose,
> E faccianvisi tante cortesie,
> Ch'a tutto 'l mondo siano graziose.

NOTES

1. My most heartfelt thanks are addressed to Professor John M. Headley and his colleagues of the Southeastern Institute of Medieval and Renaissance Studies for the opportunity to present this material in an experimental manner. My gratitude also goes to Professor J. C. Sloane, chairman of the Department of Art, and his colleagues and staff for their help and hospitality. The subject treated here has never been seen as an entity. The references to the literature are held to a minimum through the use of key books which contain extensive bibliographies and source indices. See especially Helen Waddell, *The Wandering Scholars* (New York, 1955; originally published 1927) and Otto Pächt, "Early Italian Nature Studies and the Early Calendar Landscape," *Journal of the Warburg and Courtauld Institutes*, Vol. 13, No. 1-2 (1950), 13-47, in which animal portraiture and pictorial botanical studies are treated. A more complete discussion of the historical and social background might include: Marc Bloch's *French Rural History* (Berkeley, 1966) and *Land and Work in Medieval Europe* (Berkeley, 1967). See also Sir Frank Crisp, *Medieval Gardens*, single volume edition (New York, 1967); Bridget A. Henisch, *Medieval Armchair Travels*, (State College, Pa., 1967); and Aldo D. Scaglione, *Nature and Love in the Late Middle Ages* (Berkeley, 1963). The important study of James Carney, *Medieval Irish Lyrics* (Berkeley, 1968), appeared too late to be used in this study.

2. See for instance the description of Master Messerin by Rustico di Filippo (*ca.* 1230-90)

> When God had finished Master Messerin,
> He really thought it something to have done;
> Bird, man, and beast had got a chance in one,
> And each felt flattered, it was hoped, therein.
> For he is like a goose i' the windpipe thin,
> And like a cameleopard high i' the loins;
> To which, for manhood, you'll be told he joins
> Some kinds of flesh-hues and a callow chin.
> As to his singing, he affects the crow;
> As to his learning, beasts in general;
> And sets all square by dressing like a man.
> God made him having nothing else to do;
> And proved there is not anything at all
> He cannot make, if that's a thing He can.

Trans. D. G. Rossetti. See H. Creekmore (ed.), *Lyrics of the Middle Ages* (New York, 1959), p. 153.

3. If I were fire, I'd burn the world away,
   If I were wind, I'd turn my storms thereon;
   ....
   If I were God, I'd sink it from the day;
   ....
   If I were Cecco (and that's all my hope),
   I'd pick the nicest girls to suit my whim,
   And other folk should get the ugly ones.
Trans. D. G. Rossetti; see Creekmore, *Lyrics* p. 156.

4. See H. Waddell, *Wandering Scholars*, Appendix pp. 281 ff., and J. F. Benton "The Court of Champagne as a Literary Center," *Speculum*, 36 (October, 1961), 551-91. For Gothic plans see F. Bucher, "Design in Gothic Architecture," *Journal of the Society of Architectural Historians*, Vol. 27, No. 1, (March, 1968), 49-71.

5. Carmina, VIII, 6. See H. Creekmore, *Lyrics*, p. 13, trans. J. Lindsay. Educated in Ravenna, Venantius Fortunatus (*ca.* 530-600) met Radegunde in Poitiers. He died having been ordained a bishop.

6. Passio Sanctorum Thebeorum, Epilogue II, 1054-77. See H. Waddell, *Scholars* pp. 108, 247. The Latin is elegant as witnessed by these lines:

> Quod solum potui studio ludente socordi
> alba ligustra mihi iam sponte cadentia legi,
> pollice nec pueri dignata nec ungue puelle,
> inde rudi textu, non coniuncto bene textu
> conserui parvas has qualescunque coronas.

7. On the *Latinitas* of Sigebert of Liége see E. Dümmler in *Abhandlungen der königlichen Akademie der Wissenschaften zu Berlin* (1893) and for texts see *Poetae Latini Carolini Aevi,* 2 vols. (Monumenta Germaniae Historica [Berlin, 1881-84]).

8. See for instance Carmina Burana 37, H. Waddell, *Scholars*, pp. 248-50, XVII. The text here is clearly nonclassical as witnessed in the closing lines:

> Fronde sub arboris amena,
> dum querens canit philomena,
> suave est quiescere,
> suavius ludere
> in gramine
> cum virgine
> speciosa.
> Si variarum
> odor herbarum
> spiraverit,
> si dederit
> thorum rosa,
> dulciter soporis alimonia
> post Veneris defessa commercia
> captatur,
> dum lassis instillatur.

The translation by G. F. Whicher quoted by Creekmore, *Lyrics*, pp. 18-20, differs from that given by H. Waddell, *Scholars* pp. 160-61.

See also T. G. Bergin, *The Poems of William of Poitou* (New Haven, 1955), p. 12, and A. Jeanroy, *Les chansons de Guillaume IX* (Paris, 1927), both with the original texts. An excerpt follows:

> No sai en qual hora'm fuy natz:
> No suy alegres ni iratz,
> No suy estrayns ni sui privatz,
> Ni no'n puesc au,
> Qu'enaissi fuy de nueitz fadatz,
> Sobr' un pueg au.

On Raymond Vidal, *Las Razos de Trobar* (*ca.* 1200) and Provençal poetic doctrines see W. F. Patterson, *Three Centuries of French Poetic Theory* (Ann Arbor, 1935), I, 34.

For the almost surrealistic statement of Arnault:

> Ieu sui Arnautz qu'amas l'aura
> E chatz la lebre ab le bou
> E nadi contra suberna.

See H. Davenson, *Les Troubadours* (Paris, 1961), p. 74.
See H. Waddell, *Scholars*, pp. 217-18.

9. For a translation by Owen Masters of Crazy Sweeney's "Song of the Woods," see H. Creekmore, *Lyrics* pp. 204-8. and J. Carney, *Lyrics*.

10. See R. Delisle, *Les Ecoles d'Orléans au XIIᵉ et au XIIIᵉ siècle* (Paris 1869), p. 8.

11. Ausonius, *De Rosis Nascentibus, 15*. See H. Waddell, *Scholars*, p. 6.

12. Adapted from a translation by A. Cowley, see Creekmore *Lyrics*, p. 9.

13. Vatican Library, lat. 3867, fol. 44ᵛ. See P. du Bourguet, *Early Christian Painting* (New York, 1965), Ill. 175. This manuscript is commonly called Vergilius Romanus. Similar but more sophisticated country scenes and landscapes appear in the Vergilius Vaticanus presumably of the early fifth century. The MS is Vatican Library lat. 3225. See Bourguet, Ills. 172-74, and for the bucolic mosaics in the Great Palace and Town Hall in Constantinople, see Ills. 145-50.

14. Prudentius, "De Novo Lumine Paschalis Sabbati," *Cathemerinon*, II, ll. 113-17, 121-25. See Migne, P. L. 59 col. 826. For a translation see H. Waddell, *Scholars*, p. 20.

15. Sigebert of Liége, Passio Sanctae Luciae," 19. For a translation see H. Waddell, *Scholars*, p. 107.

16. See H. Creekmore, *Lyrics*, p. 12, with a translation by J. M. Neale, revised by Chambers.

17. See H. Waddell, *Scholars*, pp. 17-18.

18. The literature on Hagia Sophia has most recently been indexed by W. MacDonald, *A Selected Bibliography of Architecture in the Age of Justinian*, American Association of Architectural Bibliographers, No. 16 (Spring, 1960). For the description of the Palace Church of Our Lady of the Pharos, *ca.* 846, in the Homilies of Patriarch Photius and the text by Nicholas Mesarites, *ca.* 1200, see R. J. H. Jenkins and C. A. Mango, "The Date and Significance of the Tenth Century Homily of Photius," *Dumbarton Oaks Papers*, No. 9-10 (Cambridge, Mass., 1956), pp. 125 ff.

19. See A. A. Vasiliev, "The Iconoclastic Edict of Caliph Yazid II, A.D. 721," *Dumbarton Oaks Papers*, No. 9-10 (Cambridge, Mass., 1956).

20. Ausonius (*ca.* 310-95) gave his impressions of country life in a description of the Moselle which has the same elegant immediacy reflected in the later mosaic:

> Quis color ille vadis, seras cum propulit umbras
> Hesperus et viridi perfundit monte Mosellam.
> Tota natant crispis iuga motibus et tremit absens
> pampinus et vitreis vindemia turget in undis.
> (Mosella, 192-95)

For a translation, see H. Waddell, *Scholars*, p. 6.

21. See D. T. Rice, *Islamic Art* (New York, 1965), p. 24, Ill. 15.

22. Various scholars have suggested North Italy, Egypt, Spain, Southern France, Tours, etc., as possible places of origin for this exceptional manuscript. We know that it was deposited in St. Gatien, Tours. A brief summary of the question is found in D. Diringer, *The Illuminated Book* (New York, 1958), pp. 73 ff.

23. The dating of Castelseprio is still an unsettled question, mostly because of quaint emotional overtones which have accompanied research on this exceptional postwar find from the very beginning. I was present in the early stages of cleaning without being able to form an opinion. Now I see no reason whatever why the cycle should not be dated some time after the iconoclastic controversy, even as late as the tenth century. After that date several

[165]

manuscripts show an exceptional but already more hardened treatment of figures and a restriction of their relation to space, in spite of their imitation of late classical prototypes. See, for example, the miniatures in the Theriaca of Nicander in an eleventh-century manuscript now in Paris, Bibl. Nat. Suppl. Gr. 247.

24. See Kuno Meyer, *Selections from Ancient Irish Poetry*, (2nd ed., 1913), p. 99, and for Irish poems generally, W. Stokes, *Thesaurus Paleohibernicus*, 3 vols. (Cambridge, England, 1901-10). For the English text, see Waddell, *Scholars*, p. 38.

25. On Baudry see Waddell, *Scholars*, pp. 100-104, Migne, P. L. 171 col. 1173.

26. H. Creekmore, *Lyrics*, pp. 202-3, trans. Robin Flower. Many examples throughout Europe of a two dimensional treatment of the human figure could be listed. The best known representatives are of course the Book of Kells and the Book of Lindisfarne. As C. Nordenfalk and H. Bober have proven, the latter is related to traditions formulated in the Middle East. In this connection, the problem of Armenia also has to be restudied, as well as the vision of the world of so-called primitive peoples in the South Central Pacific. The disregard for object weight and the illusion of motion of a body through space characterizes much of the art of the societies whose most immediate concerns are nature. An interesting late example of this approach is found in the frescoes of San Quirce in Pedret, where the crucifixion (?) shows a mannequin surrounded by a circle with a blue and red zig-zag pattern, the whole topped by a bird. See W. W. S. Cook and J. Gudiol Ricart, in *Ars Hispaniae*, Vol. 6 (Madrid, 1950), Fig. 8, and J. Ainaud, *Spanish Frescoes of the Romanesque Period* (New York, 1962).

In contrast to the two dimensional representations of the art of the migratory nations, it is all the more remarkable that the Byzantine artists still continued to create within the classical tradition. Even the surrealistic vision of Ezekiel in the Homilies of Gregory Nazianzus done for Basil I (867-86) still preserves a classical dignity of the figures and only the purple and blue sky transmits a visionary quality of the event. See D. T. Rice, *Art of the Byzantine Era* (New York, 1963), Ill. 69 and here Ill. 23.

27. Creekmore, *Lyrics*, pp. 194-222, and especially pp. 196-97, 262. Creekmore gives a good cross section of Irish and Old Norse poetry which includes some of the most descriptive seasonal poems. On the other hand, an eleventh-century Anglo-Saxon poem, *The Grave*, quoted by Creekmore, p. 265, describes the coffin in gruesome detail as a house "gruesome to live in" to be wasted by worms. Such awareness of death and decay speaks for an anticlassical point of view where man is part of the eternal cycle of creation and destruction. He thus comes most splendidly to life in battle as seen in the "Death Song of Haakon the Good" by Eyvindr Finsson. Observation and identification with nature are expressed in one of the most impressive descriptive poems on nature known to me. It is Crazy Sweeney's "Song of the Woods" in which typically enough he thinks of himself not as a hunter but as a stag. See Creekmore, *Lyrics*, pp. 194, 204-8. The poem comes from a prose romance *Suibne Geilt* which contains verses, and its contents were briefly discussed above.

28. J. Beckwith, *Early Medieval Art* (New York, 1964), pp. 39-42.

29. For Walafrid Strabo, see E. Dümmler in *Poetae Latini*, Vol. 2 (M.G.H.), p. 403, Carmen, 59.

30. In spite of the sophistication of Alcuin a deep pessimism pervaded him as seen from the *Disputatio Pippini* where he defines man as "the slave of death, the guest of an inn, a wayfarer passing" (Migne P. L. 101, col. 975). For

the poem of Alcuin's deserted house see *Poetae Latini Carolini Aevi*, Vol. 2, (Monumenta Germaniae Historica [Berlin, 1881-84]), p. 348.

31. See E. Power, *Medieval People* (New York, 1924) pp. 31 ff.

32. For Hrabanus Maurus see *Poet. Lat. Carol.*, Vol. 2, p. 188, Carm., XXV, and H. Waddell, *Scholars*, p. 57.

33. Migne, P. L. 145, col. 980. The statement of Peter Damianus: "How strange a thing is man! But half a cubit of him and the universe full of material things will not satisfy him" again points out the Carolingian dilemma between a Frankish sense of reality and the classical anthropocentric outlook. For the poem "Ad perennis vitae fontem mens sitivit arida" which deals with the glory of paradise, see H. Waddell, *Scholars*, pp. 92, 245.

34. J. Beckwith, *Early Medieval Art*, colorplate 32.

35. For a translation, see H. Waddell, *Scholars*, p. 80.

36. H. Focillon, *L'An Mil* (Paris, 1952).

37. See Creekmore, *Lyrics*, pp. 200-201. The tenth-century Irish poem describing May is one of the briskest and most incisively descriptive praises of spring.

38. Creekmore, *Lyrics*, p. 265, trans. C. W. Kennedy. The Anglo-Saxon eleventh-century poem on the decay in a coffin and a Danish poem, "Aager and Eliza," in which the dead bridegroom rises to claim the bride (Creekmore, p. 229) belong to the gloomiest extant descriptions of death. They find their counterpart only in a few Spanish poems which cruelly question life and even procreation. See W. S. Merwin, *Spanish Ballads* (New York, 1961) which includes "The Corpse-Keeper" describing a girl who kept her dead lover for seven years (p. 84), the fate of a prisoner (p. 82), and, above all, "The Gray She Wolf" describing a wolf's attack on a herd of sheep with an amazing realism (p. 95). See also note 33.

39. Creekmore, *Lyrics*, p. 201, trans. Owen Masters.

40. Creekmore, *Lyrics*, pp. 220-22, trans. O. L. Oliver. *Idem*, pp. 212, 226 with Danish and Old Norse poems on battle and revenge.

41. See J. Beckwith, *Early Medieval Art*, pp. 81 ff., where Reichenau, Trier, and other Ottonian centers are discussed.

42. *Ibid.*, pp. 104 ff. Professor Samuel Edgerton kindly informed me on the possible availability of Aristotle's color theory at that time. The treatise is *De sensu*, IV, 442a. See W. D. Ross (ed.), *Works of Aristotle translated into English* (Oxford, 1931) Vol. 3. But the renewed use of color perspective was not necessarily based on theory, more probably on observation of the wide panoramas available in the area of Reichenau.

43. Cambridge, first half of the eleventh century. See H. Waddell, *Scholars*, p. 109.

44. See J. Beckwith, *Early Medieval Art*, p. 194, Ill. 186.

45. Prudentius, *Psychomachia*, II, 310-30, Migne P. L. 60, col. 46. Here is the translation as given by H. Waddell, *Scholars*, p. 22:

> Come from the confines of the sunset world,
> Luxury lavish of her ruined fame
> Loose-haired, wild eyed, her voice a dying fall,
> Lost in delight . . .
> Flowershod and swaying from the wine cup,
> Each step a fragrance.

46. In the twelfth century a "man height" appears more frequently as a measurement. One instance is the description of the basilica of Santiago by

Aimery Picaud in the Codex Calixtinus (*ca.* 1140) in which he says that the church is 53 man-heights in length, 39 man-heights in width etc. See V. Martet, *Recueil de Textes* (Paris 1911), pp. 397 ff.

47. For a rediscovery of the horizon and the reintroduction of causal elements in late twelfth-century art see F. Bucher, *The Pamplona Bibles, 1197-1200 A.D.*; "Reasons for Changes in Iconography" in *Stil und Überlieferung in der Kunst des Abendlandes* (Berlin, 1967), Vol. 1, pp. 131-40, Plates I, 13-15, Ills. 1-29. The Cotton Genesis Recension is discussed by the author in the forthcoming *Pamplona Bibles*, Vol. 1 (New Haven and London, 1969).

48. An early study of successive planes creating a somewhat illogical space is found in the frescoe of the Crucifixion in the Chapel of Saints Quiricus and Julitta in S. Maria Antiqua in Rome. It is the work of an artist influenced by a long tradition of which the first preserved example is found in the Rabbula Gospels made in Syria in 586 A.D. (The fresco is dated perhaps as early as the mid eighth century and exemplifies the immense importance of paintings in Rome as a source for the Western artists. See also K. Weitzmann, "Various Aspects of Byzantine Influences on the Latin Countries from the Sixth to the Twelfth Century," *Dumbarton Oaks Papers* (1966), p. 9, Ill. 13-14.

49. The Eastern influences on Western and more specifically Ottonian art were considerable while the countercurrent from the West to the Middle East was negligible. But late eleventh and twelfth-century European painting nevertheless shows the creation of an independent, flexible, formal, and iconographic vocabulary, which served as a basis for increasingly original stylistic experiments. These developed into local styles as early as the second half of the twelfth century. See K. Weitzmann, "Various Aspects," quoted in note 48, and H. Focillon, *Fresques Romanes des Eglises de France* (Paris, 1949). The variety of expression can be explored in a comparison of frescoes in Berzé-la-Ville, St. Savin, Tavant, and Vic. The two-dimensional envelope which defined Romanesque sculpture as well was broken in the protruding legs of Christ in the Royal portal of Chartres around the middle of the twelfth century. This was a major breakthrough in the most literal sense of the word.

50. See A. Mason (ed.), *Aucassin and Nicolette and other Mediaeval Romances and Legends* (New York, 1958). In connection with the appreciation of the gifts of nature one might mention here one of the most charming clinical views of wine, its quality, and transportation found in a letter by Nicolas de Clairvaux. It refers to the wine of Auxerre. See J. Benton, "Nicolas de Clairvaux à la recherche du vin d'Auxerre d'après une lettre inédite du XIIe siècle," *Annales de Bourgogne*, Vol. 34 (1962), 252-55. For the changing attitudes toward *Stabilitas*, see G. B. Ladner, "Homo Viator, Mediaeval Ideas on Alienation and Order," *Speculum* (April, 1967), esp. pp. 240 ff.

51. For the Psalter of St. Louis, Paris, Bibl. de l'Arsenal 1186, see V. Leroquais, *Les Psautiers manuscrits des bibliothèques publiques de France* (Paris, 1940-41), Vol. 2, p. 13, Pls. 67-69.

52. See A. Hilka, O. Schumann, *Carmina Burana*, 2 vols. (Heidelberg, 1930). The dating of the illustrations varies according to authors from 1219 to "before 1300." From a stylistic point of view I would opt for the early date.

53. For extensive information on the extant manuscripts and their contents, see C. A. Wood and F. M. Fyfe, *The Art of Falconry by Frederick II of Hohenstaufen* (Stanford, 1943). The Paris manuscript follows Vatican Ms. Pal. Lat. 1071 and was commissioned by Jehan II Chevalier de Dompierre, who died in 1307, and his wife Isabel, grandniece of Yolande of Brienne, second wife of Frederick II. It is signed by Simon d'Orliens.

54. See note 1.
55. H. Creekmore, *Lyrics,* p. 169. The translation is by Morris Bishop.
56. See Bryan Stone, *Medieval English Verse* (Baltimore, 1964), p. 105. It is clear that a full treatment of the subject would have to include epics, romances, and plays which were more exposed to public scrutiny than poetry. As paintings they had to be understood quickly and thus had to be formalized in style and content. From the preserved discussions and sources we gather that the artist was advised to keep the problem of illiteracy in mind in contrast to the writer who through words could make more complex statements, which could be addressed to all levels of society. The visual arts thus present us with a more generalized view of medieval man's reaction to his environment than most of literature.

VII

Circumstances and the Sense of History in Tudor England: The Coming of the Historical Revolution

Arthur B. Ferguson
Duke University, Durham, North Carolina

It is to the use the intellectuals of Tudor England made of history that I wish to call your attention this afternoon rather than to their writing of it. You will, I hope, pardon me if, as a historian, I admit to something less than wild enthusiasm for the standard Tudor histories. Of course there are bright spots in the picture, but they stand out largely by contrast to the rest of it. Thomas More, as we all know, wrote the first "modern" English biography in his more or less innocently garbled life of Richard III; but it is conspicuous by its isolation. Polydore Vergil brought to England the mature scholarship of Renaissance Italy and domesticated it there; but he was remarkable rather for what he did not do than for what he did, for avoiding, that is, the crude and credulous handling of sources common in earlier chronicle writing rather than for any fresh insight into the meaning of the past; and anyway he was a foreigner, as his English contemporaries never let him forget. Hall carried on the good work—and the Tudor bias—with gusto and panache; but both he and Polydore share the doubtful credit of having set the pattern for that repetitious series of chronicles which culminated in Holinshed's vast compilation, a fitting climax to an essentially medieval historiography. These chronicles provided later generations with a highly colored version of British and English history, the stuff that plays are made on, as well as dreary sermons on the evils of rebellion; but they may well have done more by their very popularity to stunt historical thought than to stimulate it.

So it should not be surprising that what F. Smith Fussner has aptly termed the "historical revolution" in England,[1] implying thereby a radical change in historiography, should be found only after 1580 in the emergence of a new breed of scholars whose newness can be measured rather accurately by the formal criteria of modern historical scholarship. In this latter part of the Tudor century and during the first half of the century following, a succession of first-rate minds became interested in historical problems: Camden, Stow, Bacon, Raleigh, Selden, and Spelman—all in one way or another capable of a realistic and systematic examination of evidence, a willingness to stay within the area of what is credible and humanly knowable, and perhaps most significant of all, a recognition of cultures, customs, institutions, of society, in short as a primary objective of historical understanding.

What does seem surprising is that this recognizably modern way of thinking about history and of writing it should have made its appearance so late in an age supposedly responsible for introducing modernity in all things. Yet the problem here is more apparent than real. The aim of this paper is accordingly to demonstrate that, in the first eighty-odd years of the sixteenth century and even during the half-century preceding, it is possible to see gradually emerging a new sense of history—not a new historiography, much less a formulated philosophy of history, but an attitude toward the past which was a necessary precondition for a revolution in historical scholarship, and to show to what extent this sense of history developed in response to the challenge of events and problems in an age of even more fundamental transition than are most historical ages.

Before going any farther, let me make clear what I mean by the sense of history, or rather, the modern sense of history, for that, in its emerging form, is what we are concerned with. Obviously it means something more than the mere expertise of the professional historian. It involves the entire attitude toward the past. Today we have come to appreciate this more fully as historical thought has moved outward in all directions to form liaisons with other disciplines engaged in the study of man.

(These liaisons may sometimes be of suspiciously common law variety, and occasionally dangerous, but are usually of mutual benefit.) What we are now trying to do as a result of prolonged specialization, Renaissance thinkers did out of innocence: they had not yet learned the sad truth that in the study of man to conquer one must first divide. We at any rate should be especially prepared to understand the willingness of these men of the pre-social scientific era to invoke the aid of historical experience in answering all sorts of questions concerning man as a social creature. And it is in relation to this catechism of experience that the sense of history emerges in its most characteristic modern form. Furthermore, it is of the utmost importance to recognize that such change as took place in historical thought in this period was in attitude rather than theory, in the nature of the questions asked and in the categories of data held relevant rather than in the larger frame of philosophical reference. What passed for historical philosophy among English thinkers remained essentially conservative, either in the tradition of classical cyclism or in that of Christian Augustinianism or in some curious mixture of the two.

The sense of history also goes well beyond a mere appreciation of the didactic value of history. For centuries Europeans had paid lip-service to that belief; and heaven knows Renaissance writers placed what seems at times an exaggerated value on history, and long before the 1580's too. Indeed they rang tireless changes on the Ciceronian formula in praise of history. Elyot's version is typical: "history [is] the witness of times, mistress of life, the life of remembrance, of truth the light, and messenger of antiquity."[2] But this definition of the uses of history could mean much or little. To most people of the day it all boiled down to the notion that history taught lessons through examples of good and bad deeds; and this, in turn, depended on the further assumption either that history repeats itself or that its examples are universally applicable. Either way, insofar as it was innocent of any sense of the relation of human affairs to the contingencies of time and place, this could be considered an anti-historical point of view.

By the same token, the historical sense as it has emerged in modern times is most clearly distinguished by the ability, and the willingness, to see that the thoughts and actions of men, however much they may reveal of a universal human nature and however much they may repay study as the examples by which philosophy teaches, can be fully understood only in relation to the conditions peculiar to the society that produced them. This sense of history presumes a certain degree of self-consciousness, a consciousness, that is, of the unique character of one's own society which in turn makes it possible to recognize the peculiar character of other societies, past as well as present. The term "perspective" naturally suggests itself, if only by way of analogy. By it I mean the capacity to see both past and present from a particular point of view in relation to which events and societies arrange themselves in a certain temporal order and a certain relationship to each other. It implies a sense of anachronism, to use Erwin Panofsky's happy phrase. It is something quite analogous in the perception of time to the Renaissance artist's perception of space. Indeed the two ways of looking at things may well be related by more than mere analogy, for both arose out of the same subtle changes in the approach to reality which, more than any change in formal philosophy, separates Renaissance thought from medieval.

If, then, perspective is one of the characteristics we are looking for, a sense of process is another. In fact, the one could hardly have existed without the other; for it is by means of its peculiar course of development that a society achieves its unique position at any given point in history. Recognition of these processes, these lines of cause and effect become possible only when the experience recorded in history came to be considered as something more than a rich treasury of *exempla* to be drawn upon piecemeal for whatever didactic purpose the situation of the moment required. This directly didactic approach had in preceding ages been a source of strength to historical thought. By drawing attention to what was considered universal and unchanging, it had served to justify historical writing to the ancients who placed small value on those passing events which in themselves reflected mere flux. In medieval thought it gave the desired evidence of that timeless moral order which underlay the successive acts of the divine drama. But, by diverting attention from the fact of change, especially change in customs, institutions, and social structure, it had rendered irrelevant any attempt to discover meaningful continuity in the past. To the extent that Renaissance thought moved toward the observable and tangible it became increasingly aware of the forces, impersonal as well as moral, operating in society. Analysis of the contemporary scene made it easier to see in earlier periods and other societies something worth similar attention.

From what has just been said it would seem to follow that we are likely to find the key to the emergence of a modern sense of history in what today would be called social or cultural history rather than political. Such divisions are, however, too arbitrary to mean much today; to men of the Renaissance they meant nothing at all. And anyway, politics has always enjoyed, and will no doubt retain a central position in historical thought. But the tendency of formal historiography to be devoted almost exclusively to the actions of princes, statesmen, and generals, as it was well into modern times, did, in fact, tend to perpetuate the treatment of past events as *exempla,* quite capable of being detached from any necessary relation to time and place.[3] And if we are to put our finger on that aspect most distinctive of modern historical thought, we shall, I believe, find it in the increasing awareness of the social entity as something transcending regimes and dynasties, something at the same time more subject to discernible processes of change than the traditional, and essentially static, "body politic," something which therefore invites historical study, the questions asked determined in large part by contemporary experience.

This is the perspective which, for example, permitted the humanists to recognize an affinity with the societies of ancient Greece and Rome, yet at the same time to view them across a chasm of time bridgeable only by the historical imagination. It is what made it possible for the Elizabethans, whose own society had moved well beyond the conditions which had given rise to the culture of chivalry, to indulge in a truly romantic, which is also to say historically-minded, revival of that culture, to relish the consciously archaic, and to play at being knights of old. And, in the sphere of serious historical research, it is what eventually allowed Sir Henry Spelman to "discover" feudalism and to see in the middle ages, not a slough of despond between two eras of proud achievement, but a society peculiar in its laws, institutions, and customs.

I have been describing, of course, an end product of Renaissance learning, never indeed completely assimilated in that era. Typically medieval habits of thought continued to influence, even at times to dominate, expression throughout the sixteenth century. For example, one has only to read the cautionary tales of the *Mirror for Magistrates* to breathe the almost undiluted atmosphere of medieval didacticism and to see re-embodied the *de casibus* tradition in all its timeless melancholy. Although the *Mirror* does reveal some interest in causal relationships and their interpretation, throughout its stories runs the assumption that the actions of princes and generals (the only subject-matter worthy of the historian and his high-nosed muse) are to be judged according to a universal scheme of values and have therefore little to do with the contingencies of time and place.[4] And many of the social critics who carried on the traditions of the medieval pulpit placed their often highly realistic comment in the timeless context of man's uniformly sinful nature.[5] But here, as elsewhere, fresh winds were blowing. The weather pattern changed slowly: its effects on the ecology of English thought did not indeed become fully apparent until the following century; but by then the "historical revolution" had sunk deep and hardy roots.

What has led to a good deal of misunderstanding concerning the early Renaissance approach to history has been our own tendency, natural enough I suppose, to examine only what was *called* history rather than those works in which history was *used*. In this we have followed the Tudor writers themselves who in turn followed the lead of the classical historians in considering history as something confined to the full-dress rehearsal of the deeds of men famous in the affairs of state. But they knew better and so should we. Without bothering about formal definitions, men not engaged in the self-conscious task of writing history were beginning to use history for all the infinite variety of purposes to which it, considered as experience, could be put. Faced with the problems of a society in the process of unusually apparent change, their minds already attuned by humanistic study to the exploration of tradition, these men tended almost instinctively to place the present in some sort of working relationship with the past, and even, at times, with the future. It is therefore to writings on a variety of subjects not immediately connected with the art of the historian that we must turn—to writings which undertook to explore the problems arising in such diverse areas as religion, law, politics, scholarship, patriotic appeal, exploration, and invention. Someone once said—I think it was Carl Becker and he was speaking then of good writing—that, like happiness, it comes if at all only when one is preoccupied with something else. Changing the changeables, much the same might be said of the sense of history in Renaissance England.

Time will not permit me to go into much detail on all this. So at the risk of cultivating that commonest of academic weeds, the wild generality, I should like simply to trace for you a few rather broad outlines.

First of all, it might be well to establish the major but somewhat ambiguous role of humanism in promoting a fresh approach to the past. The new scholarship was in itself one of the most influential circumstances of the age, nor is there any meaningful dichotomy here separating ideas and events or external conditions. As we shall see, the interests of the English humanists linked their intellectual heritage inextricably with contemporary problems. (I am, by the way, designating as humanists not only those engaged more or less professionally in the study of ancient language and letters, but those also—and in England they included in their number most of the more prominent scholars anyway—who applied the results of such study, its inspiration if you will, to broader areas of thought and especially to the issues affecting the commonweal.) Surely so pervasive an influence, stemming as it did from a re-appraisal of classical antiquity and itself sensitive at every point to contemporary life, would provide a virtually sufficient explanation for the emergence of a new historical outlook. This moreover would seem an especially satisfactory assumption in the particular case of England, where the new learning (to use the original meaning of the term) came late, already mature and sophisticated, and expressed within the socially conscious context of Erasmian reform.

There is certainly no doubt about the superiority of historical writing done under the influence of humanism. One need only compare the *Anglica Historia* of Polydore Vergil with, say Higden's *Polychronicon*,[6] to see the vast distance that lay between the fourteenth-century chronicler on the one hand, learned as he was, in Higden's case remarkably conversant with the sources of classical antiquity, but credulous, uncritical, and incapable of weaving his materials into a narrative connected by lines of cause and effect, and, on the other, the imported humanist, a bit uninspired perhaps, yet shrewd and critical in his handling of authorities, and capable of telling the story of English politics with continuity and considerable interpretive insight.[7] But it is when the English humanists came to apply the inspiration derived from classical precept and example to the problems of the commonwealth, to act, that is, as they believed it the duty of the learned and wise citizen to do, that they begin to show signs of a deeper understanding of the relationship between the thoughts and actions of a past age and their historical milieu. Thus we find John Colet, for example, preoccupied as he was with the tensions attendant upon an impending crisis in the church as well as inspired by the vistas of a new scholarship, undertaking to reassess the words of St. Paul in part at least in relation to the society in which he lived and taught, as words spoken at a particular time and in a particular place.[8] Thomas Starkey, in the course of the most thorough analysis of English society made during the early Tudor period, found it necessary to point out in passing how English laws and institutions depended for their peculiar character on the peculiarities of English history itself and to rethink the speculations made by classical writers concerning the origins of civilization and the creative role of man.[9] Or, to take another kind of example, Sir Thomas Smith, in the process of a much needed attempt to bring some sort of definition into the picture his countrymen had of their government, found himself comparing English and Roman institutions, not in the unrealistic—and unhistorical—hope of getting Englishmen to act like Romans, but simply the better to understand English institutions as they existed in his own day.[10] Finally, with the advent of the Reformation, the English Reformers, most of whom had been raised in the atmosphere of Cambridge humanism, sought solid controversial ground in a more or less historical reconstruction of the primitive church. But more of this in a moment.

It would be hard to exaggerate the importance of the fact that the new historical perspective was inextricably linked with an increasing interest in social analysis. The search for cause, perhaps best exemplified in the pamphlets urging economic reform, and especially by the *Discourse of the Commonweal,* recently attributed to Smith,[11] led to a general catechism of experience. And it would appear that the English humanists had even more incentive than their counterparts on the Continent to apply their learning and the inspiration derived from it to the problems of their society. The island kingdom, like *Utopia* itself, by virtue of its relative security from the grosser forms of external danger, could afford to explore its own problems and to consider them in terms rather of social and cultural well-being than of political power. This, in turn, may help explain why these men used history rather than writing it, why the task of actual history-writing was left largely to second-rate minds prior to the last Tudor generation, and why, at the same time, the reading of histories from other lands, both ancient and contemporaneous, in the original and to a rapidly increasing extent in translations, went on apace. This same social orientation of English humanist thought may also explain why no

English humanist from More to Bacon, with the possible exception of Roger Ascham in his *Report of Germany*,[12] undertook the analytical kind of political history which was developed
to such a high degree by the Italians who had constantly before
them the problems and object lessons attendant upon the seizure
and loss of political power.

Even, however, if we grant the fructifying influence of
humanism, we must take into account the fact that circumstances more or less similar to those of Early Tudor England
also stimulated historical thought in the days well before the
golden age of English humanism and among men largely, if
not completely, untouched by the new learning. Even in that
sparsely documented period in English history a few notable
examples emerge. Responding to what he felt to be a crisis
in English government—an intellectual crisis, but to his mind
none the less real—Sir John Fortescue undertook an analysis of
English institutions and law which foreshadowed that of Sir
Thomas Smith and prompted him to historical reflection of a
kind not unlike that of the Tudor humanist.[13] Even more
significant was the work of Reginald Pecock, the maverick
Bishop of Chichester. That brilliant but politically obtuse
character narrowly escaped the heretic's stake by trying to defend the church against the anticlerical criticism and anti-
intellectualism of the later Lollards by a rigorously rationalistic
critique of the Scriptures considered in large part as historical
documents. Like Colet and the Christian humanists of a later
generation, he sought to interpret the words of the Bible in
terms of their historical context rather than as isolable texts.
But his historical sense, if not his scholarship, was really keener
than Colet's, and his critique foreshadows the higher criticism
of a still later day rather than the modest historical rationaliza-
tions of the early reformers.[14] And then there was John Rous,
a chaplain under the patronage of the house of Warwick and
part-time chronicler, antiquary, and illustrator.[15] Though distinguished neither as an artist nor as a chronicler, indeed unusually credulous in the latter capacity, his antiquarian interests
reveal a sense of society and a feeling for anachronism seldom

enough found in succeeding generations.[16] His drawings,[17] depicting the dress and armor of earlier generations of War- wicks, show how the eye of the artist could become the eye of the antiquary, its vision becoming gradually sensitive to ana- chronism. More important, he shows us that the early anti- quary, so far from being the rather fussy and myopic servant of the servants of Clio, could be in reality a pioneer in the study of social history.

This is not to deny in any way the importance of a fully developed humanism such as that which flourished in the select circle of which More was the brightest light, to which those fortunate visitors, Erasmus and Vives, contributed so richly, and which set the tone for those dedicated citizens who turned their learning to the problems of reform in church and society. The culture of classical antiquity, when reinterpreted in the light of contemporary life, presented to the educated minds of Tudor England the immensely stimulating picture of a complex, sophisticated, and, as they were coming to see, a unique society. Indeed, the more they knew of that society the less like their own it appeared, yet, paradoxically, the more worthwhile it became as an object of historical investigation, not necessarily for purposes of emulation but for such compara- tive study as is conducive to self-knowledge.

Self-knowledge also involved, for the Renaissance mind, a passionate search for origins. The feeling that what is oldest is truest or even best did not, of course, lead always to a mature historical outlook. It could, and did at times, foster that vene- ration for ancient authority which, when excessive, served to limit humanist thought. But it also prompted the kind of investigation without which anything like the modern his- torical outlook would have been a long time coming. Investi- gation of classical antiquity provided the paradigm for this search for origins, but it was not the only antiquity to which men of the day had recourse. Christian antiquity and the early history of the British people themselves became, in fact, more intimately involved in sixteenth-century English controversies than did classical.

Religious controversy was especially likely to promote a search for the kind of authority the distant past alone could provide. King Henry VIII's "great matter," together with its ecclesiastical repercussions, set both sides scurrying for historical justification. But the historical sense owes less to such more or less meretricious efforts at propaganda than to the serious attempts made to seek in the history of the early church the groundwork of both policy and belief. As soon as that point had been reached where the dialectical methods of the schools could no longer resolve fundamental differences, authority had to be sought in history.[18] History was, however, quite capable of speaking with a forked tongue, her answer depending on the interest and urgency of the questioner. To the orthodox, the church *was* in a sense the sum of its history, its history an unfolding of authority from Apostolic times through the dicta of the Fathers and the decisions of popes and councils. To counter this appeal to the authority of tradition, the reformers sought a similar authority in the early history of the church before it had developed its papal organization. This exploration of Christian antiquity could, at its worst, like the humanist study of pagan antiquity at *its* worst, lead toward a quite unhistorical interpretation of ancient society. It was only too easy for the ardent reformer to see in the primitive church, not the simple and groping beginnings of an institution, but an ideal to be restored, a society different only in its pristine purity from that to which they aspired in their reformed churches. Paradoxically, it was the revolutionaries who thus tended to drift into a reactionary position, and it was the conservative side, the apologists for an institution which prided itself on being *semper eadem,* who were often more ready to recognize the historical process involved in the unfolding of tradition.[19]

These were, of course, tendencies only, and, as far as the English reformers are concerned, there was an equally marked tendency for some of them at least to move closer to an understanding of Christian antiquity as a society separated from their own not only by time but by a process of development. Scornful of what one of them called the "chopological" interpretation of Biblical texts isolated from their context, the Henrician reformers, Tyndale, Latimer, Ridley, and Cranmer to name only the more prominent, made an honest effort to apply to the study of Christian antiquity the methods of humanistic scholarship they had learned at an earlier point in their careers in their study of classical antiquity, namely the methods of philological and historical criticism.[20] But the spirit of John Colet and of Erasmian scholarship tended too often to be dissipated in the heat of confessional controversy, and so it was not until the Elizabethan period that the architects of the Settlement were able once more to view both the early church and their own in something approaching an accurate temporal perspective.

Archbishop Whitgift, in particular, found himself confronted not so much by the claims of Roman Catholicism, now more or less safely outlawed, but by those of a Puritan fundamentalism which Thomas Cartwright sought to establish on the basis of a literal resurrection of what he took to be the Apostolic age, together with an equally absolute dependence on the Mosaic law. In the process of combatting this radically unhistorical appeal to history, Whitgift was able to turn his considerable scholarship toward an examination of the church as a developing institution.[21] In this he was aided by the adiaphoristic formula, already well assimilated in English thought. That principle had been imported early in the Reformation, partially domesticated among Cromwell's circle of intellectuals as an undergirding for his middle of the road policy,[22] and developed for similar purposes during the Elizabethan controversies with both the Catholic right and the Puritan left.[23] By distinguishing between those things necessary for salvation and things indifferent—ceremonies and the like—which are matters of human choice and hence subject to the contingencies of time and place, this principle left ample room for the relativity of institutions and customs and hence for an essentially historical approach to ecclesiastical problems.

The pressure to establish the credentials of Anglicanism in antiquity led also to an interesting, if somewhat recherché investigation of Anglo-Saxon antiquity. Acting on the assumption, questionable but at least congenial to antiquarian interests, that the old ways could be presumed to be the best ways, Matthew Parker, Elizabeth's faithful and royally bedeviled Archbishop of Canterbury, undertook to set over against the judgment of the papacy made in the days of Hildebrand and William the Conqueror concerning such things as the sacraments that of learned men in the days of the Saxons before the Conquest. All of which led him and his scholarly assistants to the study of Anglo-Saxon manuscripts long since ignored or translated into corrupt Latin. He even had a font of Anglo-Saxon type cut for use in publishing some of the numerous manuscripts he was able to collect.[24]

However effective the work of Parker and his associates may have been in clarifying the early history of the church in England, it had the more long-range, though unintentional, effect of stimulating the study of English law and government. For it was in part as a by-product of the ecclesiastical controversy and its accompanying revival of Saxon studies that Anglo-Saxon laws began, as F. W. Maitland once said, "to awaken from a long sleep."[25] William Lambarde, who studied under Parker and Nowell, the founders of modern Anglo-Saxon studies, turned his feeling for Anglo-Saxon antiquity to good account in finding a pre-Norman, and hence an unassailably English ancestry for the laws and institutions of his own England.[26] Questionable as his perspective was, especially on the origins of parliament, it was the product of a fresh and eager desire to find justification in a documentable rather than a legendary past.

It would be convenient at this point to be able to demonstrate that this revived interest in Anglo-Saxon laws was but a part of a more comprehensive renaissance of legal scholarship which in turn became, for England as for the Continent, one of the most powerful stimuli to historical thought. Unfortunately that is not quite the way things worked out, despite the well-intentioned Lambarde. Faced with the competing claims of two kinds of laws, those embodied in local customs and those borne upon the rising tide of Roman jurisprudence, Continental lawyers became historians in spite of themselves, and historians, moreover, in a very modern sense, committed to a comparative study of law in its relation to the society out of which it had grown. English lawyers, on the other hand had really only one law to worry about, once Roman law had failed to invade England in force and was left in a sort of working quarantine in the council courts. And, even though the English common law was in fact a developing body, "broadening down from precedent to precedent," the English lawyers tended to proceed on the quite unhistorical assumption that, being based on custom, it was of immemorial antiquity.[27] This attitude led at worst to a self-defeating primitivism which placed the origins of English law beyond the reach of any sensible historian, beyond the reach even of those equipped with the knowledge of Anglo-Saxon and early British antiquities. At best it fostered a highly imaginative interpretation of English history which sought to place all that was free and best, including parliament itself and the courts, beyond the Norman Conquest and to write the history of England since the Conquest in terms of the struggle for freedom from the Norman yoke and for reaffirmation of the old laws.[28]

These tendencies, this "hardening" of common law thinking, did not, however, set in until the Elizabethan period.[29] A few humanist scholars of the early Tudor period appear in fact to have achieved the kind of perspective that comes from comparative study. Though not himself a lawyer, Thomas Starkey brought back from his studies in Padua, among other things, a considerable knowledge of the civil law and from that outside vantage point was able to see English laws and institutions for what they were, the product of a peculiar historical development and one, moreover, significantly interrupted by the Norman Conquest. And, as we have seen, Sir Thomas Smith undertook to redefine the structure and character of English government to a considerable extent by comparison with Roman.[30] But it was not again until the seventeenth century that English legal thought achieved something like a mature historical perspective, and in Sir Henry Spelman's "discovery" of feudal society was able to bring history once again to the aid of law and law to history.[31]

The apparent provinciality of English legal thought in the Elizabethan period could be considered an expression of a growing national self-consciousness which, in turn, found expression not only in a heightened awareness of the national past but in its present position in a world of competing powers and diverse cultures, a world no longer reflecting more than the shadow of a universal order. Despite their commitment to the ideal of a Christendom made good and reasonable by man acting in accordance with their potentially rational nature and their natural dignity, even the early Tudor humanists found their vision for practical purposes focused on the problems of their own commonwealth. Many of those problems, as we have seen were of a social, economic, or administrative character. But the new nationalism was a state of mind. Some of the problems attendant upon it were accordingly intellectual.

For one thing, the English language itself had reached a point where even the most priggish of classical scholars could not ignore it. Much as they remained preoccupied with the language and literature of Greece and Rome, those humanists who served primarily as scholars and teachers found themselves of necessity involved with the vernacular. Not only did they tend to use it whenever they wanted a more than academic audience, as they frequently did, they were forced also to consider it seriously as a literary medium. Even Roger Ascham, toplofty as he was toward the entire medieval heritage, found it necessary to account for the peculiar development of the English language and in particular to explain what he considered to be the crudities of English verse forms by tracing them to the linguistic deterioration that accompanied the barbarian migrations in the days of the declining Roman Empire.[32] No such apologies mark the similar, but much more systematic historical interpretation made by Ascham's younger contemporary, George Puttenham. In the course of his frankly patriotic and consciously pioneering analysis of the "arte of English

poesie," he went farther than Ascham in explaining the development of the English language from its barbarian origins, glory-
ing the while in the rugged monosyllabic heritage of "Saxon
English."[33]

Of an earlier generation, but even more driven by patriotic
zeal, were John Leland, the pioneer antiquarian, and John
Bale, the scholar-reformer and most "bilious" of controversial-
ists. These men were both thrown on the defensive by the low
opinion they believed (on fairly good evidence, too) foreign
scholars had of English culture, and they were shocked by the
very real danger to English letters they recognized in the dis-
persal of the monastic libraries. Accordingly, with Bale's support, Leland urged that measures be adopted to rescue the
monuments of British antiquity, even suggesting the creation
of a sort of national archive.[34] In addition both undertook what
amounted to a pioneering survey of English writers. Though
more chauvinistic than accurate, Bale's *Summarium* (1548)
and the later and larger *Catalogus* (1557-59) nevertheless mark
the beginning of the systematic study of national literary history
in England. Of Leland's work it is difficult to speak with the
same degree of seriousness as that with which he took it and
himself. What, for instance, are we to say of the several entirely
mythical authors he dredged up from the turgid legends of
British antiquity, including, *mirabile dictu*, the eagle that,
according to Geoffrey of Monmouth, prophesied the building
of Shaftesbury, which somehow becomes Aquila the Prophet?[35]

Impelled by the same rather touchy nationalism, others, in
addition to both Leland and Bale, turned their attention to still
other aspects of the strong national tradition embodied in the
history of Britain, as it had come down from the days of Bede
and Gildas and been marvelously embellished by Geoffrey of
Monmouth,[36] with its story of Brutus and the Trojan origin
of the British people and its account of the wonderful world
of Arthurian legend. In addition, the chronicled doings of the
late medieval monarchy itself, and of England's fortunes in the
Hundred Years' War further enriched this heritage of national
history and proved a veritable widow's cruse for writers of

historical plays and such historical moralists as the authors of
the *Mirror for Magistrates.*[37]

National respectability demanded above all a pedigree, and
the longer the better. Indeed, there was no honorable stopping
point this side of the Creation, or at least the Flood. The
problem thus became simply how to determine England's particular lineage. It was in connection with this almost morbid
search for ancestry that the heightened nationalism of Tudor
England proved in the long run most stimulating to the historical sense. Once again it was controversial combustion that shed
incidental, but much needed, light on the past. Unfortunately,
the attendant heat seems also to have addled many an otherwise sober brain. For the gospel according to Geoffrey, with
all its absurdities, became for more than a century the national
historical orthodoxy.[38] But controversy also put a premium on
what passed in those days for empirical scholarship, including
the first hesitant use of archaeological data and of course the
more established methods of the philologist. A number of
scholars attacked the problem of English origins on the tempting assumption that linguistic similarities provide the truest
indication of the relationship of one people to another and hence
of national origins. If efforts to find in British, Saxon, or
"modern" English words traces of Hebrew, Phoenician, even
Scythian roots, as well as Greek and Latin, often reflect an
active imagination rather than profound learning, the fact
remains that such exercises kept English scholars at work on
their history and on lines by no means always leading to dead
ends.[39]

Controversy arose not from any new interpretation of the
documentable past—the story of the medieval monarchy and its
wars remained largely untouched—but from speculation concerning this far distant past, the origins of the British people
in particular and the historicity of the Arthurian legends.[40]
There was plenty in the medieval tradition to satisfy all those
who were willing to suspend disbelief in the cause of patriotism.
There was, first and foremost, the basic Biblical tradition:
Britain was founded by the immediate descendants of Noah

through his European son, Japhet. Then there was the story drawn from classical mythology (the latter not considered at all incompatible with the Biblical story among men expert in synthesizing what they took to be equally valid accounts) which found the eponymous hero in Brutus, a grandson of Aeneas, the refugee Trojan. (Like most European peoples the English found the story of the fall of Troy irresistible and the idea of being descended from a defeated and fugitive Trojan line oddly satisfying.)[41] Later medieval writers, probably concerned over what they considered evidence of a race of giants in Britain, interposed a still more far-out account about a king of Syria whose thirty-two daughters, in a simultaneous fit of pique, slew their respective husbands and were punished by being set to sea in a ship which somehow took them to England, there-upon called Albion for the eldest sister, after which the Devil with infernal impartiality cohabited with all of them and begot thereby a race of giants who continued to live on the island until the coming of Brutus the Trojan.

This stuff, to say nothing of the almost equally fantastic Arthurian saga, was bound to raise doubts in the minds of men whose scholarship or native common sense was at least equal to their patriotism. As early as 1529, for instance, John Rastell, a member of Thomas More's enlightened circle, suggested that this whole business of a king, of whom no reputable historian of ancient times had spoken, having all those daughters so uniformly vile of disposition and capable of navigating alone for thousands of miles, to say nothing of carrying on so fruit-fully with the Devil, was a pretty tall tale. And he had similar doubts about the Brutus story and much of the Arthurian ma-terial.[42] But, as is well known, it was poor Polydore Vergil who pulled the house down on himself by subjecting both the Brutus and Arthurian legends to the kind of dispassionate criticism based on the comparative study of documents which an Italian humanist of his repute might be expected to have performed.[43] He was accordingly attacked by Leland and by several others similarly committed to the medieval tradition.[44] The resulting controversy lasted for years, and to the end of the century patriotic English scholars continued, as T. D. Kendrick put it, with "muddle-headed deliberateness" to add "to the fantastic British history by still more fantastic guesswork."[45]

Among the few who opposed the fundamentalist line, John Twyne deserves special mention, for he illustrates just how important the whole thing could be in promoting historical thought. Well versed in the classics, and by avocation a collector of archaeological remains, he was well suited to become one of the most outspoken critics of the medieval tradition. More than that, he was a constructive thinker of unusual insight. Writing about the middle of the century, he subjected the Brutus legend to damaging criticism and was able to defend the more or less historical Arthur from the Arthurians themselves.[46] But he also advanced certain startlingly fresh theories of his own. To help explain the early migration of peoples he made use of the hypothesis that Britain had not always been an island, but had been joined to the mainland by an isthmus. Here he was relying more on analogies recorded by ancient authorities than on actual geological observation, yet he was quite ready to recognize the evidence implied in changes any Englishman could remember in the shape of England's own coastline.[47] He was also a century ahead of his time in considering the Phoenicians among the early inhabitants of Britain.[48] But what sets him off most distinctly from his conservative contemporaries was his recognition of the extreme probability that the original inhabitants were half-naked savages rather than the sophisticated Trojans usually pictured in popular accounts.[49] He was here bringing to speculation concerning the early inhabitants of Britain the view of primitive man he no doubt found in his classical studies. We shall see in a moment that this view was widely held in England; but Twyne is, as far as I know, the first to make this particular connection. Later in the century the harder anthropological data coming from the New World made it much easier for Englishmen to admit to themselves that their ancestors were in all likelihood painted savages quite analogous in social development to the American aborigines.[50]

[189]

Some such appreciation of cultural development and of the diversity it engendered is, as I have suggested, an essential ingredient of the modern sense of history, especially insofar as the latter depends on an awareness of the peculiar character of a people or a society. Now there are signs, quite clear if not as yet in the majority, that a few Englishmen of this period were beginning to appreciate the meaning of this element of cultural diversity along with something at least of the relativity it implied. This feeling for the peculiar character of other peoples was in a sense the reverse side of their own growing self-consciousness. The Elizabethan Englishman loved to talk about himself (witness the ease with which twentieth-century editors are able to compile those charming and useful books on "England through Elizabethan eyes"). In much the same spirit he generalized freely, and very loosely, about the national character of other peoples: the Spaniards were cruel and cowardly, the Germans great guzzlers, the Italians subtly vicious, and so on. Like all born romantics, he also enjoyed imitating foreign dress and customs, as Harrison reminds us.[51] To this curiosity the broadening of England's geographical and commercial horizons undoubtedly contributed. As Lyly wrote, "Traffic and travel hath woven the nature of all nations into ours."[52]

The Tudor reading public seems indeed to have had quite an appetite for the history as well as the description of other peoples.[53] The picture is not quite so clear when it comes to a question of the ability or willingness of English scholars themselves to write such histories. But events in a world order now chronically embroiled in the politics of power were bound to turn attention in this direction. His observation of Imperial politics prompted Roger Ascham to write his perceptive *Report of Germany,* and the paradox of cultural brilliance coupled with political decadence no doubt suggested to William Thomas the idea of writing his *History of Italy.*[54] But it was closer home, in Ireland of all places, that the Elizabethans seem to have found the most sustaining food for reflection. Long restless, the Irish were becoming increasingly troublesome to English policymakers and administrators, and the latter were beginning to want more knowledge of the Irish and their background. Furthermore, the Irish themselves were interesting—repulsive, but interesting, not unlike the American Indians to whom they were on occasion compared. Living as they did on the Englishman's very doorstep, yet quite alien in custom and institution, the "wild Irish" (as distinguished from the Anglo-Irish) presented a unique opportunity to study at close range a society not only at a different level of culture, but (the idea was taking shape) perhaps at a different stage of development. A sequence of writers in fact began to reflect on its origins and development and to compare it with other societies, both ancient and contemporary. Most of this literature stems, it is true, from the very late years of the century and the early part of the succeeding. But it is worth mentioning such examples as Edmund Campion's *History of Ireland* (1571) and Richard Stanyhurst's expansion of it for use in Holinshed's *Chronicles,* and above all, Edmund Spenser's *View of the Present State of Ireland* (1596) in which he analyzed the Irish problem to an unprecedented extent in terms of Irish history and a comparison of Irish customs with those of the ancient world.[55]

Comparing societies, whether contemporary or ancient, did not, of course, necessarily lead the Elizabethan Englishman at once to historical habits of thought. It could merely have confirmed the still current assumption of a static hierarchy in which cultures, like species, had their appointed place. More likely, however, it helped them to recognize the element of change in human culture and to seek an alternative principle of order in the process of social development from primitive to cultivated society. Certainly such observations contributed to the kind of self-knowledge to which Elizabethan writers gave lip service and without which men could no more have oriented themselves in time than in relation to their contemporaries. Certainly also the voyages of exploration, both in the New World and to the more exotic reaches of the Old, contributed a vast body of material for the comparative study of manners and customs.[56]

It took a while, a surprisingly long while in fact, for this new knowledge to kindle the English imagination. Except for

More's *Utopia* and Rastell's *Interlude of the Four Elements*,[57] both the product of that period of relative calm before the Reformation storm, there is little evidence of any such stirring of the imagination prior to the mid-century. Events at home proved meanwhile absorbing to the exclusion of much else. And anyway, as a recent writer has pointed out, people who had been accustomed to satisfying their anthropological curiosity with the weird accounts which had come down in full romantic flavor from the more irresponsible of the ancient cosmographers, tales of the dog-faced and umbrella-footed men, the preposterous creatures, and the troglodytes alleged to inhabit the outer fringes of the world, were hardly likely to be surprised or greatly moved by more or less factual accounts of American Indians, still less of Russians and Laplanders.[58] During the latter half of the century, however, an increasing number of English readers were satisfying their curiosity by means of the also increasing number of books available—largely in translation, for in their intellectual life they subsisted to an astonishing extent on foods processed and packaged by enterprising middlemen. Books like Boemus's ambitious work, Englished by William Watreman as *The Fardle of Fascions* or Richard Eden's translation of Muenster's *Cosmographia,* or Thomas Fortune's rendering of Mexia's *Foreste or Collection of Histories,* mixed geography, history, and ethnology with sufficient interdisciplinary abandon to bring out goose-pimples on our own curriculum reformers.[59] By the 1580's Richard Hakluyt was compiling accounts from English as well as from foreign sources which were to set the pattern for a more sober, if no more romantic, knowledge of other societies.[60]

In the process of digesting the new data, with its close interweaving of history and geography, English thinkers not unnaturally gained a deeper insight into the relationship between the two. The idea that human culture varied according to its geographical environment was, of course, very old. The ancients had noticed that climate, especially, had an effect on the nature of a people, and the notion persisted through medieval thought to be embraced with renewed enthusiasm by the Elizabethans as a shortcut toward an explanation of the cultural diversity in which they were becoming more and more interested.[61] The habits of what Bodin called "geographistorians" seemed, indeed to have changed little over the years. Most "histories" continued to begin with geographical descriptions and most geographical treatises continued to include extensive historical introductions. In this respect there is little difference between, for example, Higden's *Polychronicon* and Holinshed's *Chronicle,* except that the descriptive part of the latter had happily been entrusted to separate hands, most notably the perceptive and garrulous William Harrison, and even he found it impossible to "describe" England without frequent excursions into history. The same, by the way, can be said of such primary topographical studies as Lambrade's *Perambulation of Kent* and Stowe's *Survey of London.*[62] If, however, we look beyond formal historiography or its topographical cousin-german, we can see the beginnings of something which Higden's elaborate *mappa mundi* did not possess, and that is an understanding of the constant and positive interaction of geography and history. Higden used his geographical description, including the familiar speculation on the diverse effect of climate on peoples,[63] as a static setting, a stage of fixed props on which men acted in a sequence of events that bore little continuing relation to their social or geographical context. Geography may have conditioned the original character of a society, but it was not something which, by stirring its inventive genius, might continue to act as a factor in the history of that society.

Beginning with that curiously profound piece of fifteenth-century doggerel known as *The Libel of English Policy,*[64] a document shrewd in its analysis of England's strategic position and in its appreciation of the potentialities inherent in governmental policy for exploiting that position, geographical factors tend to appear in a new light. By the mid-sixtenth century a few advanced theorists—Sir Thomas Smith is only the most sophisticated example—were able to recognize in a mature mercantilist policy a tool not only for remedying economic ills but for exploiting England's geographical advantages. It was, in short, a dynamic element in the affairs of state, and, as such, it encouraged historical reflection.[65] A generation or so later we find Hakluyt treating geographical data and economic history as naturally related parts of the same intellectual problem. The first part of the famous *Voyages* is in reality a major pioneer effort in economic history.[66] It is not only an important archive, consciously compiled as such, but one in which a respect for traditional authority may be seen fighting a losing battle with the critical sense of the modern historian. Hakluyt appears to have become more disturbed as he went along by the marvelous elements in early accounts, much of which he recognized, and in a measure excused, as mere borrowings from Pliny or Solinus or some other ancient source; and he dropped Mandeville's *Travels* entirely from the 1598 edition. On the positive side, he was the first "modern" historian to recognize the significance in the history of English economic thought of the proto-mercantilist *Libel of English policy.*[67]

The opening up of a new world, the accumulation of knowledge about primitive peoples, the expansion of the European economy, and the technological achievements in navigation, war, and the publishing business presented to sixteenth-century observers of the human scene a pageant of intricately moving parts. To those of a realistic and analytical turn of mind—and England produced her fair share of such Renaissance types—it could be a spectacle dynamic in its implications regarding man and his capabilities and subtly destructive of the alternative, and still quite orthodox, picture of a static and hierarchical order. To that extent it raised unavoidable questions concerning the history of man's achievements. And it was in the course of providing the answers to those questions that the battle lines were first drawn between the ancients and moderns and the way opened eventually for those progressivist ideas which were to play so large a part in western thought for the next three centuries and which gave a new dimension to the sense of history.

A few of the more socially oriented of the early Tudor humanists were the first in England to face these implications at all directly. They did so by breathing new life into an old idea—as was their wont. They did so, not as an exercise in pure contemplation, but in order to lay satisfactorily deep foundations for a very practical discussion. What they were seeking was an anthropology which would give quasi-historical depth to their belief in man's capacity for acting in accord with his potentially rational nature and for shaping his environment in accord with the principles of right reason and human dignity. For evidence they turned, not so much to any new data drawn from the unfolding human geography of their day,[68] but to ancient authority, to Aristotle or Lucretius or Vitruvius or more immediately perhaps to their beloved Cicero. Starkey, for example, laid the basis for his comment on contemporary English society in the idea that mankind lived originally in caves, like animals, without arts or science, and were brought only gradually (by "little and little" was his favorite phrase) by men of superior inventiveness and "philosophy" to their present state of sophistication.[69] Old as it was, never in fact entirely out of sight in the intervening centuries, this idea had held little appeal for medieval thinkers whose hopes for man's worldly existence, where they retained any optimism at all, were confined largely to his moral and spiritual progress.[70] In early Tudor England, in the active discussion of social problems, it once again found fertile soil and, in the heightened awareness of social change, a congenial atmosphere. And so, like More in the imaginary society of *Utopia*,[71] these men were able to see in the history of their very real society, not primarily the record of dynastic fortunes, but the story of cultural achievement from simple and humble beginnings.

They did not, to be sure, imagine this process to be one of steady evolution—despite their "by little and little"—but rather one marked by occasional great leaps forward by supreme lawgivers like Solon or Lycurgus—or King Utopus—or by great inventors, more often than not euhemeristically conceived.[72] Nor should we look in their work for signs of the modern concept of progress. Willing as they were to recognize man's capability for constructive thought and action, they seem not to have thought of the process by which man civilized himself as likely, much less certain, to continue into the indefinite future. Indeed, to the extent that they accepted the cyclical theory of history common to most of their classical authorities, they may well have considered achievement up to the present as but the rising phase of a cycle which would one day have to start all over again on a downward grade. Moreover, insofar as they could see that man had in fact developed, they saw him doing so within the limits and according to the potentialities prescribed for him in a divinely ordained scheme of nature.[73] English humanists were not, however, for the most part much interested in such speculation. They remained remarkably content with what they could see and account for in human terms. And it is just this acceptance for practical purposes of the fact of man's achievement that helped create the atmosphere conducive to, no doubt necessary for, the modern concept of progress.

Their optimistic vision, this faith in the all but inexhaustible creativity of man, seems to have become clouded or distorted in the latter part of the Tudor century. Too much had been happening too fast for a generation still accustomed to the world outlook and the formulas of a more slow-moving era. With little other than this inherited and already badly depreciated capital to live on, men of learning tended to fall back in a sort of Pyrrhonistic funk, to doubt their ability to equal, much less surpass, the ancients and to react to the disturbing fact of change with a lot of melancholy musing about mutability. Resting as it did on something close to the pagan notion of Fortune (a concept, by the way, for practical purposes ruled out of rational discussion by Starkey) this attitude toward change could simply mean capitulation in the search for cause in human affairs. As such, it represented a reversal of the early humanist faith in social analysis employed in the service of constructive policy. By the same token, it implied a radically anti-historical outlook.[74]

Recent historians interested in the early expression of a progressive attitude have accordingly turned to the practical men of the middle and later sixteenth century and to the few scholars already engaged in a proto-Baconian effort to bring learning and technology into a working partnership.[75] Men like William Borough or Robert Norman, themselves engaged in the technical problems related to navigation, or like Richard Eden who translated key foreign works on the subject and had a good deal to say in his generous prefaces about their broader implications, or Robert Recorde who turned his modest literary skill and meager learning to the ambitious task of propagating useful knowledge, these were the men who were becoming quietly confident in their ability to build a world of their own, one that need not fear comparison with that of classical antiquity, however much it invited such comparison.[76] Men of the late sixteenth century, "practical" or otherwise, could in any case hardly have overlooked the significance of that trio of mixed blessings, namely firearms, the compass, and the printing press. Military thought remained, it is true, remarkably conservative, but by then it was becoming apparent even to such Old Believers as John Smythe that the day of English archery was past and that it was no longer possible to adapt Vegetian precepts directly to modern military realities.[77] The printing press, on the other hand, stood out in the minds of literary men and historians as a clearly epoch-making discovery. In John Foxe's great martyrology, for example, it marks as truly as the advent of Protestantism itself the emergence of a new society from the dark period of the pre-Reformation church.[78]

Whatever there may be to this argument, and there is a good deal, the important thing is that the sense of history grew to its early modern maturity in a stubbornly progressivist context. Those who believed that human culture was degenerating in a universe that was itself running down had, of course, their own historical perspective:[79] the quarrel between the ancients and moderns could hardly have taken place without on both sides a keener sense of temporal perspective than was likely in an earlier age, concerned with finding the answers to quite different questions. But the moderns did, after all, win the day in the long run. In any event, it is hard to over-estimate the importance of social and technological change as the circumstances prompting and conditioning so much of the *ad hoc* interrogation of the past which was taking place in Tudor England.

And it is once more to such questions that, in conclusion, I wish to direct your attention, and to the answers given, often simply as obiter dicta, by men acting as users of history rather than writers of it. These inquiries were seldom systematic nor did they deliberately transgress the limits of accepted historical philosophy. But those limits were broad and the inherited schemes of historical organization permissive. Within the old, therefore, it becomes possible to see the beginnings of things new. (That, in a sense, was the peculiar genius of Renaissance thought anyway.) Above all, it is possible to recognize in a variety of quarters a new awareness of society, and what is more, of society considered as the constantly changing, but far from meaningless, context of man's life on earth and hence worthy of a place, with *res gestae,* as a worthy and proper subject for historical investigation.

NOTES

1. F. Smith Fussner, *The Historical Revolution: English Historical Writing and Thought, 1580-1640* (London, 1962). As far as the early Tudor historians are concerned, the literature is surprisingly sparse. See, however, Leonard F. Dean, "Tudor Theories of History Writing," *University of Michigan Contributions in Modern Philology*, No. 1 (April, 1947), 1-24; W. R. Trimble, "Early Tudor Historiography, 1485-1549," *Journal of the History of Ideas*, XI (January, 1950), 30-41; Thomas Wheeler, "The New Style of Tudor Chronicles," *Tennessee Studies in Literature*, VII (1962), 71-77. Useful material may be found also in C. L. Kingsford, *English Historical Literature in the Fifteenth Century* (Oxford, 1913); Irving Ribner, *The English History Play in the Age of Shakespeare* (Princeton, 1957); E. M. W. Tillyard, *Shakespeare's History Plays* (New York, 1946). I regret not having been able to consult F. J. Levy, *Tudor Historical Thought* (San Marino, 1967).

2. *The Boke named the Gouernour*, ed. H. H. S. Croft (2 vols.; London, 1880), I, 82.

3. Felix Gilbert, in his *Machiavelli and Guicciardini: Politics and History in Sixteenth-Century Florence* (Princeton, 1965), makes an interesting study of this problem, Machiavelli illustrating the most sophisticated use of political history considered as example, and his younger contemporary the tendency, more unusual in that age, to see such history in terms of process.

4. *Mirror for Magestrates*, ed. L. B. Campbell (Cambridge, 1938). Cf. John Lydgate, *Fall of Princes*, ed. Henry Bergen, E.E.T.S., E.S., Nos. 121-124 (4 vols.; 1924-27). This adaptation of Boccaccio's *De Casibus Virorum Illustrium* domesticated the tradition in England.

5. For a discussion of this point see A. B. Ferguson, *The Articulate Citizen and the English Renaissance* (Durham, N.C., 1965), chap. IX.

6. For the more original part of Polydore Vergil's work see *The Anglica Historia of Polydore Vergil A.D. 1485-1537*, ed., with translation, Denys Hay, Camden Soc., Vol. LXXIV (1950); see also Denys Hay, *Polydore Vergil, Renaissance Historian and Man of Letters* (Oxford, 1952). *Polychronicon Ranulphi Higden*, ed. (with Trevisa's English translation), Churchill Babington and J. R. Lumby, Rolls Series (9 vols.; 1865-1886); see also John Taylor, *The Universal Chronicle of Ralph Higden* (Oxford, 1966).

7. In his *De Inventoribus Rerum*, Polydore revealed a considerable sense of historical relativity, especially when treating the origins of religious observances. But it is significant that the translated abridgment of that work, published in England in 1546 and reissued several times later, omitted much of this material. See, for example, Thomas Langley, *An Abridgement of the notable worke of Polydore Vergile conteynying the devisers and first finders out as well of Artes, . . . as of Rites . . . commonly used in the churche . . .* (London, 1546), STC 24654.

8. E.g., *An Exposition of St. Paul's Epistle to the Romans, Delivered as Lectures in the University of Oxford about the Year 1497*, ed. J. H. Lupton (London, 1873), pp. 1-2, 91-96; *Exposition of St. Paul's Epistle to the Romans*, in *Opuscula Quaedam Theologica*, ed. Lupton (London, 1876), p. 58.

9. *A Dialogue between Cardinal Pole and Thomas Lupset*, ed. K. M. Burton (London, 1948), e.g., pp. 106-11. See also below, n. 69.

10. *De Republica Anglorum*, ed. L. Alston (Cambridge, 1906), e.g., Book I, chaps. 4, 18, Book II, chap. 15, Book III, chaps. 6-8; see also *ibid.*, introd., pp. xiii-xiv.

11. *A Discourse of the Common Weal of this Realm of England*, ed. E. Lamond (Cambridge, 1893). On the matter of authorship, see Mary Dewar, "The Authorship of the 'Discourse of the Commonweal,'" *Economic History Review*, 2nd Series, XIX (August, 1966), 388-400. On the whole subject of the search for cause in English society, see Ferguson, *op. cit.*, chaps. VIII-X.

12. See n. 54 below.

13. *De Laudibus Legum Angliae*, ed. with trans., S. B. Chrimes (Cambridge, 1942), especially chaps. xiii, xxix, xlviii, cf. chap. xviii. See also Ferguson, *op. cit.*, pp. 120-24.

14. For specific references see A. B. Ferguson, "Reginald Pecock and the Renaissance Sense of History," *Studies in the Renaissance*, XIII (1966), 147-65.

15. See T. D. Kendrick, *British Antiquity* (London, 1950), chap. II.

16. E.g., see his digression on English laws in *Historia Regum Angliae* (1489), ed. Thomas Hearne (Oxford, 1745), pp. 80 ff., and his comparison between Saxon and Norman customs and dress, *ibid.*, p. 106.

17. Illustrated in Kendrick, *op. cit.*

18. Pecock, who professed unbounded faith in syllogistic reasoning, found himself moving off at almost every point in the direction of historical investigation or speculation.

19. For example, in answer to Jewel's challenge to the Catholic apologist to prove that their institutions possessed the authority of Christian antiquity, his opponents, Rastell and Dorman, argued that the primative church represented actually the infancy of that institution and the contemporary church its mature form. See J. E. Booty, *John Jewel as Apologist of the Church of England* (London, 1963), chap. VI. The argument runs curiously parallel to the one in which, later on, the "ancients" and "moderns" were engaged. See R. F. Jones, *Ancients and Moderns* (St. Louis, 1961).

20. Examples, especially in the works of Tyndale and Cranmer, are too numous to cite. Useful references may be found in the Duke dissertation, John K. Yost, "The Christian Humanism of the English Reformers, 1525-1555: A Study in English Renaissance Humanism," see especially chaps. I, II, V, and X.

21. For both Whitgift and Cartwright see the analysis and selective reprinting of their complex and verbose exchange during the 1570's in D. J. McGinn, *The Admonition Controversy* (New Brunswick, 1949).

22. See W. G. Zeeveld, *Foundations of Tudor Policy* (London, 1948) in which much credit in this regard is given to Thomas Starkey, borrowing from Melanchthon. It should be recognized, however, that the adiaphoristic principle was present, either explicitly or by implication, in much of the Christian humanist writings. See, for example, Tyndale, *The Practyse of Prelates*, pp. 324-27, in *Works*, II, Parker Soc., XLIII (Cambridge, 1849), and *An Answer to Sir Thomas More's Dialogue*, p. 20, in *Works*, III, Parker Soc. XLIV (Cambridge, 1850).

23. E.g., *The Works of John Whitgift*, ed. John Ayre, Parker Soc. (Cambridge, 1851), I, 180, 190-1, 201; II, 523, 538.

24. *A Testmonie of Antiquitie* (London, 1566-7?), STC 159, preface. On the subject of Anglo-Saxon scholarship, see Robin Flower, "Laurence Nowell and the Discovery of England in Tudor Times," *Proceedings of the British Academy*, XXI (1935), 47-73; Eleanor Adams, *Old English Scholarship in England, 1566-1800* (New Haven, 1937); Rosamund Tuve, "Ancients, Moderns, and Saxons," *English Literary History*, VI (September, 1939), 165-90.

25. *Collected Papers of F. W. Maitland*, ed. H. A. L. Fisher (3 vols.; Cambridge, 1911), 451. See also R. J. Schoeck, "Early Anglo-Saxon Studies and

Legal Scholarship in the Renaissance," *Studies in the Renaissance*, V (1958), 101-10.

26. See especially his *Archaionomia, sive de priscis anglorum legibus libri . . .* (London, 1568), STC 15142, and *Archeion*, ed. C. H. McIlwain and P. L. Ward (Cambridge, Mass., 1957).

27. For a thorough development of this line of thought, see J. G. A. Pocock, *The Ancient Constitution and the Feudal Law* (Cambridge, 1957), chaps. II and III.

28. An interesting discussion of the "Norman yoke" theory may be found in Christopher Hill, *Puritanism and Revolution* (London, 1958), chap. III.

29. Pocock, *op. cit.*, pp. 31-36.

30. *Dialogue*, pp. 110-11; cf. pp. 22, 108, 175. See also Ferguson, *Articulate Citizen*, pp. 373 ff. For Smith's use of his civilian and humanist training see *ibid.*, pp. 386-91.

31. Pocock, chap. V.

32. Roger Ascham, *The Scholemaster* in *English Works*, ed. W. A. Wright (Cambridge, 1904), pp. 289-92.

33. George Puttenham, *The Arte of English Poesie*, ed. G. D. Willcock and Alice Walker (Cambridge, 1936), especially Book I, chaps. viii, x, xxxi; Book II, chap. xii; Book III, chaps. iii and ix. This book was published in 1589, but was largely written during the preceding twenty-odd years. Puttenham also wrote a treatise, no longer extant, entitled *The Originals and Pedigree of the English Tong*. Cf. William Webbe, *A discourse of English Poetrie* (1586), in *Ancient and Critical Essays upon the English Poets and Poesy*, ed. Joseph Haslewood (2 vols.; London, 1815) Vol. II. See also René Wellek, *The Rise of English Literary History* (Chapel Hill, 1941), chap. I.

34. *The Itinerary of John Leland*, ed. Lucy Toulmin Smith (5 vols.; Carbondale, 1964), I, xi; see also *The Laboriouse Journey and Serche of John Leylande for Englandes Antiquitees*, in *ibid.*, I, xxxvii-xliii, and Bale's preface and conclusion.

35. John Bale, *Illustrium majoris Britanniae scriptorum Summarium . . .* (Wesel, 1548) STC 1295; *Scriptorum illustrium majoris Britanniae . . . Catalogus* (2 vols.; Basle, 1557-59). Leland, *Commentarii de Scriptoribus Britannicis* (unfinished), ed. A. Hall (2 vols; Oxford, 1709). See also Kendrick's comments in his preface to Lucy Toulmin Smith's edition of the *Itinerary*.

36. A provocative treatment of this early historical literature may be found in R. W. Hanning, *The Vision of History in Early Britain* (New York, 1966).

37. It is also interesting to notice that the deeds of English captains in France during the Hundred Years' War were warmly recommended as suitable reading for young gentlemen by both Caxton and Lord Berners. A. B. Ferguson, *The Indian Summer of English Chivalry* (Durham, N.C., 1960), chap. II.

38. There is some reason for thinking that Tudor writers were more ready than their predecessors to accept the legacy of Geoffrey at its face value. Within the precocious circle of Humphrey, Duke of Gloucester, a tradition of skeptical criticism was almost begun. John Wethamstede, Abbot of St. Albans, gave several reasons in his *Granarium* for not believing the Brutus legend. The group also included the visiting scholars, Poggio Bracciolini and Tito Livio da Forli, both of whom could have contributed to this detergent atmosphere. Kendrick, p. 34. It is, incidentally, no accident that the vogue for things Arthurian in early Tudor England coincided with the presence on the throne of a self-consciously Welsh dynasty, though neither Henry VIII nor Elizabeth were apparently active in promoting it. See Sydney Anglo, "The *British History*

in early Tudor Propaganda," *Bulletin of the John Ryland Library*, XLIV, (1961-62), 17-48.

39. An excellent example of the combined use of the philological method and archaeological data may be found in John Twyne, *De Rebus Albionicis atque Anglicis . . .* (London, 1590, but largely composed before 1550), STC 24407; see especially pp. 15-16, 108 ff., 152-53. For further examples of philological method in the interests of the national history, see Humphrey Llwyd (or Lloyd), *The Breviary of Britayne*, tr. Thomas Twyne (London, 1573), STC 16636, fols. 1-5; Sir John Price, *Historiae Brytannicae defensio* (London, 1573), STC 20309, pp. 4 ff., 40 ff., 70 ff. Inquiring into the origins of history of place-names became, however, habitual. See, for example, Sir Thomas Elyot's *Dictionary* (London, 1538), STC 7659, *s.v.* "Britannia," and almost any of the later chronicles when dealing with the early history of the island.

40. Kendrick's account of this protracted controversy leaves little but detail to be added. See especially chaps. V-VII.

41. See A. M. Young, *Troy and her Legend* (Pittsburgh, 1948); S. K. Heninger, "The Tudor Myth of Troy-novant," *South Atlantic Quarterly*, LXI (Summer, 1962), 378-87.

42. *The Pastime of People . . .* (1529), ed., T. F. Dibdin (London, 1811), pp. 3-6, 106-8. Rastell could see nothing but didactic value in the Arthurian stories. *Ibid.*, p. 7.

43. *Polydore Vergil's English History*, ed. Sir Henry Ellis, Camden Society, XXXVI (1846), Book I, pp. 26-33. See also Denys Hay, *Polydore Vergil, Renaissance Historian and Man of Letters* (Oxford, 1952), especially pp. 106 ff.

44. *Assertio inclytissimi Arturii regis Britanniae* (London, 1544), trans. Richard Robinson (London, 1582), both reprinted in W. E. Mead, ed., *The Famous Historie of Chinon of England*, E.E.T.S., O.S., No. 165 (1925); see especially preface and chaps. x and xvi.

45. Kendrick, p. 65. Outstanding examples from the Elizabethan period are the work of Llwyd and Price mentioned in n. 39 above.

46. *De Rebus Albionicis*, e.g., pp. 9, 13-14, 46-47, 66-68, 127-29.

47. *Ibid.*, pp. 8-9, 16-31, 98-107. It is interesting to notice how close Twyne came to the time-barrier imposed on geological thought prior to the nineteenth century by the traditional Biblical interpretation of history. That he failed to break it should be no surprise. Even as acute an observer of geological change as the seventeenth-century Robert Hooke found it necessary to limit the inference his own observations made logically permissible so that they might fit the accepted time-scale.

48. *Ibid.*, pp. 41-44, 78.

49. *Ibid.*, pp. 63-65, 97.

50. See the pictures by John White, both of the aborigines he saw on the 1585 expedition to the west and of the "Picts" of early British history he reconstructed imaginatively, appended to Thomas Hariot's *A briefe and true report of the new found land of Virginia . . .* (Frankfort, 1590), STC. 12786. See also Kendrick, plates XII-XV.

51. William Harrison, *An Historical Description of the Iland of Britaine*, in Ralph Holinshed, *Chronicles of England, Scotland, and Ireland*, ed. Sir Henry Ellis (6 vols.; London, 1807-8), I, 172.

52. Quoted in Willcock and Walker, ed., *Arte of English Poesie*, p. liii, from the preface to *Midas*.

53. See H. S. Bennett, *English Books and Readers, 1558-1603* (Cambridge, 1965).

54. Roger Ascham, *A Report ... of the affaires and state of Germany* ... (London, ca. 1570, but written in 1553), in *English Works*, ed. W. A. Wright (Cambridge, 1904); William Thomas, *The Historie of Italie* (London, 1549), STC 24018, ed. G. B. Parks (Ithaca, 1963). Note, in a similar vein, Giles Fletcher, *The Russe Commonwealth* (London, 1591), ed. L. E. Berry, *The English Works of Giles Fletcher* (Madison, 1964). See also W. F. Staton, Jr., "Roger Ascham's Theory of History Writing," *Studies in Philosophy*, LVI (April, 1959), 125-37; L. V. Ryan, *Roger Ascham* (Palo Alto, 1963), pp. 58-159.

55. Edmund Campion, *A Historie of Ireland* (1571), ed. R. B. Gottfried (New York, 1940); Richard Stanyhurst, *Description of Ireland*, in Holinshed, VI, 1-69 (partially based on Campion's work); Edmund Spenser, *A View of the Present State of Ireland* (1596), ed. R. B. Gottfried (Baltimore, 1949), in *Variorum Spenser*, ed. E. A. Greenlaw *et al.*, IX, 43-231. See also the slender treatise in verse with prose commentary by John Derricke, *The Image of Ireland with the Discoverie of Woodkarne* (1581), ed. John Small (Edinburgh, 1883); this edition contains a series of woodcuts depicting aspects of Irish life and history. For further information see D. B. Quinn, *The Elizabethans and the Irish* (Ithaca, 1966).

56. On the entire subject of geographical exploration and for valuable bibliographical aids, see E. G. R. Taylor, *Tudor Geography, 1485-1583* (London, 1930) and *Late Tudor and Early Stuart Geography, 1583-1650* (London, 1934).

57. Sir Thomas More, *Utopia*, eds. Edward Surtz and J. H. Hexter (New Haven, 1965). John Rastell, *A New Interlude of the IIII Elements* (London, 1525?), STC 20722.

58. Margaret T. Hodgen, *Early Anthropology in the Sixteenth and Seventeenth Centuries* (Philadelphia, 1964), p. 114.

59. William Watreman (trans.). *The Fardle of Facions* (London, 1555), STC 3197. Another partial translation of Boemus' *Ommium gentium mores* (1520), "one of the first Renaissance collections of manners and customs" (Hodgen, 131) was made by William Prat and published in 1554, STC 191. Richard Eden (trans.), *A treatyse of the newe India, with other new founde landes* ... *after the description of Sebastian Munster in his boke of universal Cosmographie* ... (1553), reprinted and ed., Edward Arber, *The First Three English Books on America* (Westminster, 1895); see also his translation of Peter Martyr's *Decades of the New World* (1555) in *ibid.* Thomas Fortescue (trans.), *The Foreste or Collection of Histories* [by Pedro Mexia] (London, 1571), STC 17849.

60. On Hakluyt, see below, n. 66. For another example of this sort of literature, see Giles Fletcher, *The Russe Commonwealth.*

61. Denys Hay, *Europe, the Emergence of an Idea* (Edinburgh, 1957), pp. 131 ff.; Hodgen, pp. 269 ff. The idea was used, for example, with mischievous effect in support of the Black Legend of Spanish villainy. William Maltby, "The Black Legend in Elizabethan and Early Stuart England" (Ph.d. dissertation, Duke University, 1966). It is interesting also to notice how heavily Jean Bodin depended on the idea. *Method for the Easy Comprehension of History*, trans. Beatrice Reynolds (New York, 1945), chap. V.

62. William Lambarde, *A Perambulation of Kent* (London, 1576), STC 15175; John Stow, *A Survey of London* (London, 1598), ed. C. L. Kingsford (2 vols.; Oxford, 1908).

63. *Polychronicon*, I, 50-52, 266.

64. *The Libelle of Englishe Polycye*, ed. Sir George Warner (Oxford, 1926).

Arthur B. Ferguson

See discussion in Taylor, *Tudor Georgraphy, 1485-1583*, p. 4, and in Ferguson, *Articulate Citizen*, chap. IV.

65. *Ibid.*, chap. XII.

66. *The Principal Navigations Voyages Traffiques and Discoveries of the English Nation* (12 vols.; Glasgow, 1903). Note especially preface to 1598 edition. Hakluyt is here more confident and articulate—and wordy—than in the 1589 edition, but he presumably had not changed his views concerning the significance of economic history. Cf. 1589 edition, facsimile, with introduction by D. B. Quinn and R. A. Skelton, Hakluyt Society, Extra Series XXXIX (1965). The invaluable prefaces plus various obiter dicta have been collected by E. G. R. Taylor, *The Original Writings and Correspondence of the two Richard Hakluyts*, 2 vols., Hakluyt Society, 2nd series, LXXVI-LXXVII (1935).

67. *Original Writings*, II, 395-96, 442-43, 445-46.

68. More was the only one of the early Tudor humanists to be very much influenced by the discoveries. He knew Vespucci's account of the primitive people of America which he described as "in everyone's hand." He also had the advantage of his brother-in-law, John Rastell's, interest in North America. See J. H. Hexter, in *Utopia*, introd. pp. xxxi-xxxii.

69. Sir Thomas Elyot, *The Boke Named the Gouernour*, I, 117, cf. I, 83, 88-89, 213-19; Starkey, *Dialogue*, p. 60, cf. pp. 22, 27-28; Stephen Hawes, *The Pastime of Pleasure*, ed. W. E. Mead, E.E.T.S., O.S., No. 173 (1928), ll. 876-91. In his account of the origin of warfare, Erasmus draws a more pessimistic picture. *Erasmus against War*, ed. J. A. Mackail (Boston, 1907), pp. 18-25. But cf. the more complex theory of Juan Luis Vives, *Vives on Education*, trans. of *De Tradendis Disciplinis* (Antwerp, 1531) by Foster Watson (Cambridge, 1913), pp. 11-22. See also Thomas Wilson, *Arte of Rhetorique* (London, 1553), STC 25799, preface; William Forrest, *Pleasaunt Poesye of Princelie Practise*, ed. (in extract) S. J. Herrtage, E.E.T.S., E.S., No. 32 (1878), p. lxxxv. On the whole subject of the ancient heritage of primitivistic speculation, see A. O. Lovejoy and George Boas, *Primitivism and Related Ideas in Antiquity* (Baltimore, 1935).

70. See examples discussed in George Boas, *Essays in Primitivism and Related Ideas in the Middle Ages* (Baltimore, 1948). E. L. Tuveson, *Millennium and Utopia* (Berkeley, 1949) treats the millenarian visions and their promise of amelioration.

71. Despite unmistakable signs of social evolution in Hythloday's account of the learning, arts, and customs of the Utopians, their constitution was attributed to King Utopus, one of the law-givers and "inventors" the Renaissance mind preferred to hold responsible for all cultural advance. See for example, Polydore Vergil's *De Inventoribus Rerum* (1521), and discussion in Hay, *Polydore Vergil*, pp. 63-64 and Kendrick, pp. 80-81.

72. See above n. 68. But see the references to the work of Elyot and Vives in n. 69 above for partial but important exceptions.

73. This attitude is very apparent in Starkey's *Dialogue* which is shot through with a typically Aristotelian notion of teleology, but something also of the Aristotelian tendency to consider the process of becoming, the achieving of the end toward which it is the nature of a thing to move, as somehow complete or nearly complete in the existing form of an institution or a state.

74. Spenser was one of the first to express this mood. See the "mutability cantos" in *The Faerie Queene*, Variorum Ed. (Baltimore, 1938), pp. 389 ff. See also Leicester Bradner, *Edmund Spenser and the Faerie Queene* (Chicago, 1938), chap. VII; A. Williams "A Note on Pessimism in the Renaissance," *Studies in*

Philology, XXXVI (1939), 243-46; Raymond Chapman, "Fortune and Mutability in Elizabethan Literature," *Cambridge Journal*, V (March, 1952), 374-82; Herbert Weisinger, "Ideas of History during the Renaissance," *Journal of the History of Ideas*, VI (October, 1945), 415-35. For the contribution of theological thought, especially millenarian ideas, to this pessimistic outlook, see Tuveson, chap. II. On Starkey's attitude toward Fortune see *Dialogue*, pp. 65-69.

75. For recent discussion of this problem see, for example, Edgar Zilsel, "The Genesis of the Concept of Scientific Progress," *Journal of the History of Ideas*, VI (June, 1945), 325-49; cf. A. C. Keller, "Zilsel, the Artisans, and the Ideas of Progress in the Renaissance," *ibid.*, XI (April, 1950), 235-40; Samuel Lilley, "Robert Recorde and the Ideas of Progress," *Renaissance and Modern Studies*, II (1957), 3-37. For the more hubristic aspect of the late Elizabethan temper, see Anthony Esler, *The Aspiring Mind of the Elizabethan Younger Generation* (Durham, N.C., 1966).

76. William Borough, *A Discours of the Variation of the Compas . . .* (London, 1581), STC. 3389, preface and sig. F ii ff.; Robert Norman, *The New Attractive* (London, 1585), STC 18648, preface; Richard Eden, trans., [Martin Cortes], *The Arte of Navigation* (London, 1561), STC 5798, preface, and [John Taisner], *Of Continuall motions* (London, 1580-1?, but written 1574), reprinted by Arber, preface; Robert Recorde, *The Pathway to Knowledge, containing the first principles of geometrie* (London, 1551), STC 20813, pref. to reader; cf. *The Castle of Knowledge* (London, 1556), STC 20796, p. 101. Hakluyt also recognized superiority to the ancients in practical matters: *Original Writings*, II, 363.

77. John Smythe, *Certain Discourses Concerning the Formes and Effects of Divers Sorts of Weapons* (London, 1590), STC 22883. On the writers on military science, see H. J. Webb, *Elizabethan Military Science, the Books and the Practice* (Madison, 1965).

78. John Foxe, *Acts and Monuments of the Christian Martyrs*, ed. Josiah Pratt (8 vols.; London, 1870), III, 718-22.

79. For a discussion of this point of view, see R. F. Jones, *Ancients and Moderns*, and Victor Harris, *All Coherence Gone* (Chicago, 1949).

VIII

The European Significance of Florentine Platonism

Paul Oskar Kristeller
Columbia University, New York, New York

If I had given this lecture some fifty years ago, and based myself on the views then current about the Renaissance, I could have taken it for granted that Renaissance Platonism, and especially the Platonism of the Florentine Academy, was an important phenomenon in the intellectual history of the Western world, occupied the center of attention during the fifteenth century, and had wide and deep repercussions throughout the sixteenth century and afterwards. The trend of recent scholarship, however, has changed our understanding of the period in a variety of ways, and the relative importance of Florentine Platonism tends to appear more limited as other currents and developments that seem to be more or less untouched by Platonism are given greater attention: early humanism and the vernacular literatures, Aristotelian philosophy and science, the Protestant and the Catholic Reformation. In the light of recent studies on these subjects, we cannot simply reassert the traditional views concerning Renaissance Platonism and its importance, but must try to avoid excessive claims that cannot be documented, and to arrive at a balanced picture based on specific facts and precise concepts. I shall not emphasize in this lecture the intrinsic importance of the Florentine Platonists, or the coherent and systematic nature of their ideas, for this has been done several times before.[1] I shall rather discuss the diffusion and influence of the writings and teachings of the Florentine Academy. I shall base myself as much as possible on specific details such as the testimony of manuscripts and printed editions, of explicit quotations or precise terms and concepts, and avoid inferences based on vague similarities, as they have so often plagued the field of scholarship currently known as the history of ideas.

It is hardly necessary for me to repeat that the doctrine of Renaissance Platonism is not the same as that of Plato, but has many other sources and ingredients: the ancient Neoplatonists and St. Augustine, medieval Aristotelianism, Epicureanism and the Cabala have all made their contributions to a highly complex philosophical system, and the list could easily be extended, not to speak of some original ideas, or combinations of ideas, that must be credited to the Renaissance thinkers themselves. I shall not attempt in this lecture to deal with Renaissance Platonism as a whole, but shall exclude the Byzantine Platonists and Cusanus, Patrizi and Bruno, as well as many other thinkers, and shall concentrate instead on the Florentine Academy, that is on Marsilio Ficino and Giovanni Pico della Mirandola, and occasionally mention some of their friends and pupils, such as Cristoforo Landino and Francesco da Diacceto. Making due allowance for their inconsistencies and their differences of opinion, we should like to assess their influence, especially during the sixteenth century, in Florence and other Italian centers, but especially in the other European countries: France and Germany, the Low Countries, England and Spain, Hungary, Poland and Bohemia. Since I obviously cannot cover this broad subject in a short lecture, I shall merely sketch a general pattern and illustrate each point with some appropriate examples.

One obvious way that a scholar's ideas may spread is through his teaching and through his personal contacts. Ficino does not seem to have traveled outside of Florence, or to have given formal instruction at the university, but his activities included public lectures and private tutoring, and he met many visitors either in his own "Academy" or at the home of the Medici or of other friends.[2] Pico della Mirandola, on the other hand, had studied at Bologna, Ferrara, and Padua, and had visited Rome and Paris before he finally settled in Florence.[3] Much more extensive than these personal contacts was the correspondence conducted by the Platonist scholars after the fashion of their time. Unfortunately, only a small part of Pico's correspondence has been preserved,[4] whereas Ficino's extant correspondence is voluminous and provides us with rich information on the network of his personal relations.[5] We can readily see that he had patrons, friends, or pupils in many of the more important centers, such as Rome and Venice, Naples and Milan, Ferrara, Mantua and Urbino, Bologna and Padua, and that his connections, at least during the later part of his life, extended also to other countries. This impression is confirmed and strengthened when we consider the persons to whom he dedicated his writings or sent complimentary copies of them, or the contemporary manuscripts that were demonstrably owned by persons whom we know as his friends or correspondents, or as persons of scholarly or social distinction.[6] Among these persons, we find King Ferrante of Naples, Cardinal Francesco Piccolomini in Rome, Duke Federico of Urbino, and Bernardo Bembo in Venice, but also King Matthias Corvinus and Bishop Johannes Pannonius in Hungary, Duke Eberhard of Württemberg, and Germain de Ganay in France.[7] Among his correspondents we find Johannes Reuchlin and several other German scholars, Robert Gaguin and John Colet, and the Italian humanist Philippus Callimachus who occupied an important position at the Polish court in Cracow.[8] A manuscript that has recently come to my attention belonged to Bohuslav of Lobkowitz, a leading Czech humanist of the time;[9] several manuscripts containing Ficino's writings belonged to Raphael de Marcatel, Abbot of Ghent and an illegitimate son of Duke Philip the Good of Burgundy;[10] and we have Ficino's own word that a manuscript copy of his letters was sent to Spain, although this manuscript has not been preserved and its original owner is not known to us.[11] A manuscript fragment that has just come to light seems to have belonged to Archbishop Hermann of Cologne.[12] Manuscripts containing Pico's works are less numerous, but among their owners we find Bishop Guillaume Briçonnet, Cardinal Georges d'Armagnac, and a member of the Fugger family.[13]

When we pass from the manuscripts to the printed editions, we are not only impressed with the large number of printings that Ficino's and Pico's various works received, but also with their wide distribution in place and time.[14] There are three editions of Ficino's collected works that appeared between the sixteenth and seventeenth centuries, all outside of Italy, and Pico's writings that had been collected shortly after his death by his nephew Giovanni Francesco were reprinted even more frequently. The total number of printings for the different works of these authors is very large, especially during the sixteenth century, and if we wish to judge their relative popularity from the number of editions, it would seem that Ficino's translations of Plato and of Hermes Trismegistus and his three books *De vita* as well as Pico's letters were the most widely read. Many of these editions were printed outside of Italy, especially in Basel and Lyon, Paris, Strasbourg, and Antwerp, but we find also occasional imprints from Deventer, Frankfurt, Augsburg, Nürnberg, Vienna, and Cracow, and two very early ones from Leipzig.[15] I have found no English or Spanish imprints, but it is quite evident that many books printed in Venice, Lyon, and Basel or other important centers of the book trade found their way also to those countries. The evidence is supplied by a few old library catalogues,[16] and there may be similar evidence for other countries that has escaped my attention or that may still be uncovered.

A further indication of the popularity of our authors is to be found in the translations of their works into other languages. Several of Ficino's works were translated into Tuscan by himself or by members of his circle,[17] and the same is true of Francesco da Diacceto,[18] whereas a medical work composed by Ficino in Tuscan was translated into Latin by an Italian scholar living in Germany.[19] Even more significant are the translations into other languages. Most numerous and important are the translations into French. One of Pico's letters was translated by Gaguin, and there are later French versions of some of his letters and short religious writings, of his *Heptaplus,* of his *Oration,* and of his commentary on Girolamo Benivieni's *Canzone d'amore.*[20]

Ficino's commentary on Plato's *Symposium* was translated into French as was his *De vita* and his *De religione Christiana,* and there are French versions of Hermes Trismegistus and of Plato's *Symposium, Io,* and *Lysis* that were made from Ficino's Latin versions rather than directly from the Greek.[21] Significantly enough, several of these translations are associated with the court of Queen Marguerite of Navarre. Some French translations of Pico's short religious writings were made for the Court of Henry VII of England,[22] whereas some of the same texts were rendered into English by Sir Thomas More and by Sir Thomas Elyot.[23] Pico's commentary on Benivieni was translated into English by Thomas Stanley in the seventeenth century.[24] One of Pico's letters was also translated into German by Jacob Wimpheling,[25] and one of Ficino's letters, as well as his *De vita,* attracted other German translators.[26] Ficino's translation of Hermes Trismegistus, one of his most influential works, was also translated into Spanish and Dutch.[27]

Whereas the bibliographical diffusion of the works of the Florentine Platonists through manuscripts and printed editions was considerable, their influence on the teaching tradition of the universities and other schools was very slight. If we take this teaching tradition as our only criterion in assessing the relative importance of the various intellectual currents of the Renaissance, Platonism would seem to occupy a very modest place indeed, and certainly could not stand comparison with Aristotelianism or with literary humanism. Yet the scanty evidence we have is worth mentioning. Unlike Ficino, his pupil Francesco da Diacceto did teach at the University of Pisa and Florence,[28] and was once considered for a chair in Padua,[29] though we have reason to believe that most if not all of his university courses dealt with Aristotle rather than with Plato. Courses on Platonic philosophy appeared only during the second half of the sixteenth century, especially at Pisa, Ferrara, and Rome, and for a short while at Bologna, and hardly outside of Italy.[30] At some of the Italian Academies, lectures were given on the so-called philosophy of love that were based on Plato's *Symposium* and on some Platonizing poems, and the extensive literature of the *Trattati d'amore* was closely connected with this tradition.[31] Whether similar developments, though less formalized, may be found in France or England is doubtful.[32] On the other hand, it is quite evident that at the Northern universities Plato was frequently used as a text for the study of Greek, and occasionally Ficino's translations may have served as texts for the instruction in Latin or in moral philosophy.[33]

However, it is quite clear that the influence of Ficino and of Pico, during the sixteenth century and later, did not rest on any institutional tradition of Platonist teaching, but almost exclusively on the impression that their writings made upon their readers. There is every reason to believe that this impression was wide and deep, and that it affected thinkers and writers who were important in their own right and hence in a position to lend authority to the Platonist tradition and to transmit some of its ideas to their own pupils and readers. The full exent of this influence has not yet been studied, and I certainly am not acquainted even with all the facts that may be known to other scholars. I can mention only a few examples that have come to my attention and that would also require much further investigation. There are only two ways in which such an influence can be documented in a valid fashion, apart from vague similarities and empty slogans: by direct quotations, and by borrowings of terms, concepts, doctrines, or metaphors that are specific enough to exclude the assumption of a chance similarity. Moreover, there must be some evidence that the earlier authors were accessible to the later ones, to exclude the possible impact of intermediary or common older sources. Keeping these criteria in mind, I shall briefly discuss some of the contributions of the Florentine Platonists that seem to have exercised a wide influence during the sixteenth century and later, not only in Italy, but also in other European countries. I shall not always explain how these ideas were interrelated in the thought of Ficino or Pico, but rather discuss them according to their subject matter, and to the area of learning and of literature in which their impact was most directly felt.

Perhaps the greatest achievement of the Florentine Platonists, and certainly the most influential, was their contribution to learning and scholarship. Ficino's Latin translation of Plato, begun in 1463 and printed in 1484, was the first complete rendering of the entire body of Plato's dialogues into a Western language and hence constitutes a landmark in the history of philosophy. This translation was more widely read than the Greek original until the eighteenth century, and it was and still is considered excellent, although a detailed comparison with the Greek original and with earlier partial translations has never been made.[34] If Plato's writings have been as completely and as easily available to modern readers as those of Aristotle, this fact is largely due to Ficino's initiative, and it is not surprising to note that in the sixteenth century philosophical and literary authors of all opinions, including the Aristotelians, show a direct acquaintance with Plato's writings and doctrines that had been largely absent in the work of their medieval predecessors. Moreover, Ficino added to his translation short introductions, and in some instances long commentaries, for example on the *Symposium* and the *Timaeus,* that contain his own interpretations and philosophical opinions, and since these commentaries were often reprinted along with his translation, they exercised a lasting influence and determined the way Plato was read and understood.[35] We might even say that these commentaries tended to lend Plato's authority to some of Ficino's own views, and it can be shown in more than one instance that later authors discussed or endorsed doctrines which they considered to be Plato's and which in reality were Ficino's.[36]

Next in importance, if not in influence, was Ficino's work on Plotinus. This translation, completed in 1492, was the first ever made of this important thinker,[37] and it is considered quite excellent. It was accompanied by a detailed commentary, and frequently reprinted down to the nineteenth century. Ficino also translated other Neoplatonic authors such as Porphyry, Jamblichus, and Proclus. Yet even more influential was his translation of some writings attributed to Hermes Trismegistus. These writings, re-edited with a commentary by Jacques Lefèvre d'Etaples and translated into French and other languages, were a favorite source of the broad currents of occult thought that flourished in the sixteenth and seventeenth centuries. For better or for worse, Ficino was largely responsible for the common tendency to associate Hermetic and other occult ideas with the Platonic and Neoplatonic traditions.[38]

Pico della Mirandola did not make any translations from the Greek, but he mastered the language, and he even acquired some knowledge of Hebrew and Arabic, giving through his example an impulse to Oriental studies. He had many philosophical and theological writings translated from Hebrew into Latin,[39] and made much use of Hebrew sources in his study of the Old Testament.[40] He was also the first Christian scholar who studied the Cabala,[41] and since he was convinced that the Cabalistic writings were of early origin and in basic agreement with Christianity, he inaugurated a trend of Christian Cabalism that found a number of followers, including Reuchlin and Giles of Viterbo.

These scholarly efforts of Ficino and of Pico were obviously indebted in their scope and method to the work of the earlier Italian humanists, but their specific content and aims reflected certain historical, philosophical, and theological ideas that were alien to the earlier humanists and peculiar to the Florentine Platonists. Ficino was convinced that the philosophy of Plato and his school was true and sustained by reason, and that the tasks of interpreting Plato and of setting forth a valid philosophical doctrine were basically the same. This is the underlying idea of his chief philosophical work, entitled *Platonic Theology* after the example of Proclus. Moreover, in Ficino's view, the Platonic tradition extended not only in a nearly unbroken line from Plato down to his own time, but it had its roots long before Plato, back in Biblical times, in the wisdom of Hermes Trismegistus, Zoroaster, Orpheus, and Pythagoras whose purported writings he eagerly studied. The Platonic tradition thus represented for him a kind of *philosophia perennis* (the term was to be coined by one of his sixteenth-century followers), and it was his providential task to revive this ancient doctrine both through his translations and through his teaching.[42] Finally, he believed that this perennial Platonic philisophy was not only as old as Hebrew and Christian theology, but in basic agreement with the latter. Hence the Platonic wisdom was itself a kind of theology and was able to lend rational support to Christian theology against its philosophical opponents such as the Averroists.

This attempt at harmonizing Platonic philosophy and Christian theology that has been called syncretistic by recent historians was further broadened and deepened by Pico. He wanted to assign a share in truth not only to the Christian theologians and the Platonic philosophers, but also to Aristotle and to all his ancient, Arabic and Latin interpreters as well as to the Jewish Cabalists. This was the underlying idea of his nine hundred theses as we learn from his famous *Oration,* of his Cabalistic studies and of his projected, but never completed, work on the agreement between Plato and Aristotle.[43] Ficino also insisted that religion was natural to man, and that all different religions in varying degrees approximate the one true religion.[44] Neither Ficino nor Pico had the slightest doubt that Christianity was the most perfect and the only true religion, yet I cannot help thinking that their ideas exercised some influence on later conceptions of religious tolerance and of natural religion as we find them in Postel, Bodin, and Herbert of Cherbury.[45]

The contribution of Florentine Platonism to the history of metaphysics is a broad and complex subject which we could not even hope to describe in this paper. At many points, Ficino and Pico merely transmitted older ideas to their readers and followers, or adapted and transformed these ideas in a more or less subtle fashion. The conception of the universe of being as a hierarchy is still fundamental with Ficino, but his special way of conceiving the great chain of being represents a Christian adaptation of Plotinus rather than a repetition of medieval schemes.[46] In some details, his system has been modified to suit his own preoccupations, and the traces of his scheme do occasionally reappear in later thinkers.[47] Even more important is the fact that Ficino emphatically restated on purely rational grounds, as Cusanus had done before him, the doctrine of the Platonic ideas. In placing the ideas and the intelligible world inside the essence of God, and in attributing to the human mind its own copies of the divine ideas, the innate formulae,[48] Ficino followed Plotinus and Augustine rather than Plato himself, but he succeeded in making this doctrine again respectable after centuries of terminism. No wonder that we find its traces in Galileo and Descartes, and in many other thinkers of the seventeenth century.[49]

However, the most influential doctrine of Ficino in the field of metaphysics was his conception of the immortality of the soul. This doctrine occupies the center of his thought, and constitutes the theme of his chief work, the *Platonic Theology*. In trying to prove the immortality of the soul by rational arguments, Ficino used and developed the arguments offered by Plato, Plotinus, Augustine, and other predecessors, and he also added some characteristic arguments of his own.[50] If we want to understand why the problem of immortality was so central for Ficino, we must remember that the debates of the Aristotelians about Averroes' doctrine of the unity of the intellect had undermined among professional philosophers the belief that individual immortality could be maintained on rational or Aristotelian grounds. On the other hand, the deep preoccupation of the humanists with man's personal experiences and his concrete moral problems made the quest for immortality and the belief in it especially relevant. The debate about immortality continued even more vigorously during the sixteenth century, and the philosophical arguments against it were forcefully developed by Pomponazzi. Yet Ficino supplied an arsenal of positive arguments that Pomponazzi was to face, and that his opponents including Nifo were to utilize. If the Lateran Council of 1512 gave dogmatic sanction to the immortality of the soul, Ficino's influence on the Council decree cannot be proven by direct evidence, but it can be plausibly assumed on more than one ground. The matter is of more than casual interest, especially since many modern theologians agree that the doctrine has but a tenuous basis in Scripture and is primarily derived from Platonist metaphysics.[51]

In the field of cosmology and of the natural sciences, the Florentine Platonists largely followed the traditional views of Aristotle and Ptolemy. Their possible contributions to specific scientific problems have not yet been fully investigated. They were familiar with Plato's views on mathematics and on physics (and Ficino wrote a long commentary on the *Timaeus* that has not yet been studied in detail), but unlike Cusanus or Kepler they did not stress the superiority of mathematical quantities over physical qualities. If the Platonist views on mathematics played a role in the rise of mathematical physics (as I think they did), the credit goes to some sixteenth-century Platonist philosophers and mathematicians, but not to the Florentine Academy which merely made the relevant texts of Plato and of other ancient authors available.

Of greater interest to the historian of science is Pico's radical attack against astrology. It has been shown that Pico was primarily prompted by moral and religious considerations to reject astrology: no spiritual being can be determined by a corporal being.[52] Yet he did state very clearly that the stars act only through light and heat, and not through any occult qualities, and his arguments did make a profound impression on Kepler, although curiously enough, Kepler did not go as far as Pico in his critique of astrology.[53]

Even in Pico's case, it has been doubted that he meant to reject all the occult sciences.[54] In his early theses, he endorsed natural magic, and he never explicitly abandoned it. Moreover, while his rejection of predictive astrology is firm and unqualified, he may have retained a belief in general astrology, that is, in an inner harmony and affinity between celestial and terrestrial beings. Ficino's position on the occult sciences is far more complex and on the whole more favorable to them. He revived the Neoplatonic doctrine of the world soul and was followed in this by most sixteenth-century philosophers of nature. He had his doubts about predictive astrology, but did not hesitate to practice it on occasion, falling back on the statement of

Ptolemy that the stars influence our body but not our mind, and on that of Plotinus that the stars signify earthly events without producing them.[55] Ficino was a trained physician, although apparently without a doctoral degree, and in his medical writings, especially in his *De vita,* he made extensive use of astrological correspondences and of their magical applications, and these ideas became quite popular especially in France and Germany.[56] His Hermetic translations furthered the same tendencies. The wide area of Renaissance magic and occultism, long despised by modern historians as contemptible superstition, has recently been rehabilitated as a courageous attempt, undertaken with inadequate means and theories, to subject physical nature to the reign of man. The Renaissance magician thus appears as the predecessor of the modern technician.[57]

I do not think that Florentine Platonism contributed to the study or revival of Plato's dialectic, a subject that had been neglected also by the ancient Neoplatonists. When Peter Ramus invoked Plato's authority for his reform of logic and his critique of Aristotle, the appeal to Plato was more verbal than substantial. Also Plato's political views were neglected by the ancient Neoplatonists and their Florentine followers alike. Yet Machiavelli seems to know and criticize Plato's *Republic,*[58] and Thomas More could hardly have written his *Utopia* without Plato.

The influence of the Florentine Academy on the various arts and on the theories concerning them has been widely studied in recent years. I must limit myself to a few general points. Ficino was a practicing musician and wrote repeatedly on musical theory, but his specific influence on later theorists remains to be explored.[59] Much more work has been done on the impact of the Florentine Academy on the visual arts. Ficino shared the high esteem for these arts that was common at his time, and he personally knew some of the leading artists. Some of Ficino's and Pico's philosophical concepts, and especially their metaphors and their allegorical explanations of ancient myths, appealed to the artists of their time, and the iconography of several works of Botticelli, Raphael, Michelangelo, and others has been elucidated with the help of the writings of the Platonists.[60] Ficino also revived and transmitted the ancient view that the visual work of the painter and sculptor expresses an idea in the mind of the artist, and ultimately an intelligible essence, and this notion was to recur in various adaptations in several treatises on the arts during the sixteenth century.[61] Equally important was the doctrine of the divine madness of the poet which Ficino took from Plato's *Phaedrus* and *Io*.[62] Ficino's friend Landino applied the doctrine to Dante in a commentary that was to remain very popular through the sixteenth century. Thanks to this commentary, and to Ficino's Tuscan version of Dante's *De monarchia,* the great Florentine poet became associated with Platonism.[63] The extensive critical literature of the sixteenth century was largely dominated by Aristotle and Horace, to be sure, but several Platonist notions, especially that of divine madness, are frequently cited and utilized, and there is at least one long and important poetical treatise, that of Francisco Patrizi, that tends to reject Aristotle and to follow Platonist principles.[64]

When we turn to the ethics and anthropology of the Florentine Platonists, we must begin with the place they assign to man in the universe. The notion that man occupies a privileged place in the order of things, and that human problems should be our central concern, is frequently found in ancient and early Christian writers, and it had a great appeal to the Renaissance humanists who liked to call their fields of study the *Studia humanitatis.* For Ficino, the dignity of man became an important topic in his *Platonic Theology.* Going beyond traditional conceptions, he tries to assign to man a central position in the universal hierarchy of beings.[65] Through his intellect and his will, man participates in all things above and below, and thus he is universal in his thought and aspirations. Moreover, he links all other things in a kind of dynamic unity and becomes the bond and center of the world. This idea is further modified in Pico's famous *Oration* where man is said to be outside the hierarchy of things and to choose freely his own nature and life. Pico did not mean to question the doctrines of sin and grace, as some historians have thought, and there is no doubt that he considered it to be man's task and duty to choose the highest form of life among those accessible to him, that is, the pursuit of the union with God.[66] Echoes of this doctrine of Ficino and Pico appear even in thinkers otherwise unsympathetic to the Platonic school such as Pomponazzi or Vives,[67] and the low opinion of man's estate expressed by the Protestant Reformers or by Montaigne may well have been a conscious reaction against these views.

The real key to the ethical doctrine of the Renaissance Platonists, and especially of Ficino, is their theory of the contemplative life. The goal of human life is the union with God, and this goal is pursued through a gradual ascent of the soul that turns away from all things external and through contemplation moves inwards and upwards. This ascent is accomplished by the two wings of the soul, will and intellect, through ever higher acts of loving and knowing that culminate in the direct enjoyment and vision of God. The ultimate union is attained during this earthly life only by a few persons and for a fleeting moment, but it must be postulated as an eternal possession in a future life for all those who have made an earnest effort in this present life.[68] This doctrine which is central to Ficino's ethics and metaphysics and which also supports his doctrine of immortality is in many ways related to medieval mysticism, and this may have enhanced its appeal to Renaissance readers, but it shows many Plotinian and original features, and it appeals to spiritual experience rather than to faith or revelation. In a way, it bridges the gap between Aristotelian science and Christian theology, without contradicting either.

It remains for us to discuss in conclusion the doctrine of Platonic love, which among all doctrines of Florentine Platonism was probably the one that had the widest appeal during the later Renaissance, especially among the poets. Ficino's own doctrine is rather complex and inextricably linked with his other ethical and metaphysical views. In his followers, the idea becomes increasingly detached from its original philosophical context and hence more and more diluted. Ficino's commentary on Plato's *Symposium,* a work which he himself later translated into Tuscan, was the fountainhead of all later poets and theorists of Platonic love. He also deals with the problem in some of his other writings, especially in his letters, the *Platonic Theology,* and the commentary on Plato's *Philebus.* These various treatments show some oscillations, for example, on the relative superiority of will and intellect, but there is a core of consistent doctrine.[69] Love is an act of the will, not of the intellect, and it may be directed downwards, toward things corporeal, or upwards, toward God who is the ultimate end of human life. Ficino then proceeds, and this is an important development, to interpret the love between two human beings on the basis of man's spiritual love for God. Whereas earthly love leads to procreation and is by no means rejected, celestial and divine love is wholly spiritual. It treats the beloved as an image of God, and actually loves another human being for the sake of God. This divine love which Ficino occasionally calls Platonic or Socratic love presupposes a kind of spiritual community. Each lover participates in the life of contemplation that has God for its ultimate object, and thus God becomes the third lover, or the link between the partners of divine love. In this sense, Ficino treats love as the bond that links all his friends and pupils with him and with each other, and that constitutes the basis of the Platonic Academy as a spiritual community.

This doctrine is evidently derived from Plato's *Symposium* and *Phaedrus,* but it also contains many other ingredients. Ficino draws on the interpretation given to Plato's love theory by Plotinus and Dionysius the Areopagite. He consciously equates love and friendship, drawing on the linguistic affinity between *amor* and *amicitia* in Latin, and utilizes ancient theories of friendship as he found them in Plato and Aristotle, in Cicero, and in the tradition about Epicurus. He also attempts to equate love and *charitas,* through the intermediary of divine love, citing St. Paul and especially St. Augustine whose doctrine of love and of the good had a great impact on his thought. Finally, whereas the medieval notion of courtly love was quite different in origin from that of Platonic love, Ficino noticed that Dante, Guido Cavalcanti, and other early Tuscan poets had given to human love a spiritual meaning, and he liked to repeat some of their phrases and paradoxes that seemed compatible with his own doctrine of divine love. The resulting synthesis was anything but consistent, and far more complex than it appears in later writers. Yet the way in which Ficino tried to combine these different notions in his theory of divine love may explain why it appealed to some theologians and especially to many poets and theorists of love. If many sixteenth-century poets, and some of their modern critics, merged and confused the Platonist conception of love with that of Petrarch and his predecessors, Ficino himself is partly to blame. But as historians we must try to disentangle the various ingredients of the theory, and this task, though admittedly difficult, has been accomplished to a certain degree in recent studies of the subject.[70]

I have tried to discuss, in a somewhat sketchy and superficial manner, some of the ideas and sources which Florentine Platonism, and especially Marsilio Ficino, transmitted or contributed to the rich intellectual ferment of the sixteenth century.[71] The writings and translations of the Florentine Platonists were so widely known, and some of their leading ideas had such an appeal, that we must be prepared to encounter their traces in all European countries and in all branches of thought and of literature. Some of these influences have been known and identified for some time, and others will no doubt be discovered as our study of the more obscure writers and thinkers of the period progresses. The end of the Renaissance and the beginning of the seventeenth century represent a watershed in the intellectual history of the West, especially in the sciences and in philosophy. After the physics of Galileo, Descartes and Newton, there is no room left for the fantastic cosmologies of the Renaissance, except where they survive in the realms of poetry and of occultism. In the field of metaphysics, and in other philosophical disciplines, the influence of Renaissance Platonism was to continue for several more centuries, at least to the end of the eighteenth. Some of this influence was disguised under the name of Plato or Plotinus whom scholars continued to read in Ficino's translations and with his commentaries. Thus we may find the traces of Florentine Platonism not only in Kepler and the Cambridge Platonists, but also in Descartes and Spinoza, in Shaftesbury and Berkeley,[72] and in Goethe, Kant, and Coleridge. Some of these influences have been investigated, and many more remain to be explored. I have no doubt that in the further study of the seventeenth and eighteenth century, aside from medieval and Aristotelian influences that are now so frequently emphasized, also the impact of Renaissance thought, and especially of Florentine Platonism, will become increasingly apparent, and will have to be taken into account. And I am convinced that there is enough truth mixed in with its fancy to make such a study worthwhile and truly satisfactory.

NOTES

1. P. O. Kristeller, *The Philosophy of Marsilio Ficino* (New York, 1943); *Il pensiero filosofico di Marsilio Ficino* (Florence, 1953). E. Garin, *Giovanni Pico della Mirandola* (Florence, 1937). P. O. Kristeller, "Giovanni Pico della Mirandola and His Sources," in *L'Opera e il Pensiero di Giovanni Pico della Mirandola, Convegno Internazionale,* I (Florence, 1965), 35-133.

2. A. Della Torre, *Storia dell'Accademia platonica di Firenze* (Florence, 1902). R. Marcel, *Marsile Ficin* (Paris, 1958). In an undated letter written before 1473 Ficino mentions his intention of going to Rome, but we know nothing else about this journey (*Supplementum Ficinianum,* ed. P. O. Kristeller [Florence, 1937], II, p. 89; cf. I, p. CXLIII. The original of this letter was recently acquired by Mr. William Schab, New York).

3. *Convegno,* p. 37.

4. E. Garin, *La cultura filosofica del Rinascimento italiano* (Florence, 1961), pp. 254-76. Another letter of Baptista Mantuanus to Pico was published from MS Selden 41 *supra* (3429) of the Bodleian Library by Benedictus Zimmerman O.C.D., *Monumenta historica Carmelitana* (Lirinae, 1907), pp. 493-95.

5. Marsilius Ficinus, *Opera Omnia* (Basel, 1576; reprinted Turin, 1959), I, 607-964. *Supplementum* I, 25-72; II, 79-96. For an index of the correspondents, see *ibid.* II, 357-67.

6. For a list of the manuscripts containing Ficino's writings, see *Supplementum* I, pp. V-LV; II, pp. 368-69. P. O. Kristeller, *Studies in Renaissance Thought and Letters* (Rome, 1956), pp. 158-69.

7. Ferrante: British Museum, MS Harley 3481 and 3482 (*Suppl.* I, p. XXXII; *Studies,* p. 159). Francesco Piccolomini: Vatican, MS Chigi E IV 122 (*Suppl.* I, p. XLV). Federico of Urbino: Urb. lat. 185, 226 and 1249 (*Suppl.* I, pp. XLII-XLIII). Bernardo Bembo: Bodleian, MS Canonic. lat. 156 (*Suppl.* I, pp. XXXVI-XXXVII; *Studies,* pp. 160-61); Leyden, MS BPL 160 a (*Suppl.* I, p. XXXI; *Studies,* p. 159); Cornell University, MS B 13 (*Studies,* pp. 166-67; I have recently identified the coat of arms as that of Bernardo Bembo); cf. Ferrara II, 162 (*Suppl.* I, p. VIII). Matthias Corvinus: Wolfenbüttel, MS 73 Aug. fol.; 2 Aug. 4°; 10 Aug. 4°; 12 Aug. 4° (*Suppl.* I, pp. LI-LII). Johannes Pannonius: Vienna, MS lat. 2472 (Suppl. I, pp. L-LI). Eberhard of Württemberg: Stuttgart, MS HB XV 65 (*Suppl.* I, p. XLVIII). Germain de Ganay: British Museum, MS Harley 4695 (*Suppl.* I, p. XXXII; *Studies,* p. 159); cf. Vatican, MS Regin. lat. 1619 (*Suppl.* I, pp. XLIII-XLIV). Ganay also corresponded with Diacceto (*Studies,* pp. 314, 316, 321-22). For other dedication and complimentary copies, see P. O. Kristeller, "Some Original Letters and Autograph Manuscripts of Marsilio Ficino," *Studi di Bibliografia e di Storia in onore di Tammaro De Marinis* (Verona, 1964) III, 5-33.

8. Reuchlin: *Opera,* 926; cf. *Suppl.* II, 222, 290, 306. British Museum, MS Arundel 195 was owned and annotated by Johannes Pirckheimer (*Studies,* p. 160). Vienna, MS lat. 12466 was copied and annotated by his son Willibald Pirckheimer (*ibid.* p. 163). Munich, CLM 956 b was copied by Hartmann Schedel (*Suppl.* I, p. XXXV). Gaguin: *Suppl.* II, pp. 242-43. Colet: Sears Jayne, *John Colet and Marsilio Ficino* (Oxford, 1963), based on Oxford, All Souls College, h. infra 1.5, a copy of Ficino's printed *Epistolae* (Venice, 1495), owned and annotated by Colet, that contains among its manuscript additions two previously unknown letters of Ficino to Colet and two drafts of Colet's reply. Philippus Callimachus: *Opera,* 865, 870, 891, 956; *Suppl.* II, pp. 224-30. Another copy of

Callimachus' *Questio de demonibus ad Ficinum* and *Questio de peccato ad Picum* is found in Olomouc, Státní Archiv, CO 306, f. 181-84v and 186-203.

9. Prague, Narodni a Universitni knihovna, MS VI E f 11 (from Roudnice). The coat of arms of Bohuslaus a Lobkovitz was kindly identified for me by Dr. Emma Urbankova.

10. Ghent, University Library, MS 1 (*Suppl.* I, p. XXIX); Haarlem, City Library, MS membr. in fol. 13 and 21 (*Studies*, p. 166); Holkham Hall, Earl of Leicester, MS 448 (*ibid.*). For Marcatel, see now K. G. Van Acker in *Nationaal Biografisch Woordenboek* II (Brussels, 1966), col. 507-12.

11. "sed etiam in Hispaniam iamdiu . . . pervolarunt" (sc. epistolae): *Opera*, 926. The Escorial once had a manuscript of Ficino's letters that was destroyed by fire in 1671 (*Suppl.* I, p. VII).

12. *Katalog der mittelalterlichen Handschriften und Einzelblätter in der Kunstbibliothek Berlin* (Berlin, 1967), p. 36, no. 49 (shelf mark 4005-03,185). The fragment of which Prof. Stephan Waetzoldt kindly sent me a photostat was written in Germany and contains a coat of arms that has been tentatively identified as that of Archbishop Hermann of Cologne. Ficino met an envoy of the archbishop in 1494 (*Opera*, 955). The following Ficino MSS were copied by foreign scribes: Brussels, MSS 4645-47 (*Studies*, p. 158). Burgo de Osma, MS 25 (*Studies*, p. 164; not seen). Cracow, Polish Academy, MS 1717 (excerpts made by Bernardus Lublinius in 1505). Florence, Marchesa Serlupi, MS 2 (written in Bruges 1475; *Studies*, p. 165). Glasgow, Hunterian Museum, MS U.1.10 (206) (*Studies*, p. 159). Hague, Royal Library, MS 130 E 8 (*Studies*, p. 165). London, British Museum, MS Burney 126 (owned by Thomas Traherne; *Studies*, p. 160; cf. Carol L. Marks, "Thomas Traherne and Cambridge Platonism," *PMLA* 81 (1966), 521-34; I am indebted for this reference to Prof. Joseph Houppert). Paris, MS lat. 652 (*Suppl.* I, p. XXXVII; *Studies*, p. 161). Paris, MS Suppl. grec. 212 may have come from the library of Beatus Rhenanus in Schlettstadt (*Studies*, p. 162). Pesaro, Oliveriana, MS 620, apparently written by a Spanish hand (*Iter Italicum* II [Leyden, 1967], p. 65).

13. Briçonnet: Paris, MS lat. 7858 (*Convegno*, p. 117). Armagnac: Chantilly, MS 102 (*Convegno*, p. 109). Friedrich Fugger: Munich, CLM 485 (*ibid.*, p. 116).

14. For Ficino, see *Suppl.* I, pp. LVII-LXXV; *Studies*, pp. 169-71. For Pico, see G. Pico della Mirandola, *De hominis dignitate . . .* , ed. E. Garin (Florence, 1942), pp. 89-99. I also refer to such standard bibliographical sources as the catalogues of the Bibliothèque Nationale and the British Museum, and the works of Panzer, Brunet, and Graesse.

15. For the Leipzig editions, ed. Paulus Niavis (Reichling 1322 and Copinger 4765), see *Studies*, pp. 172-73. For the Basel editions of Ficino's works, see P. Bietenholz, *Der italienische Humanismus und die Blütezeit des Buchdrucks in Basel* (Basel and Stuttgart, 1959), pp. 117-19, and *passim*. The edition of Ficino's *Opera*, published in Paris in 1641, is historically important, but I do not know who edited it. Gabriel Naudé, who published in 1643 Cardanus' *De propria vita*, in 1645 Augustinus Niphus' *Opuscula*, and in 1648 Hier. Rorarius' *Quod animalia bruta ratione utantur melius homine*, was still in Italy in 1641 (R. Pintard, *Le libertinage érudit* [Paris, 1943]), p. 268. For Pico, see Bietenholz, pp. 124-26. Also Diacceto's *Opera* was printed in Basel in 1563. *Ibid.*, p. 126.

16. For England: *The Lumley Library*, eds. Sears Jayne and Francis R. Johnson (London, 1956), p. 83 and *passim;* some of the Ficino editions were also owned by Henry VIII, Elizabeth I, and James I. For Spain: Biblioteca Colombina, *Catalogo de sus libros impresos* (Seville, 1888 ff.), III, 83; IV, 122-23;

V, 336-37; VI, 18-19, 23). The catalogue of the Bibliothèque Nationale lists a copy of Ficino's *De religione Christiana* (Paris, 1510; shelf mark Rés. D. 80186) that contains the signature and notes of Guillaume Postel.

17. Ficino's commentary on Plato's *Symposium* was translated into Tuscan by himself (*Suppl.* I, pp. CXXV-CXXVI and 89-92), as were his *De Christiana religione* (*Suppl.* I, pp. LXXVIII-LXXIX and 7-15); *De raptu Pauli* (*ibid.*, pp. CX-CXI and 71), cf. E. Garin, *Prosatori latini del Quattrocento* (Milan, 1952), pp. 932-69, and eleven selected letters (*Sermoni morali, ibid.*, pp. CXI and 71-72). The Latin translation of Hermes Trismegistus was retranslated into Tuscan by Tommaso Benci (*ibid.*, pp. CXXXI-CXXXII and 98-103). There are contemporary anonymous versions of the first book of the letters (*ibid.*, pp. CX and 70) and of the letter *De furore divino* (*ibid.*, pp. 68-69).

18. Diacceto made Tuscan versions of his *De amore* and *Panegyricus in amorem* (*Studies*, pp. 308-11).

19. *Suppl.* I, pp. LXXXVI-LXXXVII and 24-25. The translator, Girolamo Ricci, was the son of the Jewish physician and Cabalist, Paolo Ricci. A fragment of an earlier Latin version, probably made by Ficino's German student Johannes Streler, is found in Augsburg, MS quarto 121.

20. See the catalogues of the Bibliothèque Nationale and those of the British Museum. For Pico, see also *De hominis dignitate*, ed. Garin, pp. 96-99.

21. *Ibid.* Cf. J. Festugière, *La philosophie de l'amour de Marsile Ficin et son influence sur la littérature française au XVIe siècle* (Paris, 1941), pp. 143-44. W. Moench, *Die italienische Platonrenaissance und ihre Bedeutung für Frankreichs Literatur und Geistesgeschichte* (Berlin, 1936). Louis Le Roy's translations of Plato were made directly from the Greek, but made some use of Ficino's Latin version. Cf. W. Gundersheimer, *The Life and Work of Louis Le Roy* (Geneva, 1966), p. 42.

22. British Museum, MSS Royal 16 E XIV, XXIV, and XXV. Cf. *Convegno*, p. 114.

23. More's translation of Pico's tracts was printed twice in the sixteenth century along with his version of Gianfrancesco Pico's life of Giovanni Pico (STC 19898 and 19899) and republished by J. M. Rigg (1890). Sir Thomas Elyot's translation of Pico's *Rules of a Christian Lyfe* appeared with Cyprian in 1534 (BM).

24. *Platonick Discourse upon Love*, 1651; republished by E. G. Gardner (Boston, 1914). *An Oration Concerning the Dignity and Excellency of Man*, English, *ca.* 1660 (Columbia University Library, Gen MS 1).

25. *Ein Sendtbrief*, Strassburg s.a. (Graesse). Wimpheling also edited an edition of Pico's *Opera* (Strassburg, 1504).

26. *Ein Sendbrief ainem Cardinal*, trans. Michael Spylberger, 1521 (BM). *Das Buoch des Lebens*, trans. Johannes Adelphus Muelich (Strassburg, 1505) (*Suppl.* I, pp. LXXXV-LXXXVI and 23-24). This covers only the first book. German versions of books I and II also in Heidelberg, MS Palat. germ. 730 and 452 (*Suppl.* I, p. LXXXVI). A Low German version of book III is in Hamburg, MS Med. (alch.) Folio 191, f. 282-348v (information verified by Dr. Rolf Burmeister).

27. Spanish: Escorial, MS b IV 29, cf. *Studies*, pp. 173-74. Dutch: Antwerp, Museum Plantin Moretus, MS 266, cf. *Suppl.* I, p. CXXX.

28. *Studies*, pp. 298-99.

29. *Ibid.* H. Jedin, "Contarini and Camaldoli," *Archivio italiano per la Storia della Pietà*, II (1952), pp. 101 and 114. Cf. F. Gilbert, "The Date of

Composition of Contarini's and Giannotti's Books on Venice," *Studies in the Renaissance*, XIV (1967), 172-84, at p. 173.

30. *Studies,* pp. 291-92. On Nov. 9, 1588, Vincenzo Mondini wrote to Cardinal Federico Borromeo, asking the cardinal to recommend him to the Bologna authorities for a Plato chair: "si degni scrivere all'Ill(ust)re Regimento di Bol(ogn)a che si contenti favorirmi della letura dell'opere di Platone, ricercando questi signori un Platonico nello studio di Bol(ogn)a et havendo giá io atteso a dette opere, et di giá havuta la letura (benche di logica)," Ambr. G 139 inf., f. 563, no. 139. On Dec. 10, Mondini thanked the cardinal for his intervention (*ibid.* f. 121, no. 31), but there is no indication that his request was granted. He appears as lecturer on logic (1588-92) and philosophy (1592-96). Cf. U. Dallari, *I rotuli dei lettori legisti e artisti dello Studio Bolognese* (Bologna, 1889), II, 230-56.

31. John Charles Nelson, *Renaissance Theory of Love* (New York, 1958), pp. 63, 132-33, 147.

32. Cf. Frances A. Yates, *The French Academies of the Sixteenth Century* (London, 1947), pp. 2-6, 63, 82, 105-11.

33. *Studies,* pp. 172-73; see above, note 15.

34. Cf. P. O. Kristeller, "Marsilio Ficino as a Beginning Student of Plato," *Scriptorium,* XX (1966, published 1967), 41-54. For a first contribution to the study of Ficino as a translator of Plato and Plotinus, see Festugière, pp. 144-52.

35. Ficino composed longer commentaries on the *Parmenides, Sophist, Timaeus, Phaedrus, Philebus* and *Symposium* (*Suppl.* I, pp. CXVII-CXXV). The commentaries on the *Timaeus* and *Symposium* appear in all manuscripts and editions of Ficino's translation of Plato, and also in the editions containing the Greek text and the Latin translation of Plato.

36. For an example from Kant, see Kristeller, *Il pensiero filosofico di Marsilio Ficino* (Florence, 1953), p. 160.

37. The translation by Marius Victorinus that was used by St. Augustine was lost soon after the time of the latter, and we do not know whether it covered all or only some selected writings of Plotinus. See P. Henry, *Plotin et l'Occident* (Louvain, 1934), pp. 46-47, 94-95. P. Courcelle, *Les lettres grecques en Occident* (Paris, 1943), pp. 161-69, 397; *Les Confessions de Saint Augustin* (Paris, 1963), pp. 537-38.

38. Frances A. Yates, *Giordano Bruno and the Hermetic Tradition* (London and Chicago, 1964).

39. To the well known translations by Flavius Mithridates preserved in Vat. heb. 189-91 and other MSS (*Convegno,* pp. 120-21), we may now add Elia del Medigo's translation, long considered lost, of Averroes' paraphrase of Plato's *Republic* in Siena, MS G VII 32, f. 158-88 (*Ibid.,* pp. 118-19).

40. Garin, *La cultura,* pp. 241-53.

41. Joseph L. Blau, *The Christian Interpretation of the Cabala in the Renaissance* (New York, 1944). F. Secret, *Le Zóhar chez les Kabbalistes Chrétiens de la Renaissance* (Paris, 1958); *Les Kabbalistes Chrétiens de la Renaissance* (Paris, 1964). G. Scholem suggests that the Jewish convert, Paulus Heredia, preceded Pico as a Christian Cabalist ("Zur Geschichte der Anfänge der christlichen Kabbala," *Essays presented to Leo Baeck* [London, 1954], 158-93). The treatise *De auditu cabalistico* long attributed to Raymund Lull was actually written by Pietro Mainardi (Paola Zambelli, "Il 'De auditu kabbalistico' e la traduzione lulliana nel Rinascimento," *Atti dell'Accademia Toscana di Scienze e Lettere 'La Colombaria',* 30 [1965], 115-249).

42. Charles B. Schmitt, "Perennial Philosophy: From Agostino Steuco to

[226]

Leibniz," *Journal of the History of Ideas,* 27 (1966), 505-32. P. O. Kristeller, *The Philosophy of Marsilio Ficino* (New York, 1943), pp. 25-27; *Renaissance Philosophy and the Mediaeval Tradition* (Latrobe, Pa., 1967), pp. 75-78, 100-101.

43. *Convegno,* pp. 62, 67-68. E. Anagnine, G. *Pico della Mirandola* (Bari, 1937).

44. Kristeller, *Philosophy,* pp. 318-20.

45. Postel, see above, note 16.

46. Kristeller, *Philosophy,* pp. 74-91, 100-108. Cf. Arthur O. Lovejoy, *The Great Chain of Being* (Cambridge, Mass., 1936).

47. Francesco Patrizi follows Ficino in treating quality as a separate degree in the hierarchy of substances; cf. P. O. Kristeller, *Eight Philosophers of the Italian Renaissance* (Stanford, 1964), p. 121.

48. Kristeller, *Philosophy,* pp. 236-38.

49. Galileo: cf. Kristeller, *Renaissance Thought* (New York, 1961), pp. 68 and 151. Descartes: Matthias Meier, *Descartes und die Renaissance* (Münster, 1914), pp. 14-37. Newton: J. E. McGuire and P. M. Rattansi, "Newton and the 'Pipes of Pan,'" *Notes and Records of the Royal Society of London,* 21 (1966), 108-43, at p. 141, note 38 (I am indebted for this reference to Prof. Charles B. Schmitt). E. Cassirer, *The Platonic Renaissance in England* (Austin, Texas, 1953).

50. Kristeller, *Philosophy,* pp. 324-50.

51. E. Garin, *Cultura,* pp. 93-126. G. Di Napoli, *L'immortalità dell'anima nel Rinascimento* (Turin, 1963). P. O. Kristeller, "Pier Candido Decembrio and His Unpublished Treatise on the Immortality of the Soul," in *The Classical Tradition, Literary and Historical Studies in Honor of Harry Caplan,* ed. L. Wallach (Ithaca, 1966), pp. 536-58.

52. E. Cassirer, "Giovanni Pico della Mirandola," *Journal of the History of Ideas,* III (1942), 123-44, 319-46.

53. *Convegno,* p. 82.

54. *Ibid.* See also Frances A. Yates, "Giovanni Pico della Mirandola and Magic," *ibid.,* pp. 159-96.

55. Kristeller, *Philosophy,* pp. 310-12.

56. D. P. Walker, *Spiritual and Demonic Magic from Ficino to Campanella* (London, 1958).

57. This seems to follow from the studies by Frances Yates and D. P. Walker, and in a different way, from those of Lynn Thorndike.

58. *Il Principe,* ch. 15.

59. *Studies,* pp. 464-67.

60. E. Panofsky, *Studies in Iconology* (New York, 1939); E. H. Gombrich, "Botticelli's Mythologies," *Journal of the Warburg and Courtauld Institutes,* VIII (1945), pp. 7-60. E. Wind, *Pagan Mysteries in the Renaissance* (New Haven, 1958). A. Chastel, *Marsile Ficin et l'art* (Geneva, 1954); *Art et humanisme à Florence au temps de Laurent le Magnifique* (Paris, 1959). Ch. De Tolnay, *Michelangelo,* 5 vols. (Princeton, 1943-60). For Ficino's concept of melancholy and its influence, see E. Panofsky and F. Saxl, *Dürers 'Melencolia I'* (Leipzig and Berlin, 1923). Raymond Klibansky, Erwin Panofsky, and Fritz Saxl, *Saturn and Melancholy* [London, 1964]; this is a revised and enlarged English version of the preceding book).

61. E. Panofsky, *Idea* (Leipzig and Berlin, 1924; 2nd rev. ed., Berlin, 1960).

62. B. Weinberg, *A History of Literary Criticism in the Italian Renaissance,* 2 vols. (Chicago, 1961). B. Hathaway, *The Age of Criticism* (Ithaca, 1962).

63. Landino's commentary on Dante was published first in 1481, with a

laudatory prologue of Ficino *(Suppl.* I, p. LXXIV). On Ficino's version of Dante's *De monarchia,* see *Suppl.* I, pp. CLXI-CLXII; II, pp. 184-85. In his preface, Ficino praises Dante as full of "sententie Platoniche" (p. 184).

64. Weinberg, pp. 272-73, 765-86. A critical edition of Patrizi's *Poetica* is being prepared by Danilo Aguzzi.

65. Kristeller, *Philosophy,* pp. 104-20.

66. *Ibid.,* pp. 407-10. *Convegno,* p. 53.

67. Pomponazzi: *The Renaissance Philosophy of Man,* ed. E. Cassirer *et al.* (Chicago, 1948), pp. 282-83. Vives, *A Fable about Man, ibid.,* pp. 387-93. Cf. Marcia L. Colish, "The Mime of God: Vives on the Nature of Man," *Journal of the History of Ideas,* XXIII (1962), 3-20.

68. Kristeller, *Philosophy,* pp. 206-55.

69. *Ibid.,* pp. 256-88. Kristeller, "A Thomist Critique of Marsilio Ficino's Theory of Will and Intellect," in *Harry Austryn Wolfson Jubilee Volume, English Section* (Jerusalem, 1965), I, 463-94; *Le Thomisme et la pensée italienne de la Renaissance* (Montreal, pp. 104-23). In a letter to Colet, written shortly before his death, Ficino again discusses the relation between intellect and love or will. Here Ficino seems to treat the intellect as superior, but the entire treatment is different from Ficino's earlier discussions of the subject. See Sears Jayne, *John Colet and Marsilio Ficino* (Oxford, 1963), pp. 82-83, cf. 56-76. I was reminded of this last problem by Prof. James Devereux.

70. Nesca A. Robb, *Neoplatonism of the Italian Renaissance* (London, 1935). John Charles Nelson, *Renaissance Theory of Love* (New York, 1958). For the influence in France, see Festugière and Moench (above, note 21). For Spain: M. Menendez y Pelayo, *Historia de las ideas esteticas en España* (Santander, 1947), II, 7-76. Otis H. Green, *Spain and the Western Tradition* (Madison, 1963), I, 123-60. Joseph Vinci, "The Neoplatonic Influence of Marsilio Ficino on Fray Pedro Malón de Chaide," *Hispanic Review* XXIX (1961), 275-95. For England: Sears Jayne, "Ficino and the Platonism of the English Renaissance," *Comparative Literature,* 4 (1952), 214-38. William Nelson, *The Poetry of Edmund Spenser* (New York, 1963). For Denmark: The humanist Christiern Pedersen owned a copy of Ficino's *De Christiana religione,* cf. E. Jørgensen, *Historieforskning og Historieskrivning i Danmark* (Copenhaguen, 1931), p. 69 (communication of Dr. Jan Pinborg). For Sweden: Georg Stiernhielm shows in his writings a strong influence of Florentine Platonism *(Filosofiska Fragment,* ed. J. Nordström [Stockholm, 1924], pt. II, p. 5 and *passim).* Johannes Bureus repeatedly quotes Ficino and especially Pico (Sten Lindroth, *Paracelsismen i Sverige* [Uppsala, 1943], pp. 82-252). A copy of Pico's works (Basel, 1557) has been in the Skokloster Library since the seventeenth century. I am indebted for these data to Prof. E. N. Tigerstedt. For Portugal and the United States, see the next note.

71. The examples could be multiplied easily. Cardinal Giles of Viterbo, a professed admirer of Ficino, wrote a commentary on Peter Lombard's Sentences *ad mentem Platonis (Suppl.* II, 314-16 and 354). Erasmus, not usually considered a Platonist, shows specific traces of Ficino's influence in the *Enchiridion* and the *Praise of Folly,* as I hope to show in the near future. For the influence of Ficino and Pico in France, see also A. Renaudet, *Préréforme et Humanisme à Paris* (Paris, 1916). Rabelais, in a chapter that has many Platonist references (Pantagruel 18) cites a fictitious title of Plotinus, and also Proclus, *de magia,* which he could have known only in Ficino's translation *(Studies,* p. 170; my attention was called to this passage by Miss Alice Fiola). The Franciscan Luis Carvajal repeatedly praises Pico in his *Apologia monastica*

religionis diluens nugas Erasmi [Salamanca, 1528]; see M. Bataillon, *Érasme et l'Espagne* [Paris, 1937], pp. 347 and 352-53). The Portuguese friar Heitor Pinto composed a series of dialogues which contain mentions of Ficino and Steuco and which on the whole imitate Plato whom the author presumably knew through Ficino's translation. See A. J. Saraiva, *Historia da Cultura em Portugal* (Lisbon, 1955), II, 671-87, esp. at p. 684; E. Glaser, "Frei Heitor Pinto's Imagem da Vida Cristã," *Portugiesische Forschungen der Görresgesellschaft*, III (1962-63), 47-90. I am indebted for some of these references to Dr. Elizabeth Feist Hirsch. The Spanish Platonist Sebastian Fox Morcillo was treated in a monograph (U. Gonzalez de la Calle, *Sebastian Fox Morcillo* [Madrid, 1903]), but his relation to Ficino has not been studied. He published several commentaries on Plato's dialogues, and at least for his commentary on the *Republic* he used Ficino's translation ([Basel], 1556), see the catalogue of the Bibliothèque Nationale.

72. Many years ago, the late Prof. William Ladd called my attention to the fact that some editions of Ficino were among the books given by Berkeley to Yale. With the help of Miss Dorothy Bridgewater, I have been able to identify the editions. There are three volumes: one edition of Plotinus in Greek and Latin (Basel, 1580), and two editions of Plato in Greek and Latin (Lyons, 1590, and Francford, 1602). They are preserved in the Beinecke Library and have the shelf marks 1742 Library 2.1.11; 1742 Library 3.2.3; and 1742 Library 5.1.3. Cf. Bishop George Berkeley, *A Catalogue of Books for Yale College sent by Bishop Berkeley, 1733* (MS vault Sec. 17:1), where the three volumes are listed on pp. 7, 9, and 10. A. Keogh, "Bishop Berkeley's Gift of Books to Yale in 1733," in *Overbibliotekar Wilhelm Munthe, Fra Fagfeller og Venner* (Oslo, 1933), pp. 128-47. The Harvard Library owned in 1723 the collected works of Ficino (Basel, 1576) and of Pico (Basel, 1601), and Plotinus in Greek with Ficino's translation (Basel, 1580), but Plato only in Greek with the translation of Serranus. Cf. *Catalogus Librorum Bibliothecae Collegii Harvardini* (Boston, 1723), pp. 13, 25, 27. The *Continuatio* of 1735 lists an edition of Plato's works, printed in Lyons, 1590 (p. 114), and this must have contained Ficino's translation (*Suppl.* I, p. LXII).

Appendix

Statement of Objectives

The Southeastern Institute of Medieval and Renaissance Studies is established for the advancement of scholarship and the improvement of teaching in the southeastern region. Through the Institute the resources of Duke University and The University of North Carolina—particularly library holdings—are made available to scholars and teachers throughout the region. Participation is invited from students of all areas of medieval and renaissance studies, including (among others) art, aesthetics, history, literature, music, philosophy, and religion.

The Institute consists of eight informal seminars, each one concerned with a topic of special interest to students of the medieval and renaissance periods. Each seminar is led by a Senior Fellow and has an enrollment of not more than six participants, designated Fellows. The typical seminar meets twice a week for one to two hours, but schedules are flexible to permit arrangements adapted to the needs of the seminar. Each Fellow participates in one seminar and has ample free time to devote to his own research. In addition to the seminars, the Institute sponsors a public lecture by each of the eight Senior Fellows and holds a daily coffee hour for those Institute members who wish to attend.

The Institute alternates annually between the campuses of Duke University and The University of North Carolina at Chapel Hill. The third session, from July 17 to August 24, 1967, was held on the Chapel Hill campus.

Seminars of the Third Session, July 17-August 24, 1967

1. THE CREATION OF A CHRISTIAN REALITY IN MEDIEVAL ART

Senior Fellow: DR. FRANÇOIS BUCHER, Professor of the History of Art, Princeton University. Yale University 1954-1960, Brown University 1960-1962. Fellow, Institute for Advanced Study, 1962-1963. Guggenheim Fellow 1958. Member, Mediaeval Academy, College Art Association; Director, Society of Architectural Historians; Councellor, Academy of Spoleto; Editor of GESTA; Committee member, Index of Christian Art. Author: *Notre-Dame de Bonmont and the Earliest Cistercian Abbeys of Switzerland* (1957); (with J. Albers), *Despite Straight Lines* (1961); *The Pamplona Bibles* (to appear in 1969); "The Palace of Theoderic (?) in Spoleto," *Gesta*, Vols. III, IV, 1964-65.

Scope: Art history, aesthetics, history of architecture, history of ideas.

Description: The second commandment and the Augustinian emphasis on humility remained major obstacles in the path of Christian artistic expression well into the twelfth century both in the East and in the West. Negation expressed in iconoclastic movements or strict architectual precepts stood against the propagandistic and didactic intentions of Christian rulers and of the church. The urban societies were eventually able to create a visible Christian Universe which found its climax in Hagia Sophia in the East and in the Gothic cathedrals of the Latin West. The seminar will be concerned with the foundations of medieval art with a stress on architecture, especially the Gothic cathedral. Members should have a reading knowledge of either French or German.

II. THE SENSE OF HISTORY IN LATE MEDIEVAL AND RENAISSANCE ENGLAND

Senior Fellow: DR. ARTHUR B. FERGUSON, Professor of History, Duke University. Contributor to the first three volumes of the *Army Air Forces in World War II* (1943-48); Member of the Renaissance Society of America, of the Conference on British Studies. Author, *The Indian Summer of English Chivalry* (1960), *The Articulate Citizen and the English Renaissance* (1965).

Scope: Interdisciplinary: cultural history, law, and historiography.

Description: The seminar will seek to define the emerging sense of history in such areas as law and the social thought of the age. It will not concern itself with the formal historiography present in the chronicles and "histories," but will focus rather upon the historical implications and overtones in the works of such men as More, Starkey, Fortescue, Reginald Pecock, and Sir Thomas Smith. The seminar will consider the problem of that change in perspective on both past and present which is coming to be recognized as one of the most characteristic features of Renaissance thought.

III. ASPECTS OF CONTINENTAL FEUDALISM

Senior Fellow: DR. FRANÇOIS L. GANSHOF, Professor emeritus of medieval history and legal history, University of Ghent; Dr. *honoris causa* of various British and French universities; member or corresponding fellow of various academies, amongst which are the Académie des Inscriptions et Belles Lettres, the British Academy and the Medieval Academy of America. Author: *Études sur les ministeriales* (1926); *Recherches sur les tribunaux de châtellenie* (1932); *Étude sur le développement des villes entre Loire et Rhin* (1943); *La Flandre sous les premiers comtes* (3rd edit. 1949); *Recherches sur les capitâlaires* (1958); *La Belgique Carolingienne* (1958); *Le Moyen Age (Histoire des Relations Internationales*, I; 3rd edit. 1964); *Feudalism* (3rd English edit. 1964); *Les institutions de la monarchie franque* (in *Karl der Grosse*, I, 1965).

Scope: Interdisciplinary: medieval history, history of religion, history of law, etc.

Description: The Seminar will study texts related to institutions of feudal law, chiefly in France and Germany during the tenth, eleventh, and twelfth centuries. Knowledge of Latin will be essential for the study of the primary sources. Knowledge of German and French will be useful.

IV. RENAISSANCE LITERATURE IN ITS COSMOLOGICAL CONTEXT

Senior Fellow: DR. S. K. HENINGER, JR., Associate Professor of English, Duke University. Fulbright Scholar, Oxford University (1949-52); Folger Library Fellow (summer, 1961); Guggenheim Fellow (1962); Duke Endowment Faculty Fellow (1966). Executive secretary, Southeastern Renaissance Conference, 1960; Shakespeare Anniversary Committee, 1964. Co-editor: *Renaissance Papers 1963, Renaissance Papers 1964*. Author: *A Handbook of Renaissance Meteorology* (1960). Editor of Thomas Watson, *The Hekatompathia* (1964); Edmund Spenser, *Selected Poetry* (1966).

Scope: Interdisciplinary: esp. literature, philosophy, and history of science.

Description: The seminar will reconstruct the cosmological thought of the Renaissance and will consider various intellectual activities within this context. It will examine schemata which had been devised to describe the universe, trace the acceptance of the Copernican hypothesis, and consider the effect of heliocentrism on intellectual history. Large topics to be developed in discussion will include the concept of poem as microcosm and the concept of metaphor as cosmic correspondence. Each participant, however, will be expected to work closely with a particular literary work, philosophical system, or scientific theory.

V. RENAISSANCE PLATONISM

Senior Fellow: Dr. Paul Oskar Kristeller, Professor of Philosophy, Columbia University. Visiting Professor, Scuola Normale Superiore, Pisa (1949 and Fulbright 1952); Member, Institute for Advanced Study, Princeton (1954-55 and 1961); Secretary of a co-operative research project entitled "Medieval and Renaissance Latin Translations and Commentaries," sponsored by the Union Académique Internationale; Fellow of the American Academy of Arts and Sciences (1955-), and of the Mediaeval Academy of America (1959-); Corresponding Fellow of the Accademia dei Sepolti (Volterra, 1949-), of the Arcadia (Rome, 1959-), of the Monumenta Germaniae Historica (Munich, 1962-), of the Académie des Inscriptions et Belles-Lettres (Paris, 1965-). Recipient of the Serena Medal of the British Academy (1958); Doctor of Philosophy (honorary degree), Padua, 1962. Author, *Der Begriff der Seele in der Ethik des Plotin* (1929), *Supplementum Ficinianum* (1937), *The Philosophy of Marsilio Ficino* (1943), *The Classics and Renaissance Thought* (1955), *Latin Manuscript Books before 1600* (1960), *Iter Italicum*, Vol. I (1963), etc.

Scope: Interdisciplinary: intellectual history; history of philosophy, of theology, of literature, and of the sciences.

Description: Study of the role and significance of Renaissance Platonism, and its impact on the various branches of the thought and civilization of the period. Emphasis on its doctrinal content, and the specific theories as discussed by the writers of the period. Special attention will be given to its ancient and medieval (including Byzantine) sources. Attention will also be paid to regional differences, to chronological developments, and to the impact of philosophical Platonism on literary, religious and scientific thought. Among the theories important in Platonism, such doctrines as the Ideas, Love and Immortality will be emphasized.

VI. MEDIEVAL ARTHURIAN LITERATURE: CHIEFLY ENGLAND AND FRANCE

Senior Fellow: Dr. Robert M. Lumiansky, Professor of English, University of Pennsylvania. Member of Advisory Committee, National Defense Fellowship Program; Member of the American Council of Learned Societies, Modern Language Association, Medieval Academy of America (council 1957-). Editor of the Bulletin of the South Central Modern Language Association. Author, *Chaucer's 'Troilus and Criseyde' in Modern English* (1952), *Chaucer's Canterbury Tales in Modern English,* revised edition (1954, 1960), *Of Sundry Folk: The Dramatic Principle in the Canterbury Tales* (1955).

Scope: English and French literature, comparative literature, medieval studies.

Description: This seminar invites applicants concerned with one or more of the following: Geoffrey's *Historia,* Wace's *Roman de Brut,* Layamon's *Brut,* Chrétien's romances, the Old French *Vulgate Cycle,* fourteenth-century English Arthurian writings, and Malory's *Morte d'Arthur.* The Senior Fellow's approach will be more historical and analytical than anthropological. Applicants should have competence in the relevant languages. Anyone doing research in the relation of the Arthurian story to the medieval Tale of Troy will be most welcome.

VII. MEDIEVAL LATIN PALAEOGRAPHY AND LITERATURE

Senior Fellow: DR. BERTHE M. MARTI, Professor of Classics, The University of North Carolina. Professor of Latin and Medieval Latin, Bryn Mawr College, 1951-63; Visiting Professor of Classics, American Academy in Rome, 1961-62; Senior Fulbright Fellow in Italy; Fellow of the American Academy in Rome, Guggenheim Fellow; Board of Directors, American Philological Association, 1958-63; Editorial Board and Executive Committee, Medieval and Renaissance Latin Translations and Commentaries. Author, articles on

Lucan, Seneca, the transmission of the Classics, etc.; *Arnulfi Aureli-anensis Glossulae super Lucanum* (Monographs of the American Academy in Rome XVIII [1958]) ; *The Spanish College at Bologna in the Fourteenth Century* (University of Pennsylvania Press, 1966).

Scope: Interdisciplinary: classical and medieval Latin literature; palaeography and textual criticism; history of medieval education.

Description: The work of the seminar will be concentrated on the medieval commentaries upon classical authors. The Senior Fellow will be particularly concerned with an unpublished commentary by Anselm of Laon on Lucan's *Pharsalia* and the preparation of an edition of this text. The manuscripts will be collated and the sources of the quotations and references investigated. Members who wish to prepare editions of other Latin texts and to work on other palaeographical topics of their choice may do so. Microfilms and photostats of medieval manuscripts will be used for practical exercises in reading the handwriting of different periods. A survey of recent work on palaeography will be made.

VIII. CRITICAL THEORY IN RENAISSANCE FRANCE

Senior Fellow: DR. W. L. WILEY, Kenan Professor of French, The University of North Carolina. Advisory Council, Renaissance Society of America (1955-63); President, Southeastern Renaissance Conference (1957) ; Folger Traveling Fellow (1951) ; Litt.D., *honoris causa*, University of Chattanooga (1961) ; Visiting Professor, Brown University (1964-65); Société des Amis de Montaigne. Author, *Pierre Le Loyer's Version of the 'Ars Amatoria'* (1941), *Literature of the French Renaissance: A Bibliography* (co-editor, 1937-57), *The Gentleman of Renaissance France* (1954), *The Early Public Theatre in France* (1960).

Scope: The French Renaissance, with excursions into classical antiquity and Italy.

Description: The seminar will seek to trace an evolution of critical theory in sixteenth century France through an examination of selected texts. Some emphasis will be placed on dramatic criticism. An effort will also be made to look at the mores and milieu in which the critical mind of the period functioned. The participants in the seminar will be given adequate time to present their own projects of research.

[236]

Appendix

Fellows of the Southeastern Institute of Medieval and Renaissance Studies, 1967

SEMINAR NO. 1: Purvis E. Boyette (Tulane University)
Don W. Denny (University of Maryland)
Patricia M. Gathercole (Roanoke College)
John Howett (Emory University)
Rhea T. Workman (Columbia College)

SEMINAR NO. 2: Walser H. Allen, Jr. (Wilmington College)
Charles O. Burgess (Old Dominion College)
Walter Cane (Shippensburg State College)
Vincent H. de Paul Cassidy (University of Southwestern Louisiana)
Thomas V. H. Wheeler (University of Tennessee)

SEMINAR NO. 3: William S. Thurman (Asheville-Biltmore College)
Jerrald L. Townsend (Washington University)
Ralph V. Turner (Ohio University)
Ernest C. York (University of Alabama)

SEMINAR NO. 4: Christopher M. Armitage (Duke University)
Robert J. Bauer (University of Oklahoma)
George W. Boyd (Millsaps College)
Frank Brantley (Memphis State University)
Norma J. Engberg (George Washington University)
Robert E. Lucas (The University of North Carolina at Greensboro)
Amy Sparks (State University College, New York)

SEMINAR NO. 5: Carey S. Crantford (Furman University)
James A. Devereux (The University of North Carolina at Chapel Hill)
Donald J. Edge (Vanderbilt University)
Ann M. Gossman (Texas Christian University)
Joseph W. Houppert (University of Maryland)

SEMINAR NO. 6: Wilfred L. Guerin, Jr. (Centenary College of Louisiana)
Philip H. Kennedy (University of Tennessee)
John V. Myers (Campbell College)

Frieda E. Penninger (Westhampton College, University of Richmond)

George F. Reinecke (Louisiana State University)

Rosemary Sprague (Longwood College)

SEMINAR NO. 7: Calvin M. Bower (University of Tennessee)
Robert G. Cook (Tulane University)
Norman F. Gienapp (St. Paul's College)
Julian W. Jones, Jr. (College of William and Mary)
Phillip D. Thomas (Wichita State University)
Curt J. Whittlin (Union College)

SEMINAR NO. 8: James R. Beeler (College of William and Mary)
Jacqueline C. Freeman (Trinity College)
Julia Y. Lee (Virginia Union University)
Deirdre M. Southall (Western Carolina College)